W9-ABC-898

COTTONWOOD *and the* RIVER OF TIME

COTTONWOOD
and the RIVER OF TIME

ON TREES, EVOLUTION, AND SOCIETY

REINHARD F. STETTLER

UNIVERSITY OF WASHINGTON PRESS   *Seattle & London*

This publication was made possible in part by a generous grant from
The Pendleton and Elisabeth Carey Miller Charitable Foundation.

University of Washington Press
PO Box 50096, Seattle, WA 98145
www.washington.edu/uwpress

Library of Congress Cataloging-in-Publication Data
Stettler, R. F. (Reinhard Friedrich), 1929–
Cottonwood and the river of time : on trees, evolution, and society /
Reinhard F. Stettler.
p. cm.
Includes bibliographical references and index.
ISBN 978-0-295-98880-1 (pbk. : alk. paper)
1. Poplar—Adaptation. 2. Poplar—Evolution. 3. Poplar—Genetics. 4. Trees—
Evolution. 5. Trees—Economic aspects. 6. Human-plant relationships. I. Title.
QK495.S16S74 2009
583'.65—dc22
2008050753

Cover drawing and illustrations by the author, unless otherwise indicated.

FOR

Däni, Andrea & Nico

Biology is the study of complicated things that give
the appearance of having been designed for a purpose.

—RICHARD DAWKINS, 1986

Nature has linked her kinds into a net, not into a chain;
men are incapable of following anything but a chain, since
they cannot express in words more than one thing at a time.

—ALBRECHT VON HALLER, 1768

CONTENTS

PREFACE AND ACKNOWLEDGMENTS

Cottonwood, Cottonwood Creek, Cottonwood Fishing Camp, Cottonwood Motel, the Town of Cottonwood—what is so magic about cottonwoods? What draws people to cottonwoods? Is it the promise of a cool stream, some shade, and shelter? Indeed, water, the mainspring of life, is at the heart of it. And if there is a tree whose life cycle is hooked to water, it is cottonwood. From the germination of its seedlings to the dispersal of the next generation, all stages of its life are attuned to the seasonal dynamics of the water cycle. It's an intriguing connection and a revealing one: It lets us in on how a tree species has found its niche in nature's diversity, how it has found ways to meet the critical demands of that setting, and how—over evolutionary time—adaptation has molded a suite of characteristics to match the physical contingencies that set constraints on the species' existence.

Tree adaptation is a wonderful chapter of biology—and one largely unknown to most. We know about the birds and the bees, about flowers and pollinators, about ants and their social structure, but how trees relate to their environment seems of little concern. Trees are there, large, immutable, apparently permanent, an archaic life form that has been around for a long time. But isn't this remarkable in itself? How can they stay young while growing old? How can they keep up with an ever-changing environment for hundreds, even thousands of years? How can they keep one step ahead of rapidly evolving pests while staying rooted in the same place? Genes have much to do with it. Genes are at the heart of adaptation, the agents of adaptive mechanisms natural selection has favored over time. It is genes that regulate patterns of variation and respond to the environment's pressure. Remarkably too, genes are an archive of the evolutionary history of an individual's ancestry. Genes reflect the past, act in the present, and set the stage for the future.

We have learned much about the genetics of trees during the past twenty years, and cottonwoods, poplars, and aspens, trees of the genus *Populus*, have figured prominently in these studies. We can learn from cottonwoods what would take three times as long with other trees. We can genetically manipulate poplars in ways that as yet won't work with other trees. Poplar hybrids are now among the fastest growing stock in intensively managed plantations for lumber and pulpwood. They also may provide a new source of cellulosic biofuel and show promise in the cleanup of industrial pollution sites. Most recently, poplars have joined the inner circle of accepted biological model systems as the first tree species to have its complete genome sequenced. A large research community, linked across the globe, now shares information on all aspects of poplar biology, from adaptation of natural populations to the promise of genetically engineered clones for specific purposes.

Poplars have been the main focus of my own research for the past forty years. They have given me countless days of discovery in the field, challenging questions, headaches and sleepless nights, occasional successes in the greenhouse, exciting insights, and also the needed grant money without which research is impossible. Importantly too, they have served to forge close collaborations with numerous graduate students, postdoctoral fellows, visiting scientists, and colleagues from many different disciplines at my home institution and beyond. Poplars have also lured me to remote corners of the world and given me a taste of distant rural cultures. Altogether, it shouldn't be surprising that I have chosen poplars to form the central thread throughout the book—although here and there I will diverge where oaks or pines or chestnuts offer better examples to help us understand the arboreal world. It is a world of endurance, not splash, of persistence, not floral extravagance, yet rich in hidden mechanisms that help trees conquer space, hold on to it, and cope with time.

The book takes us to a West Cascade river where we follow black cottonwood's life cycle from seed dispersal to seedling establishment to the tree's growth and vegetative propagation—all in tune with the river's dynamics and periodic flooding. This life history raises a number of questions, such as: How important is sexual reproduction and what are its constraints? What defines a species and maintains its integrity? And why is natural hybridization so common in poplars and many other trees? We learn to appreciate the large reservoir of genetic diversity within species of trees and how that bears on their adaptability to continual change. A detour through conifer land shows how molecular tools are used to trace the migratory history of tree species after the last glaciation and to help us interpret the genetic legacy it has given them today. How closely can these populations track a changing environment, given the constraints of evolutionary mechanisms, and how will they be able to keep pace with global change?

In the final part of the book we examine poplars, and trees in general, in the context of human society. We briefly delve into the early history of plant domestication and see how poplars have long served changing human demands. We learn how recent insights into genes and their expression offer novel approaches in tailoring poplars to new needs. Broadening the perspective, we address the conflicting services expected from trees and forests, given their diverse roles as renewable production systems, as recreational playgrounds, and as residual remnants of natural ecosystems conserving biological diversity—all of this in a world where true nature is something of the past. How will we be able to integrate these different functions in our landscapes of the future?

This book is aimed at anybody interested in nature, but especially toward those with an affinity to plants who are intrigued by such questions as: What makes a seedling a good competitor over others? How long have native trees been at their current location and how well adapted are they? What happens to them when we transfer them to a new environment? How do the opposite processes of asexual propagation and natural hybridization affect diversity in natural populations? Are species real biological entities or mere taxonomic constructs? How do we distinguish them from races and varieties? Should we be worried about gene flow from non-native trees into local populations? How does genetic engineering differ from conventional plant breeding? And finally, how can we explain the paradox that plants as diverse as a tiny annual weed and a towering tree have so many genes in common?

More than anything, this book is about connections. Connections between ecology, evolution, and genetics, between rivers and their riparian vegetation, between reproductive systems and biological diversity, between climate and adaptation, between wild populations and their domesticated relatives, between natural form and its ornamental derivatives, and between plants and humans—or, in sum, connections among the physical, biological, and social worlds. The narrative also offers a glimpse of a brief but significant period in the history of biology and the approaches scientists have used to unravel some of the puzzling mysteries of the natural world.[1]

Many have contributed to this book, directly and indirectly. I greatly benefited from my longtime collaboration with Tom Hinckley, Toby Bradshaw, and Paul Heilman. Each in his own way opened my eyes to dimensions of poplar biology way beyond my imagination. They also provided leadership to a research program that over time included the expertise of Milton Gordon, Benjamin Hall, Judson Isebrands, Eugene Nester, George Newcombe, Kyösti Sarkanen, Barbara Smit, Elizabeth Van Volkenburgh, Helen Whiteley, John Bassman, Alan Black, Gary Chastagner, and their coworkers. Important early inputs were also made by European poplar experts Robert Koster, Horst Weisgerber, Victor Steenackers, and Stefano Bisoffi, later augmented by joint work with their younger colleagues, Reinhart Ceulemans, Giuseppe Scarascia, Marc Villar, and Lars Christersson.

Collaboration with the forest products industry became essential when realistic field testing had to be scaled up. Key people in making this possible were Robert Miller (Mt. Jefferson Farms); Donald Lester, Donald Rice, and Brian Stanton (Crown Zellerbach Corp., now Greenwood Resources, Inc.); Charles Wierman (Boise Cascade Corp.); Robert Rogers and Cees van Oosten (MacMillan-Bloedel Corp.); and John Olson and Jake Eaton (Potlatch Corp.). Their inventive approaches to the culture of a new crop tree and their openness in communication added significantly to the current knowledge base on poplar.

Further and able allies in probing the inner secrets of poplar were Steve Strauss, Richard Meilan, Amy Brunner, Stephen DiFazio, and their coworkers at Oregon State University. Their group, well founded on the principles of responsible ecological stewardship, turned into one of the leading powerhouses in poplar genetic engineering worldwide.

I thank Robert Naiman, Stewart Rood, and especially Jeffrey Braatne for introducing me to the world of rivers and the riparian ecosystem. Jeff was also instrumental in helping me make use of a reach of the Snoqualmie River as a study object for high school science classes. With the added expertise of Philip Hurvitz, Stewart Pickford, Luke Rogers, Sarah Reichard, Jon Honea, Joan Dunlap, and Nicholas Wheeler we were able to engage in a productive collaboration with teachers and students of several advanced-placement science classes at Mt. Si High School in Snoqualmie and the International School in Bellevue, Washington. During that time, and ever since, Isadora's Café in Snoqualmie has been serving as an unofficial laboratory for the study of public perception of science.

It was Linda Brubaker who introduced me to past climates and vegetations. Having our offices next door to each other and co-teaching dendrology provided for a longtime exchange of ideas on plant evolution and on how to convey science to students.

Carl Riches helped me with the electronic world and showed his competence in developing and running the comprehensive database of the poplar research program. Michael, his son, was equally helpful in setting up my computer base at home.

Financial support for my research came from many sources, but the sustained funding from the U.S. Department of Energy was especially helpful. It is a tribute to one of its talented scientific administrators, Gerald Tuskan, that poplar worked its way into the upper strata of biological model systems.

I greatly benefited from many colleagues who willingly contributed their expertise to specific chapters: Bruce Bare, Stefano Bisoffi, Jeff Braatne, Gordon Bradley, Toby Bradshaw, Linda Brubaker, Reinhart Ceulemans, Jake Eaton, Tom Hinckley, Jud Isebrands, Arthur Kruckeberg, Marty Main, Connie Millar, Stewart Rood, Giuseppe Scarascia, Brian Stanton, Nicholas Wheeler, and Tom Whitham.

I am deeply indebted to Don Dickmann and Steve Strauss, who reviewed the entire manuscript and made numerous valuable suggestions toward its improvement.

Let me also acknowledge the most helpful editorial advice I received. If the book has turned out to be accessible to a general reader, it is so thanks to Beth Fuget, who—with a perceptive eye and patient insistence—guided me in turning a technical narrative into common

English, and who succeeded in making the experience thoroughly enjoyable. An equally dedicated copy editor, Sigrid Asmus, and a talented graphic designer, Ashley Saleeba, contributed another layer of expertise toward a much-improved end product. And Mary Ribesky guided the whole process through its many instars.

Daniel and Andrea Stettler were a continual source of technical and moral support during my work on this book. They also gave me expert advice on graphics and artwork. And the prize for keeping my optimism in the future goes to Nico and his observant eye.

COTTONWOOD *and the* RIVER OF TIME

PART I

The Tree and the River

The setting is a floodplain of a river on the west side of the Cascade Range, the home turf of black cottonwood. It is a fleeting turf, a temporary home in the ever-changing environment of an active river. Periodic flooding, summer drought, bank erosion, shifting sand and gravel, deposition of woody debris, and channel migration keep setting a new stage season after season, and year after year. Only trees that can seize the moment and have flexible growth and reproduction can match this fickle environment. Through its pioneering existence, cottonwood also prepares the habitat for other species to follow in the natural succession of riparian vegetation. Over the next five chapters we will follow cottonwood through its life cycle and learn about the many mechanisms that have equipped it to find its niche under conditions that defy most other trees.

1 / THE TREE

The old cottonwood has lost its leaves during the last November storms. It stands there like the Statue of Liberty in the midst of the grove, the one remaining part of its crown reaching above the surrounding trees. Two other segments had come down in storms several years ago and are decomposing at its foot amid hazel shrubs and salmonberry. The tree is nearing the end of its upright existence; it's perhaps 130 years old but still impressive with its tall, cylindrical trunk. Even last spring it shed thousands of seed from its few live branches and sent them flying away in their cottony tufts. Some had landed on freshly deposited sand at the nearby river, the possible beginning of a new generation. In fact, the old matriarch is the last member of its age group in that forest and is now surrounded by younger bigleaf maples, some bitter cherries, and a few conifers. They have come up in the half shade of the disintegrating cottonwood stand, followers in the footsteps of the original pioneers, forest succession in full progress.

Is a tree really old at age 130? Aren't those the best years, years when life continues for centuries, in some trees even for millennia? True, but what is normal for Douglas fir or a bristlecone pine is not the rule for cottonwood or alder. Some species are sprinters, whereas others are marathon runners, and each has characteristic features that seem to be geared to its pace. Cottonwoods, as all members of the genus *Populus* (poplars and aspens), are early-successional pioneers, stake their claim in raw, inhospitable territory, rapidly build up expansive populations, disperse their seed in large quantities to new locations, and then yield their ground to other species. Our old matriarch is actually a black cottonwood (*P. trichocarpa*) native to western North America, a coastal species that ranges from Alaska to California and extends inland to the Rocky Mountains. This individual has spent its life at the foot of the Cascade Range in the floodplain of a river that drains into Puget Sound. It has experienced wet winters and dry summers, occasional windstorms, and regular floods in its early life, but fewer of them later as the river moved its channel away over the years. Why matriarch? Do trees come in males and females? Actually, in most species trees are bisexual, but in poplars and willows, members of the Family Salicaceae, the two sexes are in separate individuals. And thanks to wind pollination, this old female, last member of its local age group, was able to receive pollen from males of younger cohorts closer to the river. Thus, even with a much-reduced crown it was able to again participate in the competition for genetic representation among the youngest set of seedlings that got started this year.

Cottonwoods can be deceptive: they look older than they are. Their rapid growth builds a trunk of a size that other trees take twice as long to achieve. And among poplars, black cottonwood is the champion, regularly reaching heights of 110 to 130 feet and diameters of 25 to 30 inches within 50 to 60 years. By that time, many of the older branches have broken off and the bark begins to develop deep furrows and cracks, reminiscent of an old, weathered face. It's as if they sped up the aging process in order to become respectable. You could say it's a youth culture in reverse, namely one in substance but not appearance, living fast and getting out, a tree geared for action and adapted to change. We will see these qualities expressed in many traits as we look in greater detail into its vital profile in later chapters. Not surprisingly then, black cottonwood is less celebrated in the tree lore of the Pacific Northwest than the longer-lived conifers, especially western red-cedar, the tree of life. Which is not to say that this prominent hardwood was ignored by the native people. Its trunks were often converted to small dugouts, its wood used for smoking salmon, its bark and branches for building sweat lodges and temporary cabins. And many different uses were found for the copious gum in its fragrant buds, from applying it as glue to fix arrowheads and feathers to shafts, to waterproofing of baskets, to seeking medicinal benefits from it in preparations against baldness, sore throats, rheumatism, and tuberculosis.[1] But there is no question that the cottonwoods of the western plains (*P. deltoides* and *P. fremontii*) have received considerably more attention in native mythology and poetry. In the dry expanses of the western prairies they often were the only trees to be seen and would be typically growing along watercourses and moist draws. Thus, to the weary traveler they were the welcome symbol of water, fuel, and a protected campsite—guarantor of survival.[2]

What attracts us to trees? Size for sure: trees are hard to ignore. And even more so if they stay there for a long time. In other words, we are drawn to the permanence of a large living structure that remains in one place, offers shade and shelter, changes only in small increments, and doesn't threaten us. Oaks, more than any other hardwoods of the temperate zone, are the embodiment of these characteristics and, as a consequence, have held symbolic value in many cultures from earliest times. Oak groves or individual trees, hundreds of years old, have served as communal sites for pagan and sacred rituals, for signing treaties, for festivities as well as for the meting out of justice.[3] What exactly do oaks do to achieve such status? Oaks tend to choose well-developed, stable habitats that increase the probability for a long life. Once established, they grow slowly and invest much carbon in wood of high specific gravity and great strength, developing a solid structure that can outlast storms and snow. They also divert a considerable amount of photosynthates to form defensive chemicals that protect their biomass from fungi and insects. Finally, they delay puberty until they can afford it; it may take an oak thirty to forty years to begin sexual reproduction, by which time it will be well established and likely to have a permanent position in its forest. (In my enumeration of key features I have portrayed oaks as if they willfully chose them in order to better succeed in their struggle for existence; the reader should realize that this teleological shorthand is another way of saying that mutants with such features tended to leave more offspring in subsequent generations of oak evolution—thus making them more favored by natural selection in the long term.) In sum, oaks are just about the antithesis of poplars and willows, which are found in transitory habitats, where they grow as rapidly as possible, reproduce early and copiously, and invest just enough in their woody structure to gain dominance while expending little to preserve it. Not surprisingly then, these pioneers don't have an aura of timelessness. If anything, they are destined to share the fate of revolutionaries in history, relegated by succeeding generations to the transitory role of initiators and innovators but seemingly incapable of sustaining a lasting legacy. Yet these trees have been eminently successful for a long time and exist in large numbers in many parts of the world.

If our old matriarch may thus be barred from the club of venerated trees, it deserves an honored place nonetheless because it seems to emphasize the *process* rather than the *product*. Its fleeting existence draws attention to the ever-changing process of ecosystem evolution and reminds us of the underlying forces at work. After all, the seeming permanence of an oak, as comfortable as it makes us feel, is an illusion, a mere delay of the inevitable change to come. What drives our planet are processes, and the products are incidental and temporary. What drives our riparian ecosystem are the physical processes of river dynamics and their biological consequences. What drives the adaptation of vegetation to these dynamics are the processes of evolution through natural selection, combined with chance. Process is what deserves our attention if we want to understand how what we find in nature has come about, and how it is likely to function and change. True, a process needs something to work on, or work with. Erosion can only take place on something erodible. Evolution will only manifest itself in something evolvable, a string of DNA, a beak on a finch, a leaf on a cottonwood. So in the end we need the products, the structures by which to study the processes.

In the meantime, our old tree is impressive and inspirational in its own right. It is an ecosystem in itself. Its huge biomass has miles of roots in the ground, drawing water and nutrients from deep horizons and transporting them to the youngest twigs at great heights; it builds up the soil, is host to symbionts and epiphytes, offers roosting and nesting sites to birds, feeds countless species of invertebrates, and creates a unique microclimate for all the organisms around it. And short as its life may be in the world of trees, it will outlive us all. Who knows, perhaps it already has sent a broken branch or two downriver in its earlier years, which rooted and took hold and now exist as clonal copies along a lower reach. After all, there is the process of vegetative propagation—another process—and the tree's DNA may be perpetuated *in absentia* of the original carrier. In fact, we may have to revise our admiration for the towering and lasting piece of biomass in one place and recognize how equally impressive may be the existence of a successful genotype that is thriving in many disconnected individuals across the landscape. It even opens the possibility that such a genotype could be perpetuated sequentially for hundreds and hundreds of years, offering a new angle on a "short-lived" pioneering species.

2 / THE RIVER

Puget Sound dwellers will remember the Thanksgiving weekend of 1990. It had rained for five solid days, and this after some heavy snowfall in the Cascades. Rain-on-snow is a common sequence of weather conditions in the Northwest when a cold Canadian air mass is met with a moist storm front moving in from the Pacific. But this time the five-day rainfall on Cascade passes had exceeded 15 inches, with half of that occurring on November 23 alone. It led to floods of all west-side rivers and widespread inundation across the Puget Sound lowlands. What actually happened was that a loosely fallen blanket of wet snow in the mountains hadn't had time to settle and solidify before being rapidly melted by the heavy rain. The large amount of water resulting didn't have time to filter into the soil of the steep, wooded slopes of the Cascades, but rushed down as surface runoff into the creeks, streams, and rivers, raising them at the rate of one foot per hour or more and soon beyond the capacity of their channels. Our River's discharge was measured at 79,000 cubic feet per second (cfs; or 2,200 m³s), almost four times its official flood volume (20,000 cfs).[1] It exceeded the previous peak flow of another November 23, in 1959, by almost 30 percent. Worst hit was the town below the confluence of the river's three forks where 4 homes were destroyed and 510 dwellings damaged. As reported in the local paper, the postmaster saw "mail floating on three feet of water" in the office and being left with "few dry stamps."[2] Governor Booth Gardner and President Bush declared King County and neighboring counties as disaster areas, eligible for state and federal relief.

Floods are natural events in the seasonal fluctuations of most rivers. They typically happen in spring and early summer, when winter snow-packs are transformed into meltwater, adding volume to the regular precipitation. However, the coastal rivers of the Puget Sound, such as the Snoqualmie—home of our cottonwood—Skykomish, Stillaguam-ish, Skagit, and Nooksack, have a different annual profile, as reflected in their characteristic hydrographs. *Hydrographs* are the conventional way of presenting data that depict a river's flow over time and are based on measurements taken by gages installed at strategic locations along a river's course. A typical hydrograph of a coastal river shows two highs in mean flow, one between November and February, the other between April and June (fig. 2.1).[3] But, as can be seen, the maximum flows in winter far exceed those of spring. More importantly, they are key de-terminants of changes in the riverbed through erosion as well as move-ment of sediment and large woody debris. By contrast, minimum flows are typical from July through October, the result of the low precipita-tion characteristic of Northwest summers.

Rivers are part of the hydrological cycle. Water molecules rise from the ocean surface by evaporation, are transported to the land, further enriched by transpirational moisture from the vegetation, cool down and are shed as precipitation, feeding rivers and lakes, and are then transported back to the ocean again. While this is a continual process, it shows clear seasonal trends. And the seasonal cycles in temperature and water availability have in turn imprinted the cyclic life histories of living organisms. Rivers are the conduits of water and because of their movement and dynamics are for us perhaps the most alive portion of

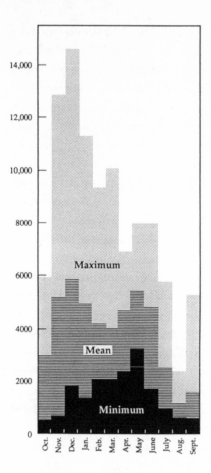

2.1 Maximum, mean, and minimum
monthly stream volumes for the
Snoqualmie River near Carnation,
King County, Washington (1931–1960).
(*From Kruckeberg, 1991, University of
Washington Press; courtesy of Arthur
Kruckeberg.*)

the hydrologic cycle. Lakes and ponds are resting, serene, and invite
contemplation—but rivers are full of action and constant change. The
foamy waves over riffles, the turbulence around boulders, the quiet flow
in pools, all are visible along the same reach and catch even the untrained eye. And when the water has receded after a high flow, it leaves
a telltale footprint: mounded gravel, streamlined sand, trapped organic
debris, bent-over saplings, and beached logs, all manifesting the hydrological forces that once again have shaped the river's channel and banks,
if only for the time being. Fascinating as this is even to the casual ob-
server, it has become a rare sight in most parts of the world. As a source
of fresh water and food, and as a means of transportation, rivers have
been a perennial attraction for humans, and as a consequence most of
them have become stripped of their vegetation, dammed, channeled,

fouled, and irreversibly turned into sterile conduits. In the many recent efforts worldwide to undo some of this damage, interest has been reawakened in better understanding riverine dynamics, untrammeled by human interference. As we will see, this also helps us better understand cottonwood and its life cycle.

In his seminal book, A *View of the River*, Luna Leopold has offered a masterly overview of rivers and their underlying processes.[4] Continual change in a probabilistic manner may be a lapidary way of summarizing these processes. But that would skip some of the elegant principles at work at the intersection of hydraulics and geology. Physicists have been known to get excited about the beauty of an equation, but even those of us in the biological end of the natural sciences admire the aesthetics of patterns brought about by the forces of fluid dynamics on erosive substrates. Who wouldn't be fascinated by the repetitive meanders rivers carve across their floodplain—named after the Maiandros River (now Menderes) in western Turkey—the unmistakable signature of a free-flowing river anywhere in the world (fig. 2.2)? Would fly-fishers be drawn to a stream that stretched out for a mile in a straight line?

How do meanders arise, and what forces maintain them? Careful and detailed measurements of rivers at varied flow levels have largely clarified the process. Let's assume that a stream runs in a straight line, both in planar view and in profile. Its bed is composed of a heterogeneous mix of particles of different sizes moving at different speeds and interacting with each other. This results in an uneven distribution of particles along the channel, bunching them up in bars or riffles, followed by pools with lesser concentrations of particles (similar to the clumping effect of vehicles moving on a freeway). These bars tend to deflect the flowing water toward a bank, and with this slight departure from the straight line a proto-meander has been initiated. What follows is the systematic accentuation of the curve through the higher flow velocity of the water on the outside than on the inside of the curve. This differential is caused by the centrifugal force pushing the water outward and carving into the outer bank while the slower-moving water on the inside of the curve has less erosive power and will deposit some of its load, adding to the point bar. As banks are eroded and point bars grow in alternating sequence, meandering becomes more pronounced. The physical processes at work also result in a more or less predictable

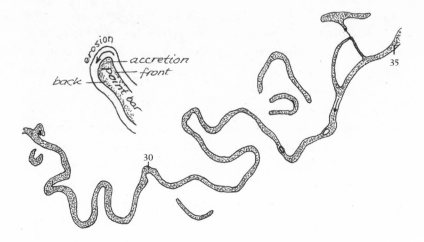

2.2 Meandering of the Snoqualmie River north of Fall City, Washington. Numbers refer to river miles from Puget Sound. (*Adapted from USGS, Fall City Quadrangle, 1993.*)

relationship between the width of a river and the size of its meanders; the radius of curvature tends to approximate 2.3 channel widths, a constant that seems to hold for meanders of all sizes, from small streams to large rivers.[5]

Are we robbing nature of its mystique in our drive to quantify one of its timeless forms? Isn't this an accountant's formula for turning an inspiring aesthetic into a metric and devaluing it in the process? Such are the occasional laments that our probing raises. To which we can only say that every one of these insights gained, be they qualitative or quantitative, heighten our marvel at the inner workings of natural processes and their intricacy. Realizing that the Fibonacci series helps explain the chambering of a Nautilus shell as well as the arrangement of florets in a sunflower and the scales on a pine cone certainly doesn't render these patterns more mundane; in fact, if anything, it lifts them to higher levels in the pantheon of natural forms.[6] Seeing meanders follow a crisp physical principle can only heighten their aesthetic appeal.

Meandering is at the heart of a river's continual change. As banks get eroded and point bars grow, the river's channel slowly migrates across the floodplain. Channel migration is the unmistakable vital sign of a healthy river. In their natural state, rivers are always on the move. And in moving they are both destructive and creative; they remove trees, shrubs, and soil, but at the same time lay down a substrate for new beginnings. And because of the differential hydraulic forces operating along a meander, point bars are not uniform across their width but differ in their physical properties along a gradient between their up-river (front) and downriver (back) side. As a result, average particle size tends to be large at the front (cobble, coarse gravel) and gradually smaller toward the back (fine sand, silt, or muck). This in turn has a bearing on the substrate's water-holding capacity and nutrient content, both of which are lower in front than in the back. By contrast, aeration and oxygen content are higher in front than in the back. These variables generate different habitats across the bar, preferred by different plants, animals, and microorganisms. They also sort out the early colonizers— for example, favoring cottonwoods in the coarser portions, while sedges and willows settle on the mucky sites. And as the river channel over the years moves away from the pioneer vegetation, allowing safe sites— sites safe from recurrent floods—and niche differentiation to develop, natural succession—the temporal sequence of plant communities— will proceed and further broaden the spectrum of species that will find a home on the bar.[7]

But then there are the spikes in the hydrograph, the floods that can violate these habitats overnight, especially those close to the main channel. This is especially true for the coastal rivers with their short, steep watersheds. Their erosive power and mass flow tend to transport and deposit large quantities of material—entire trees, logs, and coarse woody debris. Accumulating piles of this debris can shift the flow direction and result in erratic channel changes. Thus, these unpredictable, probabilistic events may have a lasting impact on the river's course. At the same time they create pulses in nutrient flow, and the piles of organic debris serve as long-term habitat for invertebrates and provide shade and pools for fish and amphibians.[8] All in all, considering simply the physical forces interacting with one another, the flowing water countered by the resisting forces of bed, bank, and transported load, Leopold sees a multitude of eventual outcomes. "The immutable physical laws of conservation of energy and conservation of mass can be satisfied by many combinations—in fact, the particular values that will exist any moment of time and place are indeterminate. Moreover, adjustment to the initial perturbation takes time and may not be completed before another chance event disrupts the condition, causing readjustment to begin anew. Indeterminacy is a principle long recognized in physics, but applicable also to fluvial science."[9] Some of this is captured in fig. 2.2, where even along this short stretch of the Snoqualmie River the meandering varies from repeatable patterns to seemingly wild departures from regularity.

There is no more graphic picture of the collective imprint left from these forces than that one can see from a plane on a clear winter day at 30,000 feet over the Delta region near Jackson, Mississippi. Below is the vast agricultural floodplain deposited by the mighty river over thousands of years. Stripped of all foliage at that time of the year, vegetation cannot hide the physiognomy of the terrain. There in the middle is Old Man River meandering southward, with active side channels looping out on both sides. Farther out are oxbows and small crescents of water, residual remnants of previous channels. Even farther out, reaching into the cropland, a vast network of distinct gray lines appear, curving through the deep brown soil, some very light, others paler, sandy memories of earlier channels crisscrossing each other and forming an intricate weave across the plain. And if we look carefully at the periphery we still can detect an occasional faded ribbon way out, miles from the current channel. If a picture is worth a thousand words, there it is on the canvas of the terrain, the cumulative history of the river's dynamics.

Our tributary to the Puget Sound is of course no match to the Mississippi. But it too has a long history of channel migration, if played out on a more modest scale. Over time it too has crisscrossed the entire width of the floodplain, touching the hills on both sides. It also has left its imprint on the land, as any farmer will tell you who is tilling his field and discovers unexpected lenses of sandy subsoil in the midst of fertile loam. More importantly, the river has left a legacy of residual woods and wetlands that form a network linking the forests on both sides of the valley and providing important corridors for migrating elk, deer, cougar, bear, and other wildlife. Thus, despite its capricious nature, despite its habit of moving its channel, or more precisely because of its recurrent disturbances, the river has maintained a permanent life zone through the valley, past all the settlements, cornfields, grazing lands, highways, gravel pits, and junkyards encroaching on it. How can this vital function be preserved for the future? This is not only a question for the Puget Sound region but in a broader sense is at the heart of all efforts now under way worldwide aimed at restoring rivers to their more natural state. We will come back to it in a later chapter and in the meantime will pursue the remarkable connection between river dynamics and the cottonwood life cycle. As we will see, the tree's life is intimately linked with the pulse of the river.

3 / REGENERATION

The point bar downriver from the old cottonwood had been essentially bulldozed by the 1990 flood. It was flat as a pool table and showed the typical distribution of substrate, with cobble at the front gradually turning to gravel, sand, and silt at the back in a smooth gradient across the bar. By the subsequent summer, a closer inspection revealed small seedlings sprouting in the crevices between the pebbles—in fact thousands, millions of them. By fall, a green sheen was covering a good part of the bar. What had happened was that the old cottonwoods on the opposite bank had shed volumes of cottony seeds, covering the freshly available substrate with their progeny. And a few months later this progeny already formed a dense thicket, with little space left for any other plant with pioneering intentions.

Black cottonwood's capability of claiming new territory hinges on a series of specialized adaptive features and the timing in which they come into play. While flowering in spring like other native trees, the cottonwood's gestation period is relatively short: seeds take only eight to ten weeks to ripen. Of course, this limits the amount of photosynthate—the product of photosynthesis—that can be allocated to the developing seed and its nutritive tissue, the endosperm. In fact the endosperm, which in bigleaf maple fills the bulk of the seed cavity, in cottonwood is a mere wallpaper lining the seed coat. Thus, in the end the seed is not much larger than the embryo inside, approximately 2 to 3 mm long. But it has one important additional feature: it is wrapped in long, silky hairs that grew out of the short stalk that supports the seed. As the capsule containing the seeds reaches maturity, it splits open and these hairs begin to fluff out, turning into the cotton that helps the seed get airborne. By now it is the end of May or the beginning of June. This means two things: The seeds will be ahead of those of other plants; and, equally important, they will find freshly scoured or deposited substrate along the river bank, as the river is now just past its peak spring flow and in the phase of gradually receding toward its summer low. Of course the process isn't as tailored as it may sound; cotton will be dispersed by the wind and its turbulence in many directions, and much of it will get hung up in shrubs or other vegetation; some of it will fall on the river and will be carried away—although a small fraction of those rafts may end up in little pools at the river's edge that may allow the germinants to set foot. As always, nature is wasteful, chance wields its scepter, and a only a tiny fraction of the original seed output will end up on a suitable substrate.

Landing on a suitable substrate is one thing, but claiming it is another, especially if you are tiny and attached to a fluffy parachute that is dragging you off with every small breeze. If the seed comes into contact with moist sand, it will instantly imbibe water and initiate the germination process within the first twenty-four hours (fig. 3.1). The seed coat will split at the radicle end and will release a small drop of a sticky fluid. A "foot" will then emerge, with a radial complement of short hairs that attach to the surface, holding the seed in place; only then does the primary root grow out of the middle of the foot—while at the same time the hypocotyl begins to elongate, raising the seed coat above the ground. The seed coat is then shed, allowing the two small cotyledons

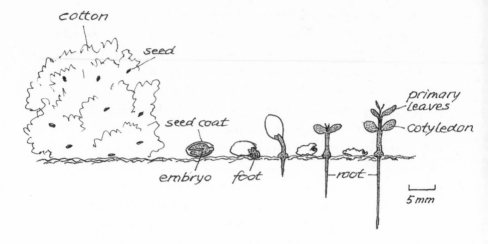

cotton

seed

seed coat

embryo   foot

primary leaves

cotyledon

root

5 mm

3.1 Germination and early seedling stages of black cottonwood.

to open up and serve as solar panels. This entire process is triggered
by moisture. In the absence of moisture, the cotton with its seed will
collect on the ground in small wads, waiting for some rain to moisten it
and press it to the substrate. Alternating sunny and rainy days, common
in spring, will thus help both the dispersal of dry cotton by the wind
and the eventual germination of the seed. But moistened seed that isn't
in contact with the substrate loses its viability in short order: another
loss of potential offspring, another price being paid for being quick and
responsive. Whereas many plants have a dormancy requirement for
their seed, in order to prevent early germination (thereby preserving it
through winter), cottonwood is opportunistic and catches the moment.
Moreover, as in most tree species, seed release and dispersal are spread
over two to three weeks for an individual tree, from the first to the last
seed, and over three to four weeks for trees within a single stand, from
the earliest to the latest tree. In this as well as in many other traits we
find a remarkable diversity packed into a local population, and as we
will see later, much of that diversity has a genetic basis and thus reflects
the process of natural selection.

But back to our successful germinant (one in a million). It has just
sent its primary root down and begun elongating its first set of leaves
above the cotyledons. No taller than 2 to 3 cm (1 inch), it keeps sinking
its root down at the rate of about 1 cm per day, maintaining contact

with the gradually receding water horizon. This contact is vital, and in order to retain it, the seedling seems to maximize root length while limiting root diameter. Thus, a month-old seedling may have a foot-long root, almost as thin as a human hair, sustaining a 2-inch shoot with five tiny leaves. A clear case of channeling juvenile growth to where it counts most.[1] It reminds me of the disproportionately long legs of young goslings, ready to meet the early demand for locomotion in water to keep up with their parents. Of course, many germinants are less lucky, especially those that got started a bit higher up on the sloped riverbank and cannot reach the receding water level. In the end, it will only be a narrow band of seedlings, paralleling the river, that will survive the first summer, those at just the right elevation: not too low to be carried away by the spring water, and not too high to miss the crucial moisture. This basic spatial geometry repeats itself in consecutive years and leaves successive bands of seedling cohorts on the slowly extending point bar as the river digs more and more into the opposite bank (fig. 3.2). And since conditions are not always favorable for seedling establishment and survival every year, there may be gaps of several years in the ages of successive cohorts.[2]

What then happens to this natural regeneration of cottonwood is best illustrated with some actual data we collected on our point bar. On a typical sandy substrate, a first-year cohort may start out with more than a million seedlings per hectare (ha), the equivalent of 400,000 per acre, or an average of 9 per square foot. In the second year, the leaf canopy of this young seedling stand closes completely and virtually prohibits any other plants getting started in its shade. But light, moisture, and nutrient supply also become limiting to those cottonwood seedlings that are not keeping up with their neighbors. Competition for finite resources above and below ground is intense and begins to eliminate slower individuals. With light being a key commodity, growth in height is now at a prime—or, as tree physiologists say, the shoot terminal becomes a strong *sink*. Sink strength determines where photosynthate is being allocated by the growing tree, and whatever goes to the terminal is not available for branches or roots. By the age of ten years, the number of live trees in the young stand has dwindled to around 20,000 per ha (8,000 per acre), or a fiftieth of the original number. This still is a dense enough stand that you'd have to squeeze your way through it.

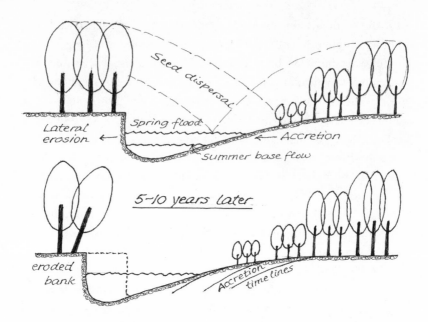

3.2 Patterns of seed dispersal, germination, and establishment in relation to micro-topographic position and river stage (spring flood, summer base flow) of a meandering river. Note the successive cohorts of cottonwoods on the growing point bar. (*Adapted from Braatne et al., 1996, with permission from NRC Research Press.*)

The survivors now are 5 to 7 m tall (~16–23 feet) and have diameters at breast height (dbh) averaging 30 mm (1.2 inches). But what is striking in these saplings is the great variation displayed among individuals, which form a continuum between what will be the likely winners and losers. If we arbitrarily divide the population in the taller or upper half (winners) from those in the lower half (losers), the winners have conquered the canopy, average 6.6 m (21.8 feet) in height and 42 mm (1.7 inches) in dbh, and have many branches. By contrast, the projected losers have fallen behind, with corresponding average measures of 3.5 m (11.6 feet) and 15 mm (0.6 inches) and very few branches. And the many dead but still standing individuals show even lesser dimensions and often excessively spindly proportions; evidently their reach for the light could not be sustained in the long run.[3]

Let's briefly reflect on what has happened so far. Of millions of seeds that were launched from an old cottonwood stand, a small subset landed at the right place at the right time; a subset of these germinated successfully and were able to keep up root growth and have access to a sustaining water source; and a subset of these were able to outdo their immediate competitors in gaining a favorable position in the canopy, increasing their chance to survive into the next phase of life. And all of this is happening among individuals of the same species, in fact among close relatives, full sibs, half sibs, cousins, stemming from the same population. What this shows is what a tough stage is set out for these seedlings on which to prove their worth, and this over ten years of fluctuating water levels, summer droughts, inundations, frosts, and other hardships. Clearly, whoever has made it has gone through many filters of intense natural selection, has shown a genotype responsive to the environmental forces impinging on it—and has been lucky.

By age twenty, within-stand competition has reduced stem numbers to around 2,000 per ha (800 per acre) or to 0.2 percent of the original number, while variation in the dimensions of individual trees is even more pronounced. Still a pure cottonwood stand, its canopy has now developed some gaps, allowing sunlight to reach the forest floor and permitting various shrub species to get started under the trees: salmonberries, snowberries, thimbleberries, and others. These shrubs have also been helped by the gradual soil formation that has taken place in the intervening years, thanks to the recurrent decomposition of organic material from falling leaves, twigs, and branches. Cottonwood stem growth in the ensuing years will keep a balance between height and radial increment until about age 30 to 40, when heights level off around 30 to 40 m (100–120 feet). But diameters will still keep expanding, reaching 120 to 150 cm (48–60 inches) or more in dominant trees of a mature stand of 80 to 100 years.[4] As a shade-intolerant, light-demanding tree, black cottonwood outgrows all its potential Northwest competitors, such as willows, red alder, Douglas fir, and Sitka spruce, during its first forty years, after which it seems to have all it needs for the rest of its modest life span. Actually, its toughest competitors are members of its own kind.

Is this type of competition unique to cottonwood? No, it is also common in alders, birches, larches, certain pines, and other early-successional trees. They all are capable of colonizing freshly disturbed sites and begin as dense, even-aged stands. Lodgepole pine carries the process even one step further: in the fire-prone interior of western North

America, it hangs on to its seed throughout its life span by having firmly closed cones that only a fire will open. The fire will also consume the trees. But from the release of that cumulative seed bank will emerge, as dense as a lawn, the next generation of seedlings—packed tighter than any cottonwood nursery. Even if subsequent competition will thin this even-aged stand to some extent, dense stocking will remain a characteristic feature of this species throughout its lifetime. In fact, tight spacing and the many dead trees resulting from it will set the stage for another hot fire, if conditions are right. Dense stocking will also keep trees to pole size—therefore the name.[5]

Darwin clearly recognized that the "Struggle for Life [is] most severe between Individuals and Varieties of the same Species," having devoted a whole section in his *Origin of Species* to this topic.[6] I'm sure he would have welcomed cottonwood to his list of examples with open arms had he ever seen it under natural conditions.

In cottonwood and other pioneers we can see a simple community of conspecific individuals—all belonging to the same species—growing up in free competition with each other. What in part determines the winners is their genetic endowment, their ability to efficiently acquire and convert resources at the expense of their neighbors. But an equally determining part must be the availability of resources and their spatial distribution. Are there any rules on how many trees of a given size can be sustained on a given site, and if so how does the natural thinning process conform to such rules? Indeed, it is in these model systems of even-aged cohorts that the changing relationships between stand density and tree size can be most easily quantified and compared. Results show a remarkable consistency among trajectories of natural thinning across species, one that can be captured in a simple equation that describes tree mass to be inversely proportionate to tree numbers. In fact, since tree mass is a function of the underlying metabolism, the equation can be extended beyond trees and plants to animal communities and ecosystems, as recently formulated by Brown and coauthors in a comprehensive metabolic theory of ecology.[7] Ultimately it shouldn't be surprising that not only are rivers subject to the dictates of physics, but that these constraints are equally binding for living systems. After all, these systems function by converting energy and transporting and distributing physical resources through their biological networks, both at the individual and community level.

What are some of the specific physical constraints a young cottonwood has to cope with? The next chapter will help us better understand these challenges and how life-history adaptations have equipped these riparian trees to meet them.

4 / WATER AND NUTRIENT RELATIONS

Having followed the characteristic development of a cottonwood stand from its inception to maturity, let's go back to our point bar and have a closer look at the environment in which these seedlings grow. It is about as forbidding as you can imagine. Squeezed between cobble and gravel, these young plants send their roots down through sand and more gravel in constant search for water and the sparse nutrients it contains. An old piece of root, exposed at the riverbank and shown above, tells the story. The above-ground conditions are no less challenging. Full sunlight is a boon for photosynthesis, but it also creates a heat buildup on leaf surfaces that needs to be cooled by transpiration. *Stomates*, the small pores on the undersurface of leaves, serve both processes, allowing for gas exchange as well as for the movement of water through the foliar tissue. But the transpirational demand requires a steady water supply that needs to be transported through the vascular tissue to the leaf. The opening and closing of its stomates allows the plant to balance these competing demands. Typically, gas exchange is high during the early morning hours and later in the afternoon but shuts down during the heat of the day. At that time, light reflection from surrounding cobble and gravel adds even more to the heat the seedling has to cope with. One way to reduce this heat load is to have smaller leaves, that is, to partition the total leaf area over many small leaves rather than a few large ones. It is transpiration, the diffusion of water through the stomates, that cools down leaves; and the smaller the leaf, the more directly it is linked to the plumbing that delivers the water.[1] This helps explain why cottonwood seedlings characteristically have narrow leaves, as narrow as those of most willows. Only later in the seedlings' life, after five or more years, when a substantial root system can provide for a sustained water and nutrient supply, will the new leaves become wider, assuming the typical ovate form— egg-shaped in outline. *Heteroblasty,* as this is called, is a good example of phenotypic plasticity, preprogrammed in the genome and responsive to the environmental cues the genotype is likely to receive.

Narrow seedling leaves are especially critical for the plant's survival during the dry summer months so characteristic of the Northwest climate. Those seedlings that make it through that period face the next challenge by fall and early winter. This is the time of rising water levels and the concomitant transport and deposition of sediment.[2] Seedlings near the front of a point bar are now exposed to the tug and abrasive forces of moving cobble and gravel. Often scoured, with their upper root system exposed, some of them may be able to hang on and make it through winter to eventually recover again in spring. Some of those that lost part of their shoot to the mechanical forces will resprout again from the base—another form of phenotypic plasticity. Exposed root tissue too is capable of sprouting shoot tissue, demonstrating the remarkable meristematic flexibility of the species. It seems that as long as some part of the root system is still anchored in the substrate, life will continue. Here let us remember that *meristems* in a plant are the growth centers where new tissues are formed. They are clusters of undifferentiated cells (like stem cells in animals) that retain the capacity to keep dividing almost indefinitely. Located at the growing tips in apical and axillary buds, and in the cambium of the stem, meristematic cells will give rise to all the different tissues of the tree.

Seedlings located more along the side and lower end of the point bar face a different challenge; they are likely to be inundated and partly or entirely covered by sediment. By the time they leaf out in spring, they may be up to their neck in sand or silt. But they don't just sit there and accept this passively. Once you start digging away, you'll find that their buried stems have sprouted small roots. This time, meristematic flexibility allows the shoot tissue to generate roots. This process may repeat itself throughout the spring floods, as more sediment settles on these seedlings, now fully in leaf. What may have been a minor problem prior to leafing out now turns into a major stress on the plant.[3] What actually happens as a result of inundation and silting is that the deeper roots begin to suffer from *hypoxia*, a shortage of oxygen, and wither away. Thus the seedlings, sitting up to their neck in water, may suffer drought stress—the ultimate paradox—because their reduced root system is unable to supply sufficient water to satisfy the transpirational demand. Here again is where the narrow leaves help make the difference that can carry the seedlings through the initial shortage of root surface until new roots have been initiated along the buried stem.

Actually, a series of specific greenhouse experiments by Barbara Smit and her coworkers have shed light on this very process.[4] When rooted cuttings of black cottonwood were subjected to flooding, the first visible reaction was a drying up of the basal (older) leaves, leading eventually to their being shed. This was followed by the withering of the lower roots. Later, new roots began sprouting higher up on the submerged stems, closer to the water surface. Then new leaves were initiated again, and shoot growth resumed. Leaves in these cuttings were those of the adult type and much larger than those of seedlings, their water demand quickly exceeding the reduced supply provided by the shrinking root system. Narrower leaves would clearly have been an advantage under these conditions. Follow-up experiments under hypoxia (where nitrogen was substituted for oxygen) showed oxygen deprivation to be a key variable in the premature death of roots. It thus appears that while running, turbulent, oxygen-rich water can sustain cottonwood root function, standing water that is oxygen-poor will not.

These experiments help explain the seeming paradox that two opposite stresses, drought and inundation, can have comparable effects on the plant's physiology, resulting in similar initial responses. The studies also support the hypothesis that narrow leaves offer a dual advantage to cottonwood seedlings in the typical environment they experience, in which they are repeatedly subjected to both types of stresses. At the same time, we may better understand why narrow leaves are also the trademark of most willows. Why should these shrubs and trees that hug the water have a leaf shape we commonly associate with plants that thrive in dry habitats? Couldn't they afford the luxury of having larger leaves that would support a more luxuriant growth, like the leaves of devil's club or those of skunk cabbage? But when we think again about the fluctuating water regime, the low water-holding capacity of sandy and gravelly substrates, and the high exposure to sunlight in a willow's riparian habitat, narrow leaves make eminent sense. In fact, these narrow leaves have enabled many willow species to also venture into harsh and dry environments in alpine and arctic regions where no poplars can be found.

The meristematic flexibility of cottonwood stem tissue and its capacity to initiate additional roots upon demand is not confined to the plant's seedling phase but persists throughout its life. As a consequence even older trees, when flooded or silted, are able to respond to this stress and tend to survive, whereas bigleaf maple and red alder don't have this capacity and will die (as is often the case at construction sites when roots of existing trees get buried by fill). Moreover, an additional, probably related phenomenon is especially prominent in black cottonwood, namely the proliferation of epicormic branches in the lower portion of its trunk. In fact, anybody who has ever climbed a black cottonwood will attest to having fought through a thicket of unruly short branches in the first eight to ten feet. *Epicormic* branches grow from suppressed buds, occasionally also from adventitious buds, which—through radial growth—become peripherally located in the bark and are then released following some stimulus, especially sunlight. These same buds can also give rise to roots if inundated or buried in silt. Thus, the lower trunk of black cottonwood has a particularly responsive zone possessing the propensity to release laterals of either kind, a flexibility presumably selected by an environment of recurrently fluctuating demands. One of the more extreme manifestations of this capability came to light after the volcanic eruption of Mount St. Helens in May of 1980. Its lateral blast caused the spillover of Spirit Lake, sending a huge debris flow down the Toutle River valley all the way to the Cowlitz River. When visiting the lower Toutle one week after the eruption, I could appreciate how massive the passing flood had been, as all the tall black cotton-woods along the river had their trunks covered with a gray mud sock up to the height of 20 feet. Later in summer, as a local resident told me, these mud socks turned green with a dense layer of epicormic sprouts. What probably happened was that the initial, temporary mud coating triggered a release of root initials which, when later exposed to light, formed adventitious buds and gave rise to lateral shoots. (But let's not infer that this was a specific adaptation to volcanic activity!)

Thus, cottonwoods have a range of means by which to balance their water demands in relation to seasonal water availability. And this pheno-typic plasticity increases as they grow taller and bulkier. From stomatal control to leaf shedding, to early budset and strategic branch dieback, they can adjust their photosynthetic demand, just as—through flex-ible root initiation and dieback—they can adjust their adsorptive sur-face and thereby regulate water supply. And the expanding trunk and branches offer an increasing body of diverse tissues in which water can be temporarily stored.

Water, of course, is also the conveyor of nutrients, whether these arrive from upstream or are already present at the site. What is avail-able at the site itself is precious little, especially for a seedling growing in scoured gravel or on freshly deposited sand. And at the time this seedling has to build up a little plant body able to face a dry summer, the waning snowmelt water is not exactly the nutrient solution needed to deliver the goods. As any gardener would ask, looking at that sterile substrate, How on earth can a plant get going in such a setting? Espe-cially since the seed didn't provide it with a generous starter kit from a rich endosperm. In the case of red alder, the explanation would be simple: alder has root nodules in which fungal symbionts (*Frankia* spp.) fix nitrogen from the air and transform it so the plant can use it and grow in frugal habitats like this.[5] But here we are dealing with cottonwood. Well, as recently discovered, cottonwood has nitrogen-fixing symbionts too. Considering how long poplars and their growth physiology have been studied, the discovery came as a total surprise. As revealed by

Sharon Doty in a series of careful laboratory and field studies, black cottonwood and its hybrids with eastern cottonwood harbor a strain of *Rhizobium tropici,* a species of bacteria capable of forming root nodules in a large range of legumes.[6] In fact, this was the first time that species was documented in a non-leguminous plant. Perhaps this is because with cottonwood, in contrast to its behavior in leguminous hosts, the bacterium doesn't form root nodules but resides in the stem—which may explain why it had escaped notice earlier. Moreover, in stems of cuttings, the bacteria are especially abundant at the nodes and in the proximity of growing buds. Further laboratory experiments have demonstrated that seedlings can be successfully grown in nutrient solutions that lack nitrogen. Apparently, the symbionts are providing the plants with the missing nitrogen in the right amount at the right time. This would be especially important during the early years of establishment and growth on low-nitrogen sites.

After what we have already learned about cottonwood seedlings and their ability to respond to immersion and silting, one detail from this recent discovery shouldn't be lost on us: the presence of the bacteria in the stem rather than in root nodules. Given the regular turnover and replacement of roots in the fluctuating riparian environment, the existence of any bacterial endophyte would be short-lived if it were tied to a root substrate. Any mutant strain capable of invading and maintaining itself in more stable shoot tissue would likely be favored by natural selection. Further mutual advantages would be reaped in asexual reproduction, as when stem fragments are shed and transported downriver to new locations; here the bacterium would benefit from transport, and the host plant by arriving with a readily functioning microflora. By contrast, as we will see later for red alder, both aspects—root dynamics and asexual reproduction—play only a minor role in that plant's life history, thus not diminishing but preserving the benefits it gains from the nodular *Frankia.*

The more we study trees with higher-resolution tools and molecular probes, the more we discover a hidden world of complexity that has remained unknown for too long. Many functions we have previously attributed solely to the expression of a tree's genome may in fact reveal themselves as interactions with the great multiplicity of microorganisms the tree harbors. And when we think of the volume of a tree and the much greater substrate on which a resident microflora may exercise its effects, we can only say that here is an underresearched domain that deserves far more intensive study. It may be that the art of being a good host is the ultimate secret of successful trees.

Having followed the fate of seedlings in their stressful riparian environment, we can better understand why, despite multiple adaptations, only a small fraction of them successfully make it through the first few years. Thus it is not surprising that cottonwoods have benefited from having a complementary second pathway—namely the flexibility of asexual propagation discussed in the next chapter—to perpetuate their existence in a constantly fluctuating habitat.

5 / PERPETUATE AND PROLIFERATE!

Cottonwood's developmental flexibility is also called into action to serve two additional purposes: to perpetuate the individual, and to make more of itself. We have already gained an appreciation of how challenging the fluctuating environment is in which this tree is growing. It seems that in its dependence on water, the tree has totally committed itself to the caprice of this vital element and its associated processes of transport, erosion, deposition, and accretion. At the mercy of hydraulic forces, cottonwood seems to make the best of it, doing so by retaining a remarkable phenotypic plasticity throughout its entire life cycle. Cloning is at the heart of this process.

It is not uncommon to see a tree that was downed by a winter flood resprout in spring. Most likely it will still have some of its root connections maintained. But a bit of digging will also show a plethora of young roots sinking into the substrate under the prostrate trunk. What then happens is that the branches on top of the trunk will become strong sinks and develop into a row of new stems, so where there was originally one tree there may eventually be a dozen of them. All of them will be clonal copies of the original, as all share the same genotype. And just like identical twins they will closely resemble each other in many traits, such as stem form, branch angle, leaf size, and sex. Most strikingly, they will all leaf out in spring in perfect synchrony with one another. In this they will stand out from neighboring trees that typically vary in the timing of bud burst. This clonal row of trees may remind us of a not-uncommon sight in old-growth conifer stands of the Northwest, namely a row of western hemlocks, nicely lined up and all of similar size. Park naturalists love to point them out and explain the role of nurse logs, fallen trees that gradually rot and then serve as a rich substrate for the next generation of seedlings to grow up on. A celebration of natural recycling, the process is often given an exaggerated spin having to do with the way a parental generation sacrifices itself for the benefit of its offspring, an anthropomorphic notion. Young hemlocks and western red-cedars are especially proficient in exploiting these logs as new nursery sites. The seedling population thus generated is, nevertheless, a collection of genetically diverse offspring from neighboring trees, often even from different species than the nurse log itself. In cottonwood, by contrast, we are looking at the perpetuation and amplification of the original individual—the ultimate in selfishness.

Of course, not all downed trees remain connected to their root system. Some get washed away by the river and end up in a pile of logs. All they will leave behind is a stump and some exposed roots. Yet here again we will see sprouts emerge, primarily around the base of the stump, the root collar, and also from surface roots radiating from the stump. As long as the tree was intact the strong sinks of the upper crown were dominating shoot growth and suppressed any such activity near the base of the trunk. But once the stem is gone, existing buds and adventitious buds at the base are released and able to exercise their meristematic potential. Thus, the original tree may extend its existence by one or more copies sprouting at the original location. A clump of trees, joined at the base, will often have originated in this fashion, especially if all members of the clump show clonal similarity as described above.

Beavers take full advantage of this resprouting capacity. After having felled a sapling or tree and removed its desirable parts, they often come back in successive years and feast on the regrown shoots. It is not uncommon to find cottonwood stumps with a history of four to five or more episodes of such subsequent harvests. And moose, elk, deer, and rabbits too depend on such a perpetual source of browse.

But why not use the river as a dispersal agent? As it turns out, black cottonwood is perfectly suited for such a fragmentation strategy, in two specific ways. Some of its twigs and smaller branches, when broken off during a winter storm, may get transported downstream by the water. If they become embedded at another point bar, they will root in the new substrate and develop several shoots in the following spring. Having a certain reservoir of nutrients and a capacity to store water, they will be even better equipped to face the first summer than will young first-year seedlings. If deposited at a relatively safe site to begin with, they will proliferate the original tree's genotype at a second location. Another mechanism, *cladoptosis*, may be a further elaboration of this process. Cladoptosis refers to the spontaneous shedding of short shoots — lateral twigs that have grown for two to three years on a branch but are then jettisoned by the tree. Rather than having broken off, these short shoots show at their base a smooth abscission surface, similar to that at the tree end of a petiole on a fallen leaf in autumn. Actively shed by the tree, some of these twigs still maintain normal rooting and sprouting functions and can again serve to asexually propagate their donor's genotype.[1]

Just how effective are these mechanisms of spontaneous clonal propagation, and how would we find out? The simplest case to assess is where multiple copies of a genotype occur together in a clump or in immediate proximity of each other. As described above, a first clue would be their similarity, a second one their sex — but with only two possibilities, that's not very diagnostic. By far the most reliable field diagnostic has turned out to be *spring phenology*, the timing of bud burst and leafing out, a trait which, in experimental studies and also in other species, has been shown to have very high heritability — that is, being under strong genetic control.[2] In other words, if members of a similar-looking clump of cottonwoods all leaf out in synchrony, they are likely to be clonal copies of each other. The ultimate test, of course, is

DNA fingerprinting, and as has been found in field and nursery studies it often will confirm the visual diagnosis.[3] Field observations of black cottonwood in spring seem to indicate that clonal clumps are more common in the hotter, drier river valleys on the east slope of the Cascades than in the moister climate west of the range. This doesn't come as a complete surprise, since under those more stressful conditions, *asexual propagules*—dispersed branch or shoot fragments—with their greater mass are more likely to persist through the first summer than the fragile seedlings. Their greater mass will store more water and nutrients and provide for a longer supply of those vital ingredients to growing tissues. With the greater tendency for cloning these propagules possess, one might therefore hypothesize that east-side populations harbor fewer genotypes per number of trees than their counterparts on the west side and, as a consequence, will show less genetic diversity from which to select new offspring. But what about the natural frequency of completely disconnected clones? After all, since branch fragments can travel there may be multiple copies of the same genotype downriver from the original. This is where field observations won't help and where DNA analysis is the only way to detect repeats. To date, no reliable frequency estimates have been made to judge how significant this form of natural cloning may be, and the question remains open.

How old could some of these clones, or genets, be? The term *genet* was coined by John Harper to refer to the collective ensemble of a genotype, including all of its clonal members that have arisen from an original zygote.[4] Thus, in black cottonwood, there may have been an original tree that gave rise to perhaps three consecutive generations of stems, all growing at the original location, plus ten additional trees downriver that resulted from dispersed propagules—all of them sharing the same genotype and therefore being the same genet. Obviously, the age of one of the current stems, which can be determined by a ring count, would underestimate the actual age of this genet by a hundred to two hundred years, and in other cases much more. How could we then determine the real age, and why would this matter? Perhaps the simplest answer is that age is one of the most basic demographic statistics of an organism, an indicator of how its life cycle relates to time and to the pulse of the environment. Obviously, we expect different features in a mouse than in an elephant, and while some of them have to do with size, others relate more directly to life span. In trees too there are differences, as pointed out earlier, between sprinters, such as poplars, birches, and alders, and marathon runners, such as oaks, beeches, and bristlecone pines. But are we justified in counting poplars among sprinters if a good fraction of them are capable of prolonging their life span through sequential cloning? And would those persistent genets, as a group among them, be genetically different from others that expire earlier? Would they harbor genes that make for greater phenotypic plasticity, allowing them to hang on through new, uncharted waters?

As it turns out, one group of poplars is actually much better suited to shed light on this question than the cottonwoods, namely the aspens. But before examining aspens, let's change course for a moment and have a quick look at another early-successional tree of the Northwest, namely red alder (*Alnus rubra*). The reason for doing so is that we now might come to the conclusion that developmental plasticity and tendencies for cloning are obligate traits of successful pioneer trees. Not necessarily. If ever you look over the western foothills of the Cascades, you see vast expanses of hardwood forests, and if they are less than sixty years old they will be solid stands of red alder. Similarly, if you hike along an old abandoned logging road, chances are you'll have to fight through a thicket of that species. Red alder is the supreme invader of disturbed upland sites of the Northwest, and for a long time the U.S. Forest Service and private woodland owners had active spraying programs against that unwanted settler in conifer country. Red alder has all the attributes of the perfect colonizer, with its rapid juvenile growth (though slower than cottonwood), early sexual maturity, and annual crops of large numbers of small, winged seeds that are widely dispersed (and don't get hung up by their cotton parachutes in branches or shrubs as do those of cottonwood). Moreover, since alders are *monoecious* (having male and female sexual organs on the same plant), every individual is contributing seed to the reproductive effort.[5] In sheer numbers of seed output, alders win the race against cottonwoods hands down. Yet we see virtually no alders in the floodplains close to the river. Why not?

Among several plausible factors, the red alder's lack of developmental plasticity ranks high. These trees have little capacity to generate a new root system when silted-in by floodwaters. They thus tend to succumb to drought stress in the following summer. Nor will they resprout from the root collar when set back by drought or mechanical damage; you virtually never see multiple stems in red alder, as are commonly found in other species of alders or in birches. Nor will stem or branch fragments set roots and turn into asexual propagules. Altogether, then, in the volatile vicinity of the river, red alder has a hard time and doesn't last very long. Add to this the lack of coordination of its seed release with the river's seasonal schedule (fall-through-spring dispersal, most of it swept away by fall and winter floods), and you can see why red alder leaves the floodplain to black cottonwood. Only on safer sites on the higher terraces, where flooding is rare, does alder have a competitive chance. And it reigns supreme in the upper watersheds, on eroding side slopes, where cottonwood's adaptive tricks have little to offer. Thus, the ultimate distribution of the two species in a watershed reveals some basic differences in their life histories. One is eminently qualified to catch the moment, instantly cover a disturbed area with seed, and then claim it (provided it won't be disturbed again); the other is tuned to the repetitive disturbances of the floodplain and uses them to perpetuate itself generation after generation.

If there is one group of poplars where the perpetuation of individual genotypes through asexual propagation will truly catch your eye, it is the aspens. Exactly how and why this comes about will be the subject of the next chapter, and our exploration will take us away from the riparian environment into more upland conditions of a northern forest belt that stretches around the globe.

PART II

Variation and Variability

In part II of this book we will meet the powerful genetic mechanisms that regulate diversity in natural populations. And poplars are ideally suited to illustrate these mechanisms at work. In plants, it is their methods of reproduction that shape the patterns of variation. At one extreme is cloning, or asexual propagation, which simply maintains the existing range of variation in a species, perpetuating the status quo. At the other is hybridization among species, which expands diversity by shuffling suites of traits beyond the species' norm—a new leaf shape, a thicker bark, or other characteristics. In between reigns a mating system in which reproductive barriers set constraints on variation and maintain the biological cohesion of the species. Over the next four chapters we will examine these processes and learn to appreciate the crucial role they play in the continual quest of trees to adapt to a changing environment.

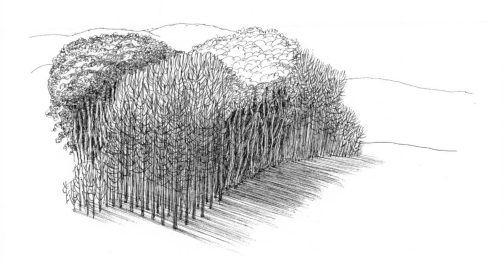

6 / CLONES

Aspen, *Populus tremuloides,* is the most widely distributed tree in North America. Its transcontinental range reaches from the Atlantic to the Pacific, and from the edge of the arctic tundra in the north to the Rocky Mountains of New Mexico in the south, in fact extending even to some isolated populations in northern Mexico.[1] And its counterpart, *P. tremula,* covers the equivalent of the Eurasian continent. Not only have these two species between themselves conquered a large tract of the Northern Hemisphere, but they are also so similar in their biology, ecology, and distribution that one might even view them as a single taxonomic entity. Evidently the ancestors of this superspecies possessed the right formula to successfully invade the emerging territory opened by the retreating glaciers and to hold onto it to this day. The only other tree that covers a similar expanse on the North American continent is paper birch, *Betula papyrifera,* with which aspen shares a good part of its range.

Linnaeus showed good sense when he named the tree *P. tremula,* after its fluttering leaves, the tree's most prominent and universal feature. That is the characteristic that seems to have drawn the greatest attention wherever the tree grows and it is the feature that has anchored it in many languages and local dialects—as quaking aspen, *Zitterpappel* (German), *tremble* (French), crann critheach (Gaelic), Nut-Ki-e (noisy leaf, Onandaga Indian), to name a few.[2] Once again, as in birdsong, a trait that has evolved purely for functional, utilitarian reasons—here, to help heat dissipation and gas exchange—has found its way into our right brain and the domain of legend, poetry, and music. And here too, knowing more about its adaptive significance from a mechanistic perspective does not diminish its inspirational value.

Within the genus *Populus,* aspens and white poplars are in a section by themselves (Table 6.1)[3] and are quite distinctive from all other poplars. One of these distinctions relates to their common occurrence in upland habitats, often in association with birches, spruces, and pines. Their adaptation to a continental climate has also equipped them to successfully cope with wildfire. In a typical burn, an aspen stand will be killed, but its extensive subsurface root system will survive and sprout a dense carpet of root suckers in the following year. These will eventually replace the old stand, and the cycle may repeat itself after another number of years. However, in the absence of disturbance natural succession will take its course, and conifers such as spruce or fir will come up under the aspen and eventually outshade it. But if a fire occurs even as late as during the transition phase, it will kill the standing trees, including the conifers, and again favor the resprouting of aspen. Thus aspen, once established, has a literal foothold on the territory. What is striking about these extensive aspen forests, covering miles and miles of the northern continent, is their clonal composition. Viewed from the air, especially in their fall coloration, they look like a colorful puzzle, a mosaic of distinctly colored patches, some yellow, some orange, some still green, and others already bare of leaves. Each of these patches is a separate genet, and closer inspection would reveal other similarities among its members in stem form, branching, bark color, and even disease incidence and browsing damage. But what is particularly striking is the size of some of these clones, which may have thousands of individual stems and cover up to several acres. And in spring, all these members will again leaf out in perfect synchrony.

Here, then, is a physical constellation that may be more amenable to providing answers to our earlier question on how to determine the real age of a genet. This growth pattern holds especially true for aspen clones that are located at the periphery of a forest and are free to expand into grassland or otherwise open territory. Here you can quantify the rate of annual expansion by measuring the incremental distance of new shoots emerging at the periphery. Given the annual rate of spread, you can then estimate how long it took a clone to reach its current size, having originated from an initial founder individual that may have long since expired. Such estimates have been made in various locations, and ages for some of the larger clones in Colorado have ranged up to 10,000 years. In fact, the claim has been made that one of these genets, the *Pando* ("I spread") clone in south-central Utah, with 47,000 stems, is the largest living organism in existence, with an estimated biomass of 6,000 metric tons.[4] Even if this may be an overestimate, it means that a particular tree genotype has been around for several thousand years and still exists happily as a stand of thousands of trees—not just a single individual, such as one of those ancient bristlecone pines that have caught all the limelight. When we think of the climate changes that have happened throughout that period and the untold number of biological challenges, this is a remarkable feat—and achieved by a poplar, a member of the supposed sprinters among trees. It is especially so in its many repetitions, distributed over two continents. Again, we may ask, How does an organism do this, and are there any common features shared by those genets that succeed? Has this to do with the perpetuation of juvenility, a retention of extraordinary meristematic capacity that may be common to all aspen trees but will come to full fruition only in a subset, or is it ordained by chance alone? Could it even be that the capacity for continual rejuvenation is sustained by the many creatures that feed on aspen, preventing its senescence?

Any walk through a northern aspen forest will show you how many appetites these trees satisfy. A series of claw marks up a stem are evidence of a black bear that climbed the tree on emerging from its winter den and fed on catkins and young leaves. Lesser marks are left by a

Table 6.1. Classification of *Populus*

(Adapted from Eckenwalder, 1996, and Dickmann and Kuzovkina, 2008)

Section	Species	Common Name	Distribution
Abaso Eckenw.	*P. mexicana* Wesm.	Mexican poplar	Mexico
Turanga Bunge	*P. euphratica* Oliv.	Euphrates poplar	Eurasia, N. Africa
	P. ilicifolia (Engler) Roul.	Kenyan poplar	E. Africa
	P. pruinosa Schr.	Desert poplar	E. Eurasia
Leucoides	*P. glauca* Haines, s.l.	Asian swamp cottonwood	E. Eurasia
	P. heterophylla L.	Swamp cottonwood	N. America
	P. lasiocarpa Oliv.	Heart-leaf poplar	E. Eurasia
Aigeiros Duby	*P. nigra* L.	Black poplar	Eurasia
	P. deltoides Marsh., s.l.	Eastern cottonwood (includes *P. sargentii*, *P. wislizenii*)	N. America
	P. fremontii S. Wats.	Fremont cottonwood	N. America
Tacamahaca Sp.	*P. angustifolia* James	Narrowleaf cottonwood	N. America
	P. balsamifera L.	Balsam poplar	N. America
	P. cathayana Rehder	Cathay poplar	E. Eurasia
	P. ciliata Royle	Himalayan poplar	E. Eurasia
	P. koreana Rehder	Korean poplar	E. Eurasia
	P. laurifolia Ledeb.	Laurel poplar	E. Eurasia
	P. maximowiczii Henry	Japanese poplar	E. Eurasia
	P. simonii Carr.	Simon poplar	E. Eurasia
	P. suaveolens Fischer	Siberian poplar	E. Eurasia
	P. szechuanica Schn.	Szechuan poplar	E. Eurasia

Table 6.1. *Continued*

(Adapted from Eckenwalder, 1996, and Dickmann and Kuzovkina, 2008)

Section	Species	Common Name	Distribution
Tacamahaca Sp. *(continued)*	*P. trichocarpa* T. & G.	Black cottonwood	N. America
	P. yunnanensis Dode	Yunnan poplar	E. Eurasia
Populus	*P. adenopoda* Maxim.	Chinese aspen	E. Eurasia
	P. alba L.	White poplar	Eurasia
	P. gamblei Haines	Himalayan aspen	E. Eurasia
	P. grandidentata Mich.	Bigtooth aspen	N. America
	P. guzmanantlensis V. & C.	Manantlan white poplar (synon. w. *P. simaroa* ?)	N. America
	P. monticola Brand.	Baja white poplar	N. America
	P. sieboldii Miquel	Japanese aspen	E. Eurasia
	P. tremula L.	European aspen	Eurasia
	P. tremuloides Mich.	Trembling/Quaking aspen	N. America

porcupine in search of the same delicacies. Clipped twigs show the activity of deer and moose or, closer to the ground, of snowshoe hares and cottontail rabbits. Careful inspection may reveal where ruffed grouse fed on winter buds. And if we get close to a lake or stream the telltale signs of the beaver will be hard to ignore. Aspen is its preferred food and its prime construction material for dams and lodges, and it has been estimated that about two hundred aspen trees will sustain a beaver for one year.[5] What will be less visible are all the removed root suckers, harvested by browsing ungulates and rabbits, and the underground herbivory of roots savored by pocket gophers. Add a host of insect species, and you get a sense of how popular this poplar is. This is not to say that the tree is happy to provide all these ecosystem services as a good citizen of the forest. It has mechanisms of its own, such as the dynamic allocation of defensive chemicals in response to browsing, to keep its herbivores at bay. But its most effective counter-strategy may well be its perpetual retention of juvenile tissues capable of releasing new shoots at every opportunity. And who knows how many of its sustaining and protective functions derive from a highly integrated and flexible resident microflora of endophytes and epiphytes?

The clonal habit of aspen, that is, the spatial spread of its clones, provides one of the most showy natural demonstrations of the power of genes in forest trees. In contrast to agricultural fields, fruit orchards, or oil-palm plantations, forests in general do not carry their heredity on their sleeve. In fact they generally hide it rather than make it evident in their appearance. A walk through a natural conifer stand will not impress you with the possibility that the size difference between two neighboring trees is the result of differences in their genetic endowment. After all, one may be younger than the other, or growing on a rockier spot, or be more shaded by a third tree, or have less access to water, or be suffering from root rot. In other words, with no genetic replication the heterogeneity of both the trees and their microenvironment is so overwhelming that genetic constitution seems like a remote cause. It's not surprising, then, that many foresters show little interest in genetics; they cannot see its relevance to silviculture. I became aware of that bias early in my role as a teacher of dendrology and tree genetics, and looked for ways to correct this misconception. And long before I had showy experiments of my own to demonstrate evidence to the contrary in field plots, aspen came to my rescue.

Thus, class field trips to the eastern slopes of the Cascades invariably involved an exercise in the study of aspen stands. It went about as follows. Students were divided into groups, and each group was assigned a pair of adjacent clones and given the task of listing and describing all possible traits by which the two could be reliably distinguished. "Reliably" meant that the particular trait was clearly evident on many individuals of a clone and that it could be discriminated from the members of its neighboring clone. With the aid of several of these traits, the group was then asked to mark the dividing line, the seam between the two clones. Usually, stem form, bark color, and branching habit got most of the initial attention and rarely failed to escape detection. In fact, even the most visually challenged student would be struck by the juxtaposition of two populations of trees, one composed of perfectly straight stems, the other of uniformly crooked ones. But what surprised the groups even more were the subtle differences that came to light simply through the number of statistical repeats and the consistency of the contrasts. Fine shades in bark color, minor differences in the patterns of branch scars, or slight divergences in branch angles emerged as highly discriminatory too, where they might have gone unnoticed by casual observation. Contrasts even became detectable in the foliage (here I have to say that these field trips typically occurred in early fall, before the leaves changed color). Leaves from short shoots (those preformed in the bud) would differ in size and shape of the leaf blade, in the proportionate length of the petiole, in the shape of leaf tips, or in the presence or absence of leaf galls[6] (the simplest way to compare these is to lay out ten leaves from one clone on a sheet of paper next to ten leaves from the other clone). In the end, dozens of traits turned out to be distinctly different between any pair of clones, and students would be proud of their long lists and their powers of observation. The ultimate message, of course, was that all these differences, so faithfully repeated, could hardly be attributed to differences in the environment—which essentially was the same for both clones. It had to have a genetic basis. We then agreed that a critical test of this hypothesis would still require several replicated trials of careful statistical design to be installed in the field and then measured. But even as a first approximation, aspen served to convince most students that genes had a powerful influence on the many traits that give the tree its distinctive appearance. (By now, I hope to have inspired a reader or two to go seek the nearest aspen stand and engage in the same exercise.)

To confirm and further elaborate on this message, I later showed students several slides I had taken in a German poplar nursery in midwinter. One of these nursery beds held half a dozen clones of one-year-old saplings, each clone in a separate row, replicated twice. As it happened, rabbits had found their way into the bed overnight and done much damage. But they showed obvious clonal preferences, chewing up one entire row, then skipping two, doing minor damage in a third, and feasting again in the replicate of the first clone. Thus, another hidden layer of genetic variation had come to surface, exposed by a selective agent. Differential palatability may escape our human olfactory sense but not that of a more discriminating rodent.

Aspen can thus be an eye-opener and may alert us to the genetic input in a tree's appearance. It is then easy to use this lesson and go to less-obvious displays of genetic variation, such as we typically find in other forest stands. Indeed, I found it necessary to take this step with Northwest forestry students (or even foresters) because of their skepticism that what may be true for aspen may have limited relevance to "real" trees—conifers. We would then look at Douglas fir (the gold standard of Northwest trees) and compare neighboring trees. Invariably, they too would differ in many subtle traits that also repeated themselves, but here in multiple branches and twigs within a tree, such as the length-to-width ratio of needles, or their color, and especially the amount of surface wax (with its bluish tinge), as well as the size and color of cones and the shape of their scales, along with many other characteristics. And as countless experimental tests with grafting or other forms of vegetative propagation in conifers have shown, many of these traits too have a strong genetic underpinning.

Two more lessons may be derived from our observations on aspen. The side-by-side occurrence of distinctive clones, each composed of hundreds or even thousands of stems, most having persisted in that location for a long period of time, yet differing in numerous characteristics that are under strong genetic control, clearly shows that multiple evolutionary solutions have succeeded in meeting the unique historical contingencies at that locale. In other words, there may be no such thing as one optimal solution to the evolutionary challenges having confronted this population over time. In fact, it is easy to envision the changing tug of selective forces operating on these stands, one year favoring drought resistance, another year height growth, a third year late bud burst, and so on—but never singling out a genotype that has it all, all the time. We may then view the resulting mosaic of clones as successful operational solutions, or works in progress, rather than as the ultimate hall of fame. And what we see here we are likely to find, and indeed do, in most natural forests almost anywhere: namely remarkable genetic polymorphisms—diversity in forms, multiple genetic variants— in adaptively significant traits among individuals of the same species.

In most tree species this variation occurs among neighboring trees, because they originated from separate seedlings (genotypes). But aspen, thanks to its clonal habit, puts these variants on amplified display.

The second lesson is how powerful asexual propagation can be in this spatially contiguous form, especially if sustained by recurrent disturbances. This becomes more obvious when sucker growth is compared with that of seedlings. Thanks to their supply of nutrients and water from existing stems and roots, suckers tend to outgrow seedlings in height by 30 to 50 percent during the first five years and may show growth superiority up to thirty years. And unless seeds land on a bare patch that will stay moist for the first month or so, they won't even have a chance to compete. Even if a sucker shoot should get disconnected from the original stem, it will be able to generate new suckers within one to three years. Needless to say, there has to be a certain output of seed, or else aspen would never spread over any distance. But here comes one further advantage of asexual reproduction. Whereas it takes seedlings ten to fifteen years before they begin to flower, sucker shoots may begin as early as six years of age.[7] Thus they have a head start, and the most expansive clones will contribute disproportionately more seed and pollen—and therefore suckering genes—to the gene pool of the next generation (assuming that there is no negative correlation between suckering and fertility). In this manner, sexual reproduction will help maintain traits that sustain the capacity for vegetative propagation in this species.

Cloning is not a human invention—nature has practiced it for millions of years. Trillions of cloned trees, shrubs, and herbaceous perennials cover our planet, especially in northern latitudes and at high elevations. In fact, the process has been so successful we may ask, What is the good of sexual reproduction?

7 / WHY SEX?

As aspen shows, asexual propagation is an eminently successful formula to hang on to life once a tree has gained a foothold in a particular place. And chances are that if this tree and all its suckers made it for a hundred years in that location, this genet has proven its stuff and has every reason to expect a happy existence for another hundred years or more. The varied physical and biotic challenges it has met should adequately prepare it for what is yet to come. So why go to the expense of sex? Why not disperse propagules that are exact replicas of its proven genotype?

Let us first remember what happens in sexual reproduction. At the age of ten years or more, a typical aspen will form floral buds on some of its short shoots. Each bud will contain the primordia of an *ament*, or catkin, composed of many floral discs that in female trees bear a single pistil, in males up to a dozen or more stamens. These tissues are all diploid, which means they have two sets of nineteen chromosomes, one set from each of the tree's parents. What then happens is that the diploid mother cells of the eventual sex cells will undergo a process called meiosis, a sequence of two divisions that (1) halve the chromosome numbers to the haploid level (to one set of nineteen chromosomes), and equally importantly (2) allow the chromosomes to recombine. This recombination not only rearranges entire chromosomes, but also involves the exchange of chromosomal segments and thereby causes a shuffling of genes. As a result, pollen and egg cells each contain a haploid set (each with nineteen chromosomes), but each sex cell will be different from every other one—in fact, thanks to the shuffling process, it is very unlikely that any two of the millions of pollen grains released by an individual tree carry the same genetic package. But, we may ask, why break up a successful genetic recipe that has proved its worth at this location for a good many years? And why then combine it in mating with another such shuffled package from a tree that may not even live in the same neighborhood? Or to put it in quantitative terms, why give up half of your genes—a loss of 50 percent of your genetic representation in your offspring—just to let them mix with those of another individual?

This conundrum has occupied some of the most fertile minds among evolutionary thinkers. After all, sex is ubiquitous in both plants and animals and also occurs in variant forms among simpler organisms. Clearly it must be successful or we wouldn't find it everywhere. Yet it comes at a steep price to the individual. What is the explanation? "Every year produces a new crop of explanations, a new collection of essays, experiments, and simulations. Survey the scientists involved now and virtually all will agree that the problem has been solved; but none will agree on the solution"—this is how Matt Ridley put it in his lucid treatment of the subject in *The Red Queen* (1993).[1] Among the many hypotheses offered over the years, the ones focused on forces of natural selection operating within species, especially parasites, seem to be the most persuasive. They posit that biotic factors are likely to be more powerful selectors than the physical environment because they are flexible and able to change in response to an organism's defenses. If so, organisms that produce varied offspring are more likely to surprise their parasites with a diversity of new problems, thereby leaving more progenies to survive in the next generation. But parasites will keep changing in turn, and so the race goes on, never really ending. That is what moved Leigh Van Valen to draw the analogy to Lewis Carroll's Red Queen, who has to keep running just to stay in the same place, when back in 1973 he elevated this hypothesis to a new evolutionary law.[2] The compelling aspect of this proposition is that, for any species, continuity is only possible via change, and that past continuity offers no guarantee for perpetuity. In addition, change need not be directional, or progressive, but may be oscillating and fall back on previous forms. So it may well be that parasites are the prime movers in the evolution of sex and, as Dawkins put it in 1990, that this idea is "promising a final solution to that problem of problems."[3]

Sex is not only an either/or mechanism—male or female—owing to the fact that it orchestrates a great variety of variables that, together, will affect the reproductive fitness of an individual.[4] Let us examine these variables in a typical poplar, for example aspen, as we follow them through the reproductive process step by step. One word, diversity, again captures what we will find among neighboring clones. In all of them, floral buds will flush long before vegetative buds, often as early as February, allowing the wind-dispersed pollen to reach the female catkins without interference from foliage. But the specifics of how many reproductive buds are developed relative to vegetative ones, how early they appear, and over what period they function, as well as how large each catkin is and how copious its pollen output, are all distinct from clone to clone. Interestingly, they will again be highly consistent among stems within a clone and remarkably consistent from one year to another. A sexy clone with great floral output will tend to be sexy year after year.

Poplar pollen is dry and light and can be carried by the wind over long distances. Once it has landed on a receptive stigma, it hydrates, acquiring fluid from the stigmatic papillae, and assumes a spherical shape. Shortly thereafter it germinates a pollen tube, which then penetrates the stigmatic surface and begins growing down into the style (as illustrated in fig. 7.1). What then happens can be nicely seen with fluorescence microscopy after appropriate histological preparation and staining of the pistil. With many pollen grains on the stigma, it looks like hundreds of luminescent roots heading down through the style toward the ovules.

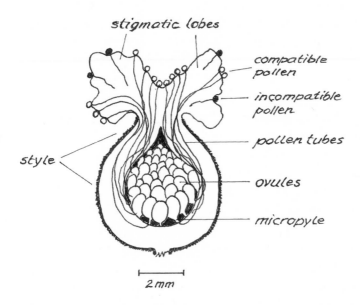

stigmatic lobes

compatible pollen

incompatible pollen

pollen tubes

style

ovules

micropyle

2 mm

7.1 Diagrammatic longisection through a female flower (pistil) of black cottonwood at the stage of pollination and fertilization.

This is a real race, and if you look as early as four hours after pollination, you can see some tubes are definitely longer than others. The first tube to reach an ovule penetrates it through a small opening, the *mycropyle*, and enters the embryo sac, where it sheds its two sperms. One sperm fertilizes the egg cell, the other the primary endosperm nucleus—in a process called double fertilization, a landmark of the angiosperms. The whole sequence, from pollen germination to fertilization, is completed within twenty-four hours and rewards the fastest sprinters. First come, first served seems to be the rule, as mycropyles, once occupied, no longer attract additional tubes.[5]

Here is where such reproductive stratagems as male competitive ability, female choice, parental investment, control of paternity, and parent-offspring conflict enter the picture. Botanists have borrowed these concepts from the fascinating insights gained in the study of animal reproduction over the last thirty years.[6] One of the commonalities of flowering plants and animals is that both spend most of their life cycle in the diploid state, with two sets of chromosomes. One advantage of that stratagem is that it allows both parental contributions to be expressed in the offspring. It also offers some protection to the offspring against random mutations upsetting the system. Any mutation disabling a gene can be compensated for by the unchanged corresponding gene (more precisely, allele) at the same location in the second chromosome since it is much less probable that two mutations will occur exactly at the same spot on two chromosomes. In both higher plants and animals the haploid phase is short but at the same time characterized by large numbers: sperm in animals, male gametophytes (pollen) in angiosperms. Selection at this stage may actually offer an opportunity to increase offspring quality. This is where the angiosperm flower may have evolved an especially effective organ, the *style,* in which the competitive value of pollen from one and the same male and from different males can be tested. As recently shown in the intensively studied model plant, *Arabidopsis thaliana,* out of 8,200 genes screened in pollen (from the 26,000 genes in its genome), 1,584 were found to be active at this haploid phase, many of these affecting metabolic rate and therefore bearing on progeny quality. Also, since the haploid phase prevents any masking of recessives, that is, making deleterious alleles unable to hide behind their normal counterparts on the other chromosome, all active genes are exposed to selection, and deleterious mutations can be purged—creating a highly effective filter mechanism.[7] Interestingly enough, there is some experimental evidence in corn that "fast" pollen generates offspring with slightly faster growth. It is easy to imagine how racing through that remarkably long silk of corn can test a pollen's worth.[8] Poplar provides a much shorter racecourse—about 5 mm in length—but even that may help to sort the wheat from the chaff.

Whereas the male strategy is to maximize the number of fertilizations, the female's is to select the best male input, as described, and to allocate sufficient but not excessive resources to the progeny. After all, in a perennial plant there is always another year in which to generate more offspring, and it may be advantageous to maximize output over a lifetime. The offspring's strategy, however, is to grab as many resources as possible, at the expense of both maternal parent and competing siblings, as happens in a clutch of nestlings. With the poplar pistil containing up to forty ovules (in black cottonwood), there is ample opportunity for competition within this clutch. Typically, only about half of the ovules will develop an embryo, and their location within the pistil will influence its size. Thus, final seed size will vary by a factor of two to three from any given pistil. This seed size is strictly a function of embryo size itself, since, as explained in chapter 3, the endosperm in poplar is almost negligible, providing a thin wrapping of little nutritious value. With little help from its endosperm the embryo will be entirely on its own in fighting for its existence once the seed germinates, so its size will matter.

Indirect evidence for the way embryos within a pistil compete for limited resources has come from an experiment with black cottonwood. We found out that pollen of this species, when irradiated with a lethal dose of 100K Rads, will still germinate a normal pollen tube, even though its nuclear material has been destroyed. Even more remarkably, this tube will grow down through the style at more or less the same rate as a normal tube and will eventually penetrate a micropyle. But since its DNA has been destroyed, it won't have any functional sperm to deliver and thus will fail to fertilize the egg cell. As a result, no embryo will form (or will do so only very rarely).[9] When such pollen was mixed with normal pollen in a 1:1 mixture and applied to stigmas, only about half the number of filled seed were obtained as compared with a normal pollination. Evidently, irradiated pollen was equally successful in gaining access to ovules, thereby preventing them from being fertilized by normal pollen. These ovules didn't develop, but the other ovules in the same pistil—which had been fertilized by the normal pollen—did develop and gave rise to embryos and viable seed. And these were significantly larger than those from pistils fertilized only with normal pollen. Apparently, fewer developing embryos meant that the larger proportion of resources available for their growth increased their size. And larger embryos would be favored in early survival after germination.[10] The experiment may have somewhat exaggerated the outcome, however, since pistils under natural conditions hardly ever get saturated with pollen, given the fickleness of wind pollination, and typically yield only few large seeds each.

The female parent has additional ways of economizing its allocation of resources to the reproductive effort. It can withdraw the supply of nutrients to non-fertilized pistils and will shed them prematurely. It will also shed entire catkins if they don't carry any fertilized pistils. Here again, sink strength determines the allocation of photosynthates, and developing embryos seem to be powerful attractors. In the final act, the dispersal of seed, it is maternal tissue that has a decisive influence on the buoyancy of the propagule, by means of the tuft of silky hairs that originate from the stalk of the ovule. The number and quality of these hairs will determine their usefulness as parachutes for the seed. When the mature capsule splits, these hairs begin to fluff out, especially on a sunny, warm day, and a small wad of a few seed will get airborne and be carried away. This process begins with capsules at the base of a catkin and will gradually proceed toward those at the tip, and may take a week or more depending on the weather. Overall, in correlation with the diversity of microclimatic conditions within a tree's crown and the staggered maturation, dispersal of its seed is spread out over two to three weeks. Given the vagaries of weather and river, it is easy to see how this hedging-your-bets approach has proved to be a successful strategy in the past and, in fact, is commonly found in other tree species.

So far, we have navigated around one basic question concerning poplars and their sex, namely, What's so good about gender and sexual dimorphism—why have separate males and females rather than packing both sexes into every individual as is true for most other tree species? The simplest answer is that all members of the Willow Family (Salicaceae) are *dioecious,* having male and female reproductive structures in separate individuals, and it may be strictly a case of historical legacy in this particular evolutionary lineage. Although this may be a sufficient explanation, let us consider some selective advantages that would maintain this condition through evolutionary time. Economically, it may be advantageous to specialize and do one thing well rather than two things adequately. For example, developing specialized flowers may allow male catkins to become much larger and occupy more positions on the tree than if some of the most favorable positions for trapping pollen were taken up by female catkins. This way, pollen output by one tree may exceed that of two bisexual trees. From an ecological perspective, such gender dimorphism allows the partitioning of niches among individuals and thereby minimizes competition for the same resources. A well documented feature in the animal kingdom, it may even apply to the Willow Family. A few studies of dwarf willows in the arctic and of aspen in the Rocky Mountains have found tendencies for male genets to be more likely to be situated on higher, drier ground, whereas more females are found in moister and resource-richer locations. The more exposed sites would favor the wide dispersal of pollen, whereas the moister, more nutrient-rich conditions would enhance a more prolonged maturation of seed and, after dissemination, the establishment of seedlings.[11] The genetic advantage of gender separation is that it makes outcrossing obligate, or unavoidable, resulting in more diverse offspring. Greater diversity of progeny may then increase genetic representation in the spatially and temporally heterogeneous environment trees commonly encounter.

The downside of separating the sexes, of course, is that the twain may not meet—a situation especially true in sessile organisms, those attached to a single spot. Although sex ratios in poplars have been generally found to be close to 1:1, local stands or populations may significantly depart from that ideal.[12] Thus, despite the airborne pollen, not every receptive female will be adequately pollinated every year. Annual flowering may compensate for this but that also happens to be true in monoecious trees such as birches and alders. In the end, we are left with an unanswered quandary and realize once again that much of our reasoning is speculative.

To add one final twist, once in a while poplar trees have been found that produced some bisexual catkins. Often they were hybrid trees, showing intermediate features of two or more species. Interestingly too, when followed over several years, some showed variable tendencies for bisexuality from year to year.[13] Apparently their genetic predisposition was sufficiently labile to be influenced by environmental factors. And in a few cases in which self-pollinations were conducted, they turned out successfully, giving viable seed. Evidently these individuals were not merely deviant but actually showed full competence in producing functional floral organs of both types. Thus, it may well be that the genetic prescriptions for both sexes exist in all poplars but that typically only one of the two is expressed in a given tree. If so, we may ask, What are the critical cues that throw the switch, and are they accessible to manipulation? Here is where genetic engineering offers intriguing new approaches that let us peek into the inner workings of sex expression and its control. We will come back to that subject in chapter 20.

Let me briefly summarize. Sexual reproduction in higher plants is a process in which a diploid individual allocates half of its genes in recombined haploid packages to sex cells, or *gametes*, and combines them with those of another individual. Among multiple explanations for the evolutionary rationale of this costly-for-the-individual process, the parasite-evasion hypothesis is currently favored. Sexual reproduction is a powerful regulator of diversity among offspring and variation within species. In poplars it is further enhanced by the two sexes being in separate trees, thereby leading to obligate outcrossing. The various stages in the reproductive act, from pollination to the dispersal of seed, open the door for natural selection, operating in both the haploid and diploid phases and in the competitive arena, where male and female stratagems may diverge, and where parent-offspring conflicts come into play.

Sexual reproduction also opens the door to pollination by invasive gametes from other species. That is especially true for pollen that is indiscriminately dispersed by wind, common in many tree species and all poplars. What could be the consequences and how can they be influenced? These questions will be the subject of the next chapter.

8 / PASSWORD?

Wind pollination, common in forest trees, makes use of a universally available agent that can be counted on almost any time of the year. It is also enormously wasteful. Pollen may be transported great distances where it won't do any good. Researchers have found major quantities of pine pollen in the Russian steppe, miles from the nearest pine stand. Other researchers trapped significant amounts of birch pollen on a Finnish light ship anchored in the Baltic far from shore.[1] All that DNA going to waste. What it means to the tree is that excessive quantities of pollen have to be produced simply to ensure that a tiny fraction will get to the intended target. And this at the right time. What it also means is that some of this pollen will land on the wrong stigma. Is there a password, some physical or chemical barrier, that will protect a female from alien pollen gaining entry? Is there a firewall that stops a "virus" from commandeering the female's genetic program and directing it toward an unwanted, perhaps inviable embryo?

What if there were no such barriers? Imagine the consequences. Suppose that wind-dispersed pollen could indiscriminately fertilize whatever stigmas happened to be receptive at that time, regardless of species—a reproductive free-for-all. Wouldn't we end up with one giga-population of continuous variation in which special adaptations would disintegrate as soon as they had arisen? Indeed, this is the very point where we come to the connection between genetics and speciation. When Darwin proposed his fundamental theory of evolution through natural selection, he hitched it to the process of species formation and published it under the title *The Origin of Species by Means of Natural Selection.* He clearly saw the importance of the cohesive unit, the ensemble of individuals that share common features and provide biological continuity in the fluid process of evolution. While he liberated the species from its divinely ordained status—still upheld by Linnaeus, the classifier of nature—and similarly saw it as a crucial unit, he couched it in biological terms. What eluded him at the time, however, was the genetic connection among a species' individuals, the physical basis of their common adaptations, and the nature of heredity. As many historians of science later mused, Darwin would have been the first to embrace Gregor Mendel's seminal work in genetics, had he known about it, as it would have given his evolutionary theory a mechanistic underpinning.

It wasn't until 1937 that the critical link was forged. Later to become known among biologists as the Evolutionary Synthesis, or Modern Synthesis, it brought together the separate fields of genetics and systematics (taxonomy, classification), the lab and the field, theoretical and empirical studies, and in the process generated the synergism of twentieth-century evolutionary biology. The key instigator was Theodosius Dobzhansky, a young Russian geneticist who ten years before had joined the *Drosophila* laboratory of T. H. Morgan at Columbia University in New York through a Rockefeller fellowship. In his 1937 *Genetics and the Origin of Species,* he digested the pioneering work of several other researchers of the period and, although not creating a new theory, developed a sufficiently coherent case to persuade his fellow scientists to join ranks—or at least respect each other's work. He soon had a partner in this effort, Ernst Mayr, a systematist and ornithologist at the American Museum of Natural History in New York, who in 1942 wrote a sequel, *Systematics and the Origin of Species*. The essential contribution they made was to frame the process of speciation in genetic terms and, at the same time, identify the mechanisms that may intervene and prevent that from happening. In contradistinction to descriptive taxonomic tradition, these scientists came up with an operational concept of the species and called it the Biological Species Concept. According to their definition, "Species are groups of actually or potentially interbreeding natural populations, which are reproductively isolated from other such groups."[2] In this view, species are not merely arbitrary taxonomic units, but real natural entities; and key elements in their continuing existence are (1) the sharing in a common gene pool, and (2) the reproductive isolation of this gene pool from other such gene pools. The duo of scientists, whose studies were rooted in the animal world, was then joined by an equally capable synthesizer from the plant world, G. Ledyard Stebbins, who initiated comparative studies in plants within this new context. His book, *Variation and Evolution in Plants* (1950), became another classic and influenced botanical research for the next twenty years and more.

So let's then return to poplar and see what concrete isolating mechanisms may actually be at work to guard the reproductive process from genetic intruders and thereby maintain the genetic cohesion of the species. A good pair of species in which to examine this are aspen and black cottonwood, which coexist on the eastern slopes of the Cascade Range. They are about as distinct from each other as poplars can be. This fact has not escaped the taxonomists, who have put them in separate sections of the genus, aspen in Section *Populus* (formerly *Leuce*), black cottonwood in Section *Tacamahaca*, the balsam poplars (see Table 6.1). And despite their joint occurrence in the interior of the Pacific Northwest, no bona fide natural hybrid between the two species has ever been documented. Careful studies in the field and the laboratory have attributed this absence to a number of reproductive isolating mechanisms that range from the visually obvious to the cryptic. For ease of reference, we will make a count of them here.

Although we find the two species in the same general area, they typi-

cally are (1) ecologically separated, with aspen doing well on drier upland sites and black cottonwood preferring moist, riparian habitats. But
every once in a while, on a moist site, the two can be found side by side.
Thus, this ecological separation is at best a leaky barrier, especially when
we think of how far pollen can be carried by wind. What now comes into
play is (2) a temporal isolation that is much firmer: whereas flowering
in aspen happens in February, it occurs in black cottonwood four to six
weeks later. Even with the usual variation in timing among individual
trees, this largely precludes an overlap between the two species, and
may be the decisive mechanism preventing hybridization. Yet in fact it
is further reinforced by additional barriers. To find them, we can place
aspen branches in the cooler and delay the timing of their flowering
until it matches that of cottonwood. When we then collect aspen pollen
and dust it onto black cottonwood stigmas, it will hydrate and grow a
pollen tube just as if it were on aspen. The tube will then penetrate the
stigmatic surface and proceed down the cottonwood style—but, about
halfway down, it will stop. According to detailed studies, what seems to
fail is a chemical dialogue between pollen and style that in compatible
matings sustains the tube's elongation.[3] Thus, (3) this barrier effectively
prevents the tube from reaching the micropyle and entering the ovule
(see fig. 7.1). However, should a tube make it all the way and deliver
the male gametes for a successful fertilization, there is a good chance
that (4) early embryo abortion will terminate the process. And in the
absence of any signal coming from a developing embryo, the pistil will
undergo (5) premature abscission and will be shed. All in all, a series of
five mechanisms together serve to prevent an illicit mating, with three
of them operating before fertilization, thereby minimizing a waste of
female resources at an early stage.

But suppose we don't take "no" for an answer and decide to probe further into how barrier No. 3 could be circumvented. Now, let's remember the remarkable properties of highly irradiated pollen, explained in
chapter 7, which seems to behave like normal pollen although it is sterile. Suppose we tried to cheat black cottonwood into accepting normal
aspen pollen by mixing it with irradiated pollen of its own. Would the
presence of familiar pollen along with the foreign one perhaps trig-
ger crucial female responses that would permit access to the foreign
gametes? (Needless to say, if we used fertile black cottonwood pollen

for this trick, it would outgrow aspen pollen and preemptively fertilize all the ovules.) This experiment was actually conducted and, remarkably, produced hybrid seedlings.[4] And, critical in scientific work, it was repeatable. Apparently, the irradiated conspecific pollen was capable of opening the door to the foreign pollen, presumably eliciting from the style a "recognition" molecule that could be borrowed by the aspen pollen tube, allowing it to proceed all the way to the egg cell and fertilize it. A true deception!

And there was no question about the hybrid nature of the seedlings obtained in this way; novel as they were, they showed the expected intermediacy between the two parent species in many traits. They were promising in their early growth, but after a few months they began to slow down and look sickly. A few survived until age ten but were no taller than 6 feet. Another isolating mechanism, (6) hybrid inviability, commonly found in distant matings, had come into play.[5] Probably the two genomes were too different from each other to allow a coordinated development of the plant in the long run. Given the taxonomic distance between aspen and black cottonwood, such developmental disharmony wouldn't be surprising. Conceivably, there might have been even one more barrier, (7) hybrid sterility, to turn this incipient path into a blind alley—but in the absence of evidence we don't really know. Altogether then, six to seven isolating mechanisms keep this pair of species from sharing their gene pools. No wonder that no bona fide natural hybrids have been found between the two.

We can see from this example that experimental matings offer a powerful tool to shed light on genetic relationships—and therefore taxonomic relationships—among species within a genus. Presumably, the farther apart two species are taxonomically, the more barriers separate them reproductively. To test this hypothesis with poplar, a careful study was conducted by Ray Guries, in which he chose seven species from three different sections of the genus (see Table 6.1) and artificially crossed them in twenty-eight mating combinations. No tricks were played with irradiated pollen; the manipulations merely optimized the mating and seed maturation conditions. His results essentially confirmed the prediction: the various isolating mechanisms were weak among closely related species and progressively stronger among distant ones.[6] Often, individual mechanisms were leaky but reinforced by others. In several cases, *reciprocal crosses* (using species A as female, species B as male, and vice versa) behaved very differently from each other. For example, whereas aspen pollen on black cottonwood stigmas had no problem penetrating the stigma in short order, black cottonwood pollen tubes on aspen stigmas seemed to aimlessly wander around on the surface, looking like twisted snakes under the scanning electron microscope.[7] In later work, another difference was found in reciprocal hybridizations between another pair of poplar species, *P. trichocarpa* (black cottonwood, abbreviated as T) and *P. deltoides* (eastern cottonwood, abbreviated as D). When using T as the female parent, many fewer viable seed (often even none) were produced than in the reciprocal crosses. What happened was that the capsules split prematurely before the hybrid embryos had ripened, although if these immature embryos were placed on an artificial nutrient medium they could be saved and turned into fully competent hybrids.[8] It's likely that what caused the problem was the shorter normal gestation period in T (6–8 weeks in the greenhouse) than in D (more than 10 weeks). A T mother would therefore jettison her seed according to her own schedule, whether they were ready or not (remember the economy of maternal investments); and since hybrid embryos took longer to mature many of them were caught unprepared. But a D mother, on a longer schedule, would carry hybrid embryos to term. What this shows is that there are different ways in which isolating mechanisms may operate in asymmetric fashion.

What we see in *Populus*, a wind-pollinated genus, gets further complicated in the many tree genera that are pollinated by insects, birds, bats, or other animals. I am thinking, for example, of acacias, basswoods, horse chestnuts, magnolias, maples, and a large number of tropical trees. Here, another layer of isolation is added, based on the discriminating power of these zoonotic agents. And hand in hand with these vectors, the evolutionary explosion of angiosperm floral diversity has further enhanced the barriers to illicit matings. What has emerged is a wide spectrum of flowers, some broadly appealing to ants, beetles, and flies, whereas others are finely tuned to bees, hummingbirds, or bats.

Dobzhansky and Mayr did more than recognize the critical importance of isolating mechanisms in the process of speciation. Their role in forging the Modern Synthesis also included bringing in the seminal work of Ronald Fisher, J. B. S. Haldane, and Sewall Wright. These three population geneticists had in the early 1930s developed the quantitative framework for the way changes in gene frequencies in populations—organic evolution—actually came about. They pinned the evolutionary process to four specific mechanisms, with their mutual interactions, and proceeded to make quantitative predictions for specific evolutionary scenarios—or, in today's parlance, they modeled the process. It was Dobzhansky's special gift in explaining the relevance of these theories to laboratory geneticists and field naturalists that led to the joining of separate research trajectories into a new synthetic effort.[9]

Since I will repeatedly refer to one or the other of these four evolutionary mechanisms in subsequent chapters, let me briefly describe them here in concise terms. Later examples will help to fill them in with more color.

1. Mutations are heritable changes in the genetic material that occur at a low frequency, more or less at random, as a result of copying errors during DNA replication, or from damage to DNA inflicted by the environment (heat, cold, UV radiation, etc.); they are the ultimate source of all biological diversity and, unless lethal to the carrier, are transmitted from parent to progeny.

2. Gene flow is the movement of genes among populations within a species via pollen, seed, or asexual propagules; it tends to increase genetic diversity in a recipient population while attenuating differences among populations. Gene flow from a neighboring population may introduce genes that confer resistance to a disease; or, conversely, it may contaminate the gene pool of a population with maladaptive genes.

3. Selection is the non-random differential reproductive contribution of genotypes to the next generation, as expressed by their individual Darwinian fitness, which is a function both of the environment and of the ensemble of genotypes competing with each other at a particular time. Individuals in a population differ in their survival and reproductive capacity, and in conveying these capacities to their progeny; this reflects their genetic endowment and how that shapes their phenotype in a given environment, as compared to their neighbors. Natural selection is the ultimate driver of adaptive change.

4. Random change, or genetic drift—that is, the erratic, unpredict-

able drifting of gene frequencies across generations—can occur when population size shrinks to small numbers; it corresponds to sampling errors in small samples and tends to result in the loss of genetic diversity. Chance, of course, is also at work during meiosis (in the shuffling of genes) and in mating (in the choice of gametes from the gametic pool). Recombination, the shuffling of genes in meiosis and mating, has sometimes been invoked as a fifth mechanism of evolution. But purists argue that it does not directly change gene frequencies. Even so, it is a powerful process in providing genetic diversity for natural selection to act upon.

All in all, it is the constant interaction of this finite set of evolutionary mechanisms with each other and with an ever-changing environment that has brought about all the organismic diversity we find on our planet today, including us humans. And even as more and more intricate details are discovered that further elaborate on the evolutionary process, the four basic mechanisms continue to serve as an adequate framework within which to accommodate its fascinating complexity.

Here let me alert the reader to the many fine writings of Richard Dawkins, an evolutionary theoretician at Oxford University, who has skillfully updated the Darwinian legacy and eloquently described it in modern terms. His *The Blind Watchmaker* (1986) and *Climbing Mount Improbable* (1996), to name just two, have turned into classics of their own and set a new standard for how to explain evolution to a general audience. They are not only exemplary in clarity of language, skillful choice of metaphors, and witty argumentation, but are also models of conveying a sense of excitement for science and discovery.

In this chapter we have gained some insight into what constitutes a species and why we should view it as a dynamic entity of interacting populations that share in a common gene pool. We also have seen, in the case of poplars, what specific isolating mechanisms are at work to maintain the integrity of the species and to prevent foreign gametes from gaining access to that gene pool. The next chapter will show that not everything is so neat and tidy and that plenty of genes seem to ignore the border patrols. This is especially true for many forest trees, and poplars will again serve as the perfect example to illustrate these effects.

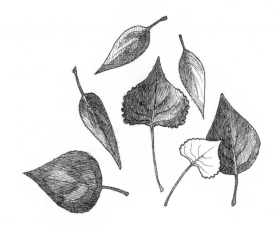

9 / NATURAL HYBRIDIZATION

It was not lost on Mayr and Dobzhansky, both zoologists, that reproductive isolating mechanisms were occasionally leaky, and that this was much more the case in plants than in animals. But it was the botanist Stebbins who pursued the topic in depth and greatly amplified the evidence. Although hybrids can be found among animals, they tend to be much rarer because of strong sexual selection; that is, behavioral mechanisms that affect mating preference (think of the peacock and its extravagant plumage). Plants, by contrast, are less constrained, especially wind-pollinated species. Even those that outsource pollen dispersal to insects are subject to delivery errors on account of distracting food sources. The probability for such events will especially increase among long-lived perennials, both as donors and recipients, because longevity allows low-probability opportunities to become real.

Furthermore, in these plants the occasional hybrid can hang around for a long time and, even if sterile, can propagate itself asexually. Eventually, a favorable mutation may occur in one of its many reproductive organs that will render it fertile. Once fertile, it may mate with both of its parental species or with others of its kind, producing novel progenies that may have a competitive edge in a changing environment. It turns out that hybridization is not only common in the plant kingdom but that it has been responsible for having generated much of its current diversity.[1]

Where would we look for hybrids, and how would we identify them? Good places would be areas where two related species of wind-pollinated perennials overlap in their distribution range. Here, just as in hybrids between horses and donkeys, we would expect intermediacy in phenotype to serve as an indicator of hybridity. Poplars, as long-lived and wind-pollinated perennials, would make a perfect choice for study. In our hunt for natural poplar hybrids we may as well start where two very closely related species come together, since, as explained in the last chapter, this is where they are more likely to interbreed. And where better to look than up in the north where humans are rarer and the forces of nature have been less compromised. In Alaska, for example, at the northern end of its distribution range, the coastal black cottonwood comes in contact with its close interior relative, balsam poplar (*P. balsamifera*). But first a word on this species. Its name refers to the resinous substance which, in all poplars of the section *Tacamahaca* (Balsam poplars), covers the buds and the preformed leaves in them. This defensive chemical the tree uses to protect itself against herbivores is very potent in balsam poplar — a single twig in a closed room can produce an overwhelming odor (in a research lab in Fairbanks I once was told about a technician who had to be reassigned from a project because she would get sick from that smell). Balsam poplar has a vast boreal distribution range that almost matches that of aspen although it doesn't reach as far south in the Rockies and the Great Lakes states.[2] It is an upland species, like aspen, but has a greater tolerance of elevated water levels and is commonly found in seasonally wet depressions. It uses the full range of vegetative propagation strategies, commonly showing root suckering even if not as abundantly as aspen, as well as stump sprouting and rooting of branch fragments. Many of its morphological features closely resemble those of black cottonwood—so much so that some taxonomists have treated the two species merely as subspecies of *P. balsamifera*.

Once on a fall trip in Alaska, driving on the Richardson Highway from the interior to the coast along the Copper River, it occurred to me that I was moving from the turf of balsam poplar to that of black cottonwood and that hybrids might be out there. So I stopped occasionally and checked the cottonwoods along the road. I knew that leaf shapes and other morphological traits wouldn't be very helpful (because too similar), so I was looking for the dried-up female catkins that had been shed under the trees. If their seed capsules were two-valved, they came from a balsam poplar, if three-valved, from a black cottonwood (one of the reliable diagnostics between the two species). And to my great satisfaction I eventually came across a number of trees that had a mixture of two- and three-valved capsules, sometimes on separate catkins, more commonly combined on the same one. Most likely, they were hybrids. But given the limited diagnostics to test for possible intermediacy, it would have taken a more careful study involving biochemical markers to verify their hybrid status. After a few miles, judging by the capsules, I was in solid black cottonwood country. Thus, the hybrid zone seemed quite narrow.

Farther south, in the eastern foothills of the Rocky Mountains in southern Alberta, opportunities for hybridization are even greater. We may call this area the great convergence zone of poplars, where balsam poplar and black cottonwood meet two additional species: narrowleaf cottonwood (*P. angustifolia*, also from the *Tacamahaca* Section) from the south, and eastern cottonwood (*P. deltoides*, from the *Aigeiros* Section) from the east. And they all interbreed and form a highly complex set of hybrid populations along the major rivers flowing out of the Rockies. In fact this zone, approximately 200 kilometers (km) in length, may well be one of the largest and most complex hybrid zones of poplars worldwide. A delight to any geneticist, it shows such a plethora of variability in any spot that you cannot help but begin to collect leaves from a group of neighboring trees and lay them out on the ground as you try to figure out the likely crosses, backcrosses, and advanced-hybrid crosses that led to them. Here we may remember that a *first cross* (F_1) between, say, the broad-leaved black cottonwood and the lanceolateleaved narrowleaf cottonwood would have a leaf blade of intermediate width; if this F_1 hybrid is fertile and crosses back with black cottonwood, the leaf width of this B_1 progeny would broaden again halfway toward the black cottonwood parent, and so on, with successive backcrosses (B_2, B_3 . . .) interpolating between the respective parents. With eastern cottonwood entering the fray, a much different leaf, of deltoid shape and prominently toothed, with a green undersurface (compared to the whitish one of the other three species) and a flat petiole (compared to the roundish one of the others) would add to the range of variation. And advanced-generation hybrids (F_2, F_3 . . .) would recombine the variable features into many new forms. Containing all these differences, the zone is a literal breeding ground for diversity. This biological treasure trove has long been recognized by researchers at the nearby University of Lethbridge, who over the years have devoted much effort toward elucidating the genetics, ecology, and eco-physiology of this population complex.[3] The group has also been instrumental in studying how natural regeneration can be successfully restored along these rivers, as we will see in a later chapter.

All along the foothills of the Rockies, on both eastern and western sides, as well as farther south, poplars hybridize. What is typical for hybrid zones is that they are narrow and tend to offer intermediate habitats between the preferred environments of two adjacent species. Thus, where eastern cottonwood will occupy the warmer, drier sites at lower elevation, black cottonwood and narrowleaf cottonwood are found higher up in cooler, more mesic conditions, and the hybrids are found in the transition zone in between. It seems plausible enough that hybrids, which carry the genomes of two or more species, or parts thereof, would be better adjusted in handling intermediate conditions than the two (or more) parental species. With that in mind, one could postulate that under ideal conditions there would be a perfect continuum of forms between two species, as one traverses a hybrid zone, with backcrosses to the two species connecting the F_1 hybrids in between. Or, to put it in formal terms, if we have species Y and Z, and if we designate backcrosses from F_1 to Y as By, and those to Z as Bz, we might expect a natural sequence of Y $\rightarrow$ By $\rightarrow$ F_1 $\rightarrow$ Bz $\rightarrow$ Z, as we go from species Y to species Z. The expected mating patterns would also favor this model. And since there would be a greater abundance of pollen from the larger species populations than from the rarer F_1 hybrids, backcrosses would likely exceed any crosses among the F_1 generation. This model may look like a geneticist's simplistic formula for nature, but today it can readily be tested with molecular tools. Interestingly enough, both conformation to and departures from the model have been found in actual hybrid zones. For example, in a closely studied area of the Weber River drainage in northern Utah, where *P. angustifolia* is in contact with Fremont cottonwood (*P. fremontii*, a close relative of *P. deltoides*), backcrosses to *P. angustifolia* were found to be abundant and in the expected zone, but those to *P. fremontii* were completely absent. Controlled mating tests with *P. fremontii* then revealed that such backcrosses resulted in inviable offspring.[4] Thus, natural hybrid zones need not always be genetically symmetric.

If poplars freely hybridize under natural conditions, as they seem to do wherever two species come together, we shouldn't be surprised to also find spontaneous hybrids where local poplars cross with introduced non-native poplars. Europe, an early center of international commerce, and having as well a great appetite for exotic species, set the stage for many tree hybrids, not just poplars, in its botanical gardens and arboreta. One good example was the introduction of *P. deltoides* in France at the end of the seventeenth century. Some spontaneous hybrids of this American species with the European black poplar, *P. nigra*, showed sufficient superiority in growth and form to the native species to receive early attention in nursery circles. Under the name of *P.* × *canadensis*, these vegetatively propagated cultivars began to be more widely planted and eventually led to the emergence of a new plantation culture that spread to other parts of Europe. By the twentieth century, specific breeding and selection programs were instituted in France, Italy, Germany, and other countries to further improve and refine these Euramerican hybrids with respect to regional needs. Many of these programs are still under way today, having originated years before when a few native pollen grains happened to land on exotic stigmas. More localized but not uncommon in Eurasia are hybrids between the various cultivars of white poplar (*P. alba*) and the native aspens (*P. tremula, P. adenopoda*). And in many parts of the world one of the most widely planted poplars, the slender, columnar Lombardy poplar (*P. nigra* var. 'Italica'), will often show its genetic contribution to native species by generating some half-columnar hybrids. To my surprise, I discovered a clump of them in my own backyard, the University of Washington campus. They were hybrids with black cottonwood and grew among native hardwoods along a former railroad track, not far from where rows of Lombardy poplar had been planted. Needless to say, they came in handy as demonstration material in dendrology courses.

What is the genetic significance of hybridization? Clearly, it opens the door to gene flow between species, at least by a crack. Even if the F_1 hybrids are less fertile and backcrosses predominate, individual genes or blocks of genes from species Y can get transferred into the genetic background of species Z (or the other way around). There, they interact with a new ensemble of genes, and their phenotypic expression will be subjected to the filter of natural selection in the new genetic environment. Even if most of these transfers end up on the evolutionary dumping ground, a few may be innovative enough and may contribute to raise the Darwinian fitness of their new hosts and their descendants in an ever-changing environment. Genetic introgression, or *introgressive hybridization,* is the term coined by Edgar Anderson (1949)[5] to describe the process. If it happens at a low rate, not overwhelming the recipient species' gene pool, we may view it as a source of genetic enrichment. Favorable genes, once having entered the new gene pool, may then gradually spread to other portions of it. That's the theory. Exactly how much this has really contributed to the adaptive evolution of a species remains unclear. With the molecular tools now available, it will be interesting to dig deeper into this process and begin to quantify the degree to which it may have already affected genetic variation patterns within and between particular pairs of species.

A second way, perhaps even more dramatic, in which hybridization may have evolutionary consequences is when, in combination with polyploidy, it leads to a new species. Here is how it works. A diploid hybrid may be sterile because its two chromosome sets are sufficiently distinct that they won't properly pair during meiosis, and thus produce dysfunctional gametes. But if its chromosomes double in number to the tetraploid level (a not uncommon error that occurs during cell division), each chromosome will now have a compatible partner with which to pair in meiosis, and so in this tetraploid fertility is restored. Self-fertilization (or mating with another such tetraploid hybrid) would then perpetuate the new hybrid line. Moreover, since this line would now be reproductively isolated from its two parent species, the two-step process would have generated a new species. This intriguing process had been discovered in the 1920s, and since then it has been experimentally duplicated by plant geneticists in many species combinations. Remarkably, a large fraction of angiosperm species have been hypothesized to have had such a hybrid origin.[6]

Now, we may ask, Doesn't genetic introgression violate the concept of biological species? And if so, how should we deal with this from a taxonomic point of view? These questions get us onto the slippery terrain of taxonomy, where no geneticist feels comfortable. As it is, even without the complication of hybridization, the idealized postulates of the biological species concept are rarely if ever fulfilled by the operational species of a conventional classification. In turn, this illuminates what an elusive unit what we call a species actually is. In fact, it was Dobzhansky himself who proclaimed that "if someone should succeed in inventing a universally applicable, static species definition, he would cast serious doubt on the validity of the theory of evolution."[7] The way we may interpret this dictum is that, in the evolutionary process of speciation, as two populations gradually diverge over time and become distinct varieties, then subspecies, then species, those taxonomic designations will in the end be arbitrary, a judgment call. And they will differ from case to case. Because who is there when the critical mutation happens, setting up an inviolable reproductive barrier that promotes a subspecies to species status? And which taxonomist will first conduct all the needed experimental crosses to test for reproductive compatibility before affording species status to a given taxon? Further, if arbitrariness of this kind clouds the species concept, how much more will it affect higher levels of classification? Thus taxonomy is part science, part art, an endeavor whose roots go way back to the earliest human efforts of looking for order in nature. No wonder the discipline is often viewed as antiquated, and that calls for its innovation are regularly voiced whenever new tools become available that allow a reexamination of past approaches to classification. Yet at the same time everybody dealing with biological diversity expects some practical taxonomic guidance for resolving day-to-day problems—at least an official list of species names that hopefully won't change throughout one's lifetime. Here once again we see countervailing forces at work—the desire for certainty versus the acknowledgment of uncertainty in a world of constant change.

The taxonomy of *Populus* has recently been revised by James Ecken-walder of the University of Toronto. He has not only conducted extensive field studies on poplars all over the North American continent, but has also brought modern evolutionary concepts to bear on the task.[8] A "lumper" rather than a "splitter," he classified the genus into six sections with a total of twenty-nine species (see Table 6.1). More recently, this was revised by Dickmann and Kuzovkina to thirty-two species. Both are significant simplifications from other classifications, which distinguished as many as eighty-five species, sixty or more in China alone. However, such a reduction is not an uncommon trend in taxonomy. It derives in part from the earlier emphasis on descriptive morphology, as well as from the historic isolation of taxonomists, most dealing with only a restricted spectrum of variation in the region under their purview. Add to this the common desire to gain recognition by the ability to designate a taxon with a new species name. And add the additional complication created in species that also have asexual propagation, producing distinctive clones that might merit taxonomic status.

Just to illustrate, I won't forget an episode in the Armenian Caucasus Minor region where an old botanist introduced me to the trees of the area. An extremely columnar poplar caught my eye, and my host gave it a scientific name I had never heard of. We kept seeing more of them over the next several hours. It was a beautiful spring day and I noticed that all of them happened to be male. When I asked this colleague, Where are the females? he explained that there were none in this species. So I thought of asking him about the reproductive continuity in this species, but knew I wouldn't get a reply (in his defense, he probably was a residual victim of the Lysenko era, when Russian genetics had been hijacked by political ideology).[9] Thus, much in a final classification hinges on how much diversity is accepted within a species, both that resulting from natural adaptation of populations to diverse environments as well as random variation. This intraspecific variation, the real stuff of evolution, as it is often referred to, will be the subject of chapter 10.

In his taxonomic treatment of *Populus*, Eckenwalder also made use of the abundant fossil record of the genus, especially the well-preserved leaves in many collections. He found sufficient evidence to suggest that hybridization between species of the *Tacamahaca* and *Aigeiros* Sections has a long history, going back to the Tertiary, a fact that may help explain why such intersectional crosses are still so successful today.[10] He also speculated that the enormous natural range of the North American aspen may have come about through ancient hybridization of several precursor species found in the fossil record but no longer extant.[11] Thus, in all likelihood, natural hybridization is not a new phenomenon in this genus but has long been an influential process in shaping the current hierarchy of diversity among its species. As we will see in chapter 20, the recent analysis of the poplar genome revealed that polyploidy too has played a role in the evolutionary history of poplars.

Before leaving the taxonomy of *Populus*, we shouldn't miss the opportunity of comparing it with that of the closely related genus *Salix*, the willows. Both poplars and willows make up the Family of Salicaceae, but the willow species outnumber those of the poplars by an order of magnitude, a difference that may well reflect the fundamental difference in pollination between the two genera. The 350 to 500 species of willows[12] are not merely a celebration of taxonomic splitting, but rather the outcome of a long history of insect pollination. Willows, like poplars, are largely dioecious, but both sexes have nectar glands and use insects as pollen vectors. And since insects are behaviorally equipped to discriminate in their foraging for nectar, they tend to visit similar plants on a given day, thereby enhancing the probability of *consanguineous* matings (matings among relatives). Such matings raise the level of inbreeding and, with that, the similarity among offspring. If continued generation after generation, populations from such matings will become internally more homogeneous as well as increasingly distinctive from other populations. If accompanied by the odd mutation that sets up an isolating barrier, new species will emerge, and this at a more rapid rate than under wind pollination, where the frequent mixing of genes will tend to blur the differences among populations. This is likely why we have in the Salicaceae Family a remarkable contrast between its two constituent genera: on the one hand the highly diverse willows, ranging from prostrate shrubs to tall trees, and with chromosome numbers varying from 2n = 38 to as high as 228;[13] and on the other the arboreal poplars, all sharing the same chromosome number, 2n = 38, and having large amounts of variation within each species, but with less distinction among them. Here is evolutionary evidence for the power of pollination systems.

For a good fifty years hybridization has been recognized as an important process in the evolutionary history of the plant world. Yet until recently little importance has been accorded to the hybrid zones themselves. Clearly these areas were the zones where hybridization happened, even if that seemed to affect only the parental species involved. Now, thanks to the studies of Thomas Whitham and his large group of coworkers at Northern Arizona University in Flagstaff, and collaborators elsewhere, our perspectives have become much broadened, with the result that these zones have been brought into the ecological limelight, in which poplars played an early leading role. Here, I will try to briefly synthesize some of the wide-ranging studies—encompassing a showcase of inter-disciplinary research, including molecular biology, chemistry, genetics, breeding, physiology, ecology, entomology, and pathology—that these scientists have conducted. Most of their studies show an exemplary integration of descriptive, analytical, and experimental approaches, combining laboratory with field trials and natural communities. Significantly too, this work has made a major contribution toward bridging the gap between genes and ecosystems and has received wide recognition.[14]

We can best begin by going back to that resinous substance of the *Tacamahaca* poplars (what resonant name!) that in black cottonwood wafts through the air as the perfume of spring, but in balsam poplar may give you a headache. It is one of several secondary compounds belonging to the group of phenolic chemicals commonly found in the Willow Family and that serve a defensive function against herbivores. These compounds (called secondary because they are side branches of primary metabolic pathways) occur in the buds, leaves, and twigs of poplars and have a bearing on the feeding, oviposition, and growth of insects as well as on herbivory by rodents, deer, and elk. While primarily defensive, they also serve as attractants to specialized chrysomelid beetles, which—in one of these evolutionary twists typical for the insect world—incorporate these chemicals to defend themselves against other insects. In the tree, concentrations of these compounds differ among different tissues; they tend to be higher in early leaf stages than in later ones, higher in juvenile than in mature twigs, and especially high in resprouts, where they may severely affect digestion in hares. Evidently they can vary quantitatively in response to the environment as well as to cues from feeding herbivores.

These compounds are under genetic control and often differ between species, just as their ingestion by specific insects can vary in intensity and protective effect. Hybrids typically contain the compounds of both parental species. For example, *P. fremontii* contains flavone glycosides, whereas *P. angustifolia* utilizes flavonol glycosides, and hybrids contain both. Now you may remember that we first met the hybrid complex of these two species in the Weber River drainage in northern Utah. There the pattern of introgression was unidirectional, with F_1 hybrids strictly backcrossing to *P. angustifolia*. It was this hybrid zone that the Whitham group studied, and they also conducted censuses of insects on these trees. What they found was a remarkable variation in the abundance and distribution of insects. With the 13 km hybrid zone at Weber River representing less than 3 percent of the cottonwood population of that drainage, they nevertheless found that it was supporting 94 percent of the population of a chrysomelid leaf beetle, and 85 to 100 percent of the population of *Pemphigus betae*, a gall aphid.[15] They subsequently expanded their survey to additional hybrid zones in six drainages and found this gall aphid to be on average twenty-eight times more abundant in hybrid zones than in adjacent pure populations of *P. angustifolia*.[16] It seemed that hybrids were the preferred hosts for these insects.

But as we know, all hybrids are not equal. The Weber River hybrid zone contains not only F_1 hybrids but also a great array of backcrosses to *P. angustifolia*, raising the question of whether the insects could tell them apart. In an elegant effort to quantify possible host preferences, these scientists made a census of fifteen common arthropods (from Insecta and Arachnida) on these trees and used the scores to classify the trees into F_1, backcrosses, and *P. fremontii* categories. In parallel, they classified the trees by using diagnostic morphological and molecular data. Remarkably, the two classifications concurred to a high degree.

Apparently the arthropods were able to track the genetic variation of their hosts. Thus, the arthropod communities on hybrids differed not only from parental species but also among different types of hybrids. The result was a heterogeneous mosaic of host-herbivore combinations that were generating a high biodiversity in this relatively narrow hybrid zone.

The findings from these studies are not unique to poplar but have many parallels with hybrid zones in other species, as found in studies recently compiled by several researchers and summarized by Whitham and coworkers.[17] There are many cases, involving species from grasses to eucalypts to conifers, in which herbivore and pathogen abundances on hybrids exceed those on parental species. And, as one might expect, species richness is further enhanced when F_1 hybrids are fertile with both parental species (termed *bidirectional introgression*), as compared to the unidirectional introgression described above. But given that herbivores and pathogens affect not only their host but indirectly also other organisms, simple cause-effect relationships can quickly become complex. In the end, the overall effect of the presence of a hybrid zone on the biological community structure—from microbes to vertebrates—is a network of interactions that reflects the complexity of the food chain. Here, numbers alone may not always be the ultimate criterion, as an occasional hybrid zone may provide critical habitat for a rare or endangered species.

Overall, natural hybrid zones have unique properties compared to the neighboring populations of parental species. They are centers of biological dynamics not only in the transfer of genes from one species to another but also in serving as evolutionary and ecological hot spots for a multitude of organisms. Yet these zones haven't received the attention they deserve, especially when it comes to forest trees. Given that wind pollination is the rule for approximately 550 species of conifers and 400 to 500 species of angiosperm trees worldwide, opportunities for natural hybridization should be abundant, even if they occur primarily among closely related species. The pines (*Pinus*, ~100 species) and oaks (*Quercus*, ~200–300 species) should be especially rich in hybrids and are indeed prominently represented among documented cases, notably on the North American continent.[18] Let's hope that the elegant and multifaceted studies described above will serve as a stimulus for other researchers to take advantage of these opportunities and shed more light on the changing biological dynamics in these hybrid zones.

The term hybrid invokes two notions: the combination of two or more entities into a new one, and the handiwork of humans. Hybrid corn, hybrid tomatoes, hybrid vehicles, hybrid technologies are a few that come to mind. Yet nature has long played with hybridization, and the plant world offers a vast arena where the play is staged. Forest trees, as conservative and long-lived as they are, have been active on that stage for ages, and to this day one can visit them in venues that offer extensive and highly accessible presentations where local actors can be observed. They even stand still for close study. Plagiarism of scripts has been rampant too—but who cares when so many different variations enliven the recurrent theme? As a longtime subscriber I never get tired of visiting another stage and seeing another version of the play, with the principals in new costumes.

PART III

From Species to Populations to Genes

Species are composed of populations, populations of individuals, and individuals of organs and genes. It is genes that set the norm for the way an individual reacts to its environment; it is the pool of genes of individuals that define a population and the way it adapts to that environment, and it is the collective pool of populations that forms the adaptive norm of a species. In the next five chapters we will study patterns of adaptation, from the population down to the molecular level, taking advantage of studies with conifers that have been especially informative. But we won't abandon poplars and will also look at oaks and chestnuts. Since adaptations are shaped over evolutionary times, we can understand current species only in the light of their recent history. That history has been strongly influenced by the last ice age and the events during a species' migration from its glacial refuges. Studies show that fluctuating climatic conditions over that period, combined with the limitations inherent in the evolutionary mechanisms themselves, have left tree populations imperfectly adapted to their current environment, let alone to an environment undergoing further rapid change.

10 / COMMON GARDENS

T his third part of the book will take us inside the species. This may be troubling for some readers since a crisp species name, especially a Latin binomial, suggests the comfortable certainty of an officially recognized unit of biological organization, a handle to nature's confusing diversity. Why probe inside? Shouldn't we be happy that someone before us has gone to the trouble of sorting things out and come up with a convincing classification and a compelling name? Can't we accept that members of a species are essentially all the same? But remember that there is some arbitrariness about classification and that even the best taxonomists wrestle with it and argue about procedures and guiding protocols. And they are the first to agree with geneticists that exciting observations and surprises reward those who look for variations within a species, their patterns, and their possible significance. After all, doesn't all of humanity belong to a single species, *Homo sapiens*, and nevertheless remain strikingly diverse?

Tree species too are rarely homogeneous. As we have learned already, many have extensive natural distributions, with some, like paper birch, ranging across the boreal belt from coast to coast, and others, like black cottonwood, from Californian latitudes to Alaska. Climatic conditions differ greatly across such spaces and will select for local trait combinations that may be apparent even to the naked eye. Aspen from Arizona will hardly be the same as its counterpart in the Yukon. We may then ask, How closely attuned are populations of a species to the local conditions, and how can these adaptations be maintained with a constant gene flow happening among neighboring populations, perhaps even neighboring species? As we will see, the only way to find out is via experiment. And forest trees have quite a story to tell. But in this chapter we will first acquaint ourselves with a series of studies that were conducted with herbaceous perennials—studies that opened a key chapter in plant evolutionary research.

"The Concept of Species Based on Experiment" was the title of a paper in the February 1939 issue of the *American Journal of Botany,* published by Jens Clausen, David D. Keck, and William M. Hiesey— the first in a series of papers that became classics in the evolutionary literature.[1] The authors, a geneticist (Clausen), a taxonomist (Keck), and a plant physiologist (Hiesey), provide another early example of the productive collaboration of scientists from different disciplines who joined their talents to shed light on evolutionary processes—in their case with the focus firmly on plants. Members of the Carnegie Institution of Washington, they conducted research at the Division of Plant Biology in Stanford, California, and the rich floristic province of California was their laboratory.

Clausen, Keck, and Hiesey—typically quoted as if they were syllables of a single word (and hereafter referred to as CK&H)—promoted a profound if simple argument, namely that taxonomy would benefit from experiment. In other words, the study of plants in situ, no matter how elaborate and detailed, offered only limited insight into their taxonomic status, let alone into the processes that led to it. Experiments, if properly designed, would add further dimensions to the information gleaned from purely descriptive observations. In fact, in the above paper, they drew attention to some crossing experiments conducted by Linnaeus that as early as 1774 had led the early classifier of nature to see the possibility of plant speciation by hybridization. Their view is well captured in this passage:

It is evident that the species problem is too complex to be solved by herbarium work alone and that the geographical and ecological methods, indispensable in all good descriptive taxonomy, are also insufficient. Cytological [chromosomal] and genetical methods of themselves are just as limited, for species and other evolutionary units are closely connected with a natural environment. Very few cytologists or geneticists study their plants or animals except in the laboratory, and the forms studied are seldom representative of those found in any natural environment.[2]

What CK&H spell out here can be put in broader terms: describing nature is one thing, explaining it is another. A plant, an animal, a biotic community can be intimately observed and described in all detail, but you have to poke it, disturb it, and peek inside to see how it functions. This may involve its transfer to another place, the removal of a predator, the withdrawal of a nutrient, or the creation of a major perturbation, and may appear to the gentle reader as violating the basic tenets of the naturalist's creed. Yet it is the only way to discover the inner workings, the underlying processes, and the controlling mechanisms that give rise to these seemingly harmonious individuals and their communities. "Do no harm" has little resonance among experimental naturalists.

Perhaps the main experimental tool with which the names of CK&H have become permanently associated is the *common-garden experiment*. Its basic purpose is to disconnect a plant from its local environment and place it side by side with plants of the same or closely related species from other locations in a common environment. In that common environment the phenotypes of plants—their appearance—will more closely reflect their underlying genotype, and the ensemble of all plants can therefore be more directly compared, unburdened from their source environments. Whatever differences are seen among them are genetic; or, more precisely, the expression of genotypes in that particular environment. If such common gardens are then established in a range of contrasting environments, say across the natural range of the taxa (units of classification), two insights can be gained. First, the variation on display may be resolved into clearly distinguishable subunits, such as coastal versus interior, low elevation versus high elevation, moist versus dry habitat, and so on. Reproductive-isolation studies, as described in chapter 8, will then suggest how to treat these subunits taxonomically, for example as species, subspecies, or ecological races (e.g., a race found only on a specific soil type). Second, some of the diagnostic characters that stably distinguish these subunits may reveal themselves as critical adaptations of plants to their respective source environments. Thus, short stature may not be merely incidental to an individual plant but common to all members of a high-elevation taxon. Finally, in the words of the authors, "When experiments have established the correlations [with the environment], such character complexes become important indicators . . . that can be used in tracing the distribution of ecotypes . . . in the field and in mapping them with the aid of herbaria."[3]

Actually, it is interesting to see how the common-garden approach emerged as an investigative tool in plant-environment relationships. As often happens in science, it came about through the confluence of parallel ideas from different people in different locations, and developed into a coherent concept in the early 1920s. Clausen had grown up as a farm boy—a curious farm boy—in Denmark. Very much an autodidact who wanted to become a competent farmer, he was inspired by his uncle and drawn to the study of the local botany, geology, and archeology. A gifted secondary school teacher then turned him toward a career in science that gained further momentum at the University of Copenhagen. Exposure to several leading botanists/plant geneticists helped him chart his course in the study of natural populations with an eye toward understanding their genetics, cytology, and ecology. He had a definite experimental bent, conducted transplantation studies and comparisons of natural and artificial hybrids, and published early results in 1921–22—just as a botanist in Lund, Göte Turesson, came out with similar papers. As Clausen later noted, "Unknown to each other, we had been working on the same subject of races of species adjusted to ecologically distinct environments at sister universities only 30 miles apart, though in different countries. From that time on, there was fairly close liaison . . . across the sound."[4]

Meanwhile, several thousand miles to the west, Harvey M. Hall, botany professor at Berkeley, California, launched a similar effort, sparked by the same idea. Having read Clausen's papers he decided to conduct transplant studies of his own, taking advantage of the diverse vegetation zones of California. To this end, and with the help of two students, David Keck and William Hiesey, he established three experimental gardens aligned between the coastal lowlands through the central valley and across the Sierra Nevada. He chose their locations at Stanford (elevation 30 m), at Mather (elevation 1,400 m) on the west slope of the Sierras, and at Timberline (elevation 3,050 m) east of the Sierra crest. Thanks to holding a parallel staff position with the Carnegie Institution at Stanford, Hall was able to confer a long-term status to these gardens.[5] Over the years, they turned into important study centers and attracted many scientists, including Dobzhansky and Stebbins, who became regular visitors. Hall and Clausen closely followed each other's work, and in 1927 Clausen was able to spend a year at Berkeley through a Rockefeller fellowship (by coincidence, the same year that another such fellowship had brought Dobzhansky to Morgan's lab in New York). Finally, in 1931, Hall was able to lure Clausen to Stanford on a permanent basis. Promising as the collaboration would have been, it was of short duration, as Hall died one year later. Clausen then became the group's leader and, thanks to the familiarity of Keck and Hiesey with the experiments, was able to continue the program.

What followed was a comprehensive series of long-term studies, covering many species complexes and integrating ecological, physiological, and genetic tests both in the field and laboratory. A central element in their research—as always in experimental botany—was the choice of plants to be studied. They had to be species that occurred along that transect, preferably herbaceous perennials that could be easily grown, cloned, and transplanted.

A good example was the choice of so-called weedy yarrows—the ubiquitous *Achillea millefolium* complex of the Northern Hemisphere and no glamour plant. In western North America, the hexaploid *A. borealis* (with six chromosome sets) occurs along the coast from the Aleutian

Islands to southern California, and the tetraploid A. *lanulosa,* to the east of it and more inland. Additional species and subspecies had been named whose biological status was unclear. Along the central California transect, the various forms occupied virtually all vegetation zones from the shores of the Pacific to the crest of the Sierra and east to the Great Basin. Given the diversity and distribution of this species complex, what guided the three scientists in their experimental study? They couldn't have stated their objectives more directly and more clearly: "to clarify the relations of the individual to the local population, of the local population to the climatic race, of the climatic race to the species and the species complex, and to extend our knowledge of the relationships between plants and their environments, thereby advancing our understanding of the evolutionary processes giving rise to these natural units."[6]

To satisfy the objectives of this particular study—one of many— seeds were collected from several individuals at each of the populations sampled along the transect (yarrows are obligate cross-pollinators), grown in a greenhouse, and random samples of seedlings transferred to the garden at Stanford. After two years, thirty of these individuals from each population were then subdivided (cloned) and transplanted, one copy at each of the three common gardens. Their identity was carefully retained throughout the subsequent three years, during which detailed measurements were taken of all key variables and their seasonal timing. Herbarium specimens were also kept for later study. And a subset of plants was later studied under controlled conditions in the greenhouse and in growth chambers to identify specific climatic variables and their physiological impact on growth and development. Whoever has found himself in the Stanford garden, let alone in the contagious presence of Jens Clausen and William Hiesey, will attest to the meticulous layout and labeling of materials in the garden, the striking contrasts among plants in size and shape, and the encyclopedic amount of data collected from all this material over the years—truly a monumental work.

Fig. 10.1 gives an example of the differences found among A. *lanulosa* plants from three different source populations, grown at the three common gardens.[7] The valley source, (c), was clearly most luxuriant and fecund when grown at the low elevation of Stanford, whereas it did poorly at Timberline. There, the alpine source, (a), was in its element,

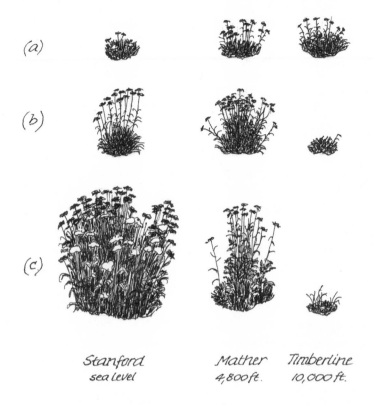

(a)

(b)

(c)

Stanford
sea level

Mather
4,800 ft.

Timberline
10,000 ft.

10.1 Yarrow (*Achillea lanulosa*) from three different source populations, (a) alpine, (b) montane, and (c) valley, grown in common gardens at three different elevations. (*Adapted from Clausen et al., 1940, Fig. 119, with permission from the Carnegie Institution of Washington.*)

but at Stanford could not take advantage of the benign environment. And the montane source, (b), interpolated between the other two. Only by growing plants from these sources side by side in three different environments could their individual genetic predisposition, or *reaction norm*, be brought to light. In addition, having clonal copies growing simultaneously at the three elevations gave further precision to the experiments, revealing the phenotypic plasticity of individual genotypes.

Based on the experiments with yarrow, CK&H distinguished four climatic races (or ecological races) in *A. borealis*, and seven races in the elevationally more diversified *A. lanulosa*. However, as pointed out in their study, since these races blended into each other along the transect, and since each race showed much variability within itself, their distinctions were not evident in the field. Only in the rigorous experimental setup, disconnecting heredity from the source environment, did statistical patterns emerge to reveal the racial stratification. And under controlled conditions, the physiological differences of certain races within species often exceeded those between races of the two species. Evidently local climatic conditions exerted selection pressures strong enough to maintain these racial differences in spite of continual exchange of pollen and seed among neighboring populations. Cryptic as it may be in the field, the report notes, "the climatic race, like other kinds of ecotypes, is therefore the basic (but usually neglected) ecologic unit, just as the species is the basic taxonomic unit."[8] Now, as any statistician will tell you, the number of such ecotypes and their discreteness may be a function of sampling. In other words, with more intensive sampling, the apparent discontinuity of ecotypes may have been revealed to actually be a continuous *cline,* or character gradient, as defined by the evolutionary scientist J. S. Huxley (1938).[9] In fact, both patterns of variation—ecotypical and clinal—have been shown to exist in many studies, both of plants and animals, as summarized by Stebbins in his classic treatise of 1950.[10]

Ultimately, the key significance of these studies was to show the reality and importance of *infraspecific variation* (variation within species) in traits related to adaptation, and to point to the evolutionary forces that maintain this variation, or force it to change in a different environment. Of course, although CK&H demonstrated that differences among ecological races are genetic, they had no way of identifying the genes responsible. That technology would not be developed until the 1980s.

There is much more to be found in the work of CK&H, as written up in their serial monographs, appropriately titled *Experimental Studies on the Nature of Species* and published under the aegis of the Carnegie Institution of Washington. Once again, their work shows how productive the synergy can be when scientists from different disciplines choose to combine their talents in pursuing a common goal. It also shows the benefits of longitudinal studies, along with their dependence on continuity in personnel, facilities, and funding. Finally, the written output in detailed monographs conveys the power of careful documentation and interpretation without regard to the number of pages—and, by the same token, the loss we have since incurred in our modern culture of short grant cycles and stenographic instant publications.

Interestingly, the idea of screening for genetic differences among populations within species had occurred to forestry-oriented experimenters long before the work of CK&H, if for more practical reasons—especially in the commercially important conifers. In fact, this interest initiated a long line of research efforts on an international scale, eventually generating information way beyond the early objectives. The next chapter will tell us more about that work and the insights gained from it.

11 / TRANSPLANTED TREES

Common-garden experiments had been initiated with forest trees almost two centuries before the work of Turesson, Clausen, and their contemporaries. And from these early studies emerged a prominent line of investigation, *provenance research,* that began to shed light on geographic variation in several major tree species. Indeed, as many forest biologists have pointed out, it is in the area of ecological genetics that forestry research may have made its earliest and most significant contribution to biology. Yet until recently this work has received little attention from the scientific community. Why? The simplest explanation is that results from these studies were often published in obscure research station reports, proceedings of meetings, or other "gray literature," or else in forestry journals, all of which fall under the rubric of applied science and are therefore easily overlooked. Science has a culture of its own, and it tends to be highly compartmentalized. With the broadening of perspectives and as much of ecological research becomes interdisciplinary, many of these gaps are now being bridged. Interestingly, as we will see in chapter 14, it is in the context of climate change that these field studies are being rediscovered by scientists and recognized as remarkably informative. It turns out that such transplant trials offer insight into the way diverse seed sources respond to new environments.[1]

The original motive for forestry provenance studies was eminently practical: namely, to find the best geographic seed sources (provenances) for planting stock of desirable quality. Of special concern was the sustained supply of naval timber for shipbuilding, especially in England and France. White oak and Scots pine (*Pinus sylvestris*) figured prominently among the preferred species. In 1745 this led a French nobleman, Duhamel du Monceau, to initiate a comparative field trial with Scots pine from the Baltic provinces and neighboring Russia, as well as from Scotland and several sources in central Europe (we must remember that this pine has an enormous distribution range that extends from Spain to northern Scandinavia, and from the Atlantic to eastern Siberia). Forty years later, it was du Monceau's nephew, Fougeroux de Blavan, who was able to see the results of the trial and to publish them.[2] Apparently they met with much interest and may have been a key element in later motivating Philippe-André de Vilmorin, brother of Louis Levêque, a well-known plant breeder, to extend the work with this species. In 1820, he began a follow-up study on his estate near Orléans, France. After growing and observing the pines for thirty-six years, he reported his findings in 1857. The results clearly showed that many of the differences in growth and form that had been observed in the regions of origin turned out to be genetically based. The best-performing sources were those from the Baltic region, collectively recognized as "Riga Pine."[3] This may not come as a surprise to those who have traveled in the Baltic region and seen those surreal pine stands, where every tree looks like an organ pipe topped by a small, fine-branched crown. A lumberman's dream. What was new was that this quality could be perpetuated via seed at other locations. A nurseryman's dream. The Vilmorin legacy in

France continues to this day in a thriving chain of Vilmorin nurseries, and documents containing his work can still be seen at the original estate in Orléans.

Interest in these findings led to several other provenance studies of Scots pine in Austria, Germany, and Sweden, and in 1908 to the first international test, coordinated by the International Union of Forest Research Organizations (IUFRO). It contained thirteen seed lots from widely dispersed sources in central Europe, which were planted at eleven locations.[4] With its documentation of bearing out the importance of heredity, the idea caught on and prompted the launching of similar studies with other important conifers, such as Norway spruce (*Picea abies*), and on this continent with Douglas fir (*Pseudotsuga menziesii*) and ponderosa pine (*Pinus ponderosa*). The European interest in exotics, especially the impressive conifers of the Pacific Northwest, provided further impetus to learning more about the pre-adaptation of individual seed sources to the intended planting environment. Even in the 1960s I was often amazed by the detailed knowledge of some British or German forester about geographic variation in Sitka spruce or Douglas fir, compared to the ignorance of a forest manager in the area where the seed had come from. Moreover, IUFRO, through its working groups, became increasingly the facilitator of this expanding provenance research and the source of technical advice on field designs, measurement schedules, and statistical analysis.

World War II interrupted these international efforts and destroyed many of the field installations. But as forestry research resumed so did these studies, both in Europe and North America. Importantly, too, the research objectives began to gain a broader genetic perspective. Increasingly, researchers were interested not only in differences in the performance and quality of provenances but also in the patterns of variation and the underlying physiological mechanisms. The study of these factors called for more intensive sampling of natural populations, larger numbers, more carefully located field tests, more sophisticated experimental designs, and more intensive monitoring. What originally had begun as an experimental approach to improve silviculture turned into an effort more closely aligned with the emergent field of genecology, a merger of genetics and ecology, a term coined by Turesson (1923), the Swedish botanist we met in chapter 10.[5] One good example of that type

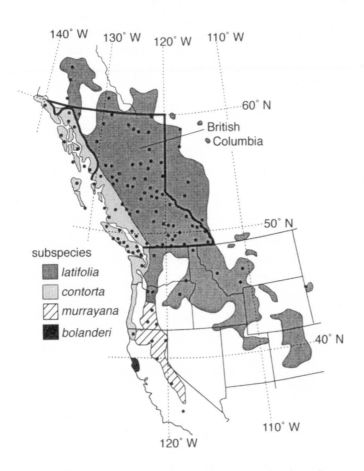

11.1 Distribution range of lodgepole pine (*Pinus contorta*) and its subspecies in western North America. Dots indicate populations sampled in the Illingworth study. (*From Rehfeldt et al., 1999, with permission from the Ecological Society of America.*)

of study is the large-scale provenance test of lodgepole pine established in British Columbia by Keith Illingworth of the B.C. Forest Service in the mid-1970s. An ambitious undertaking, it involved seed collections from 140 source populations throughout the large distribution range of the species. The seeds were then planted in sixty carefully replicated field trials across the province and in the Yukon (fig. 11.1). For more than twenty-five years, the B.C. Forest Service has maintained this large array of test plantations, regularly remeasuring them and keeping careful records. Given the vagaries in budgetary priorities and political pressures common to all public agencies, that such a program is being seen through to its fruition speaks for the foresight and persistence of these researchers and administrators. We will meet this study again in chapter 14 and will see how its data are helping to shed light on tree adaptation to a changing climate.

Actually, there are other experiments with even longer track records[6]—although owing to a lack of adequate statistical design their information has often been limited. And then there are many others that met all design criteria but were prematurely discontinued because of changing priorities, administrative neglect, or lack of funding. Tree research is by its very nature long term. While the early years of a field test may give valuable information on phenology, disease susceptibility, and response to climatic extremes—frost, drought, storms, and the like—it takes longer for patterns in sequential growth, stability, and reproduction to reveal themselves.

What was learned from this enormous body of provenance research in forestry, and what were the practical consequences? Let me try to distill the essentials. As we may well expect, species with large distribution ranges tend to harbor more genetic diversity than those with small ranges. But each species has its unique profile of genetic diversity. Even species from the same region may differ from one another, some being fine-scaled specialists (showing genetic differences over short distances), others coarser-scaled, while still others are broad generalists, showing little genetic variation even across highly contrasting environments. Another expected trend shows that a plant from the native seed source is generally attuned to the local climate but is not necessarily the best performer; progeny from some other sources may outgrow it on its home ground. Finally, in a number of species some seed sources have shown a significantly broader range of adaptability to new conditions than others—often beyond simple explanation. From a practical perspective, what has become abundantly obvious is that seed source matters. This message was heard loud and clear, and as a consequence seed collection guidelines were issued for the most important commercial tree species.[7] By the 1970s, origin-certified seed had become a widely accepted requirement for reforestation in many parts of the world.

One more insight gained in these studies was that, regardless of differences found among provenances, there always tended to be a residual amount of genetic variation on display within individual provenances, with this emerging in various traits. Evidently, some genetic diversity in forest trees exists even at a local level—offering an ultimate source of potentially adaptive germ plasm for an uncertain future.

With that general background, let us examine what is meant by a tree being attuned to the local climate. What specific traits are involved, and to which environmental variables are they geared? Here again, poplar offers a wealth of insights, as recently summarized by Robert Farmer, a long-term student of the genus.[8] One of the major variables to which trees have to adapt is the timing of their growth period so as to match the local seasonal cycle. Thus, in a species that covers a large latitudinal range, its northern populations, adapted to early fall weather, set buds under the relatively long days at that time of year; more southern populations do the same under shorter days at a later time. If northern-provenance trees are grown at more southerly sites, they will still follow their genetic program, close down their growth, and set buds early (under long days), thereby forgoing the benefits of a prolonged growing season at their new location and, as a consequence, will remain small. Conversely, southern-provenance trees grown in the north will keep up their growth too long in the fall, waiting for short days to set bud, and will get damaged or even killed by early frosts. Tests of aspen provenances, conducted in growth chambers in which several light and temperature regimes could be tested, showed that *photoperiod*—the number of daylight hours—was the critical cue that triggered budset. Bud break in spring is similarly programmed and does not yield to the new conditions in a transplant environment. The same trend holds true for differences in source elevation: high-elevation provenances tend to start growth late in spring and terminate it early, even if given mild conditions at low elevation, just as CK&H found in yarrow. Evidently, long-lasting seasonal cycles have exerted sufficient selection pressure to fit trees into the likely periodicity of their home turf by building the timing control into their genetic program. However, that doesn't mean that all trees at that source are in perfect synchrony—only that the population mean will differ from that of another provenance.

Looking further, it's clear that among the strong selectors of fitness genes are not only the timing of seasonal cycles, but also the moisture and temperature regimes of the growing season. Thus a species such as eastern cottonwood, found both in the humid climate of the southern United States and in the arid west of the prairies, is likely to reflect this in physiological and morphological traits. One such trait is leaf size, and—as smaller leaves seem to better cope with heat and drought—the geographic trend roughly follows a gradient, with large leaves in the moist southeast gradually becoming small ones in the drier west. And since leaf size and shape are often used as diagnostic features in trees, these differences led earlier taxonomists to distinguish up to five different species of cottonwoods in what today is treated as a single species, *P. deltoides*, with its three subspecies, *deltoides*, *monilifera*, and *wislizeni*. Another cottonwood that experiences sharply contrasting climatic conditions is black cottonwood, *P. trichocarpa*, and this over even shorter distances across the Cascade Range in the Pacific Northwest. These mountains separate a moist maritime climate on the western side from a dry continental climate on the eastern side. Black cottonwood grows along rivers on both sides, from their upper drainages at 3,000 foot elevations down to the lower reaches. Two such rivers, the Nisqually on the west side and the Yakima on the east, form a pair of contrasting valleys that begged the question of how cottonwoods had adapted to these divergent conditions. Interest in understanding this led to a common-garden study that is worth describing here since it is an example of many others conducted elsewhere and has revealed in great detail how, over time, selection pressures mold a species into distinctive ecological races or populations—and how we find out about that. Since the research involved only two common gardens, it is also straightforward to interpret. We will call it the Dunlap study, named for Joan Dunlap, who conducted it for her doctoral research at the University of Washington.[9]

In the Dunlap study, the two key variables that determine growth conditions along the two rivers, precipitation and temperature, are strikingly different. Along the maritime Nisqually valley, annual precipitation increases from 41 inches in the lowlands to 81 inches at the upper elevations of 3,300 feet, while along the Yakima it decreases from 71 inches east of the Cascade crest to a low of 8 inches at the lower end. The corresponding maximum July temperatures range from 75 to 79°F for the Nisqually and from 79 to 90°F along the Yakima. The native vegetations reflect these contrasts, the western slope being covered by coniferous forests, and the eastern slope in its upper portion by conifers, which then change into an open shrub-steppe at the lower elevation, where evaporation and transpiration rates are high. Cottonwood stands along the two rivers traverse these different vegetation zones, offering many sampling populations for experimental study. The Dunlap study involved cuttings taken from forty-two individual trees sampled along the length of each river and over elevational differences of 3,000 feet. Cuttings were first grown in one location for one year (in order to equalize their condition) before being outplanted in twelve replicates (repeats) at two test sites (common gardens), one at Puyallup in the Puget Sound lowland, the other near Wenatchee in the dry interior. Both sites were managed to control weeds and rodents and were irrigated so as to assure survival. Intensive measurements were taken during the first two years and these were then complemented with studies of selected traits on cuttings grown under highly controlled conditions in growth chambers.

Results at the Puyallup test site west of the Cascades showed that clones from the maritime Nisqually valley were larger in stem, branch, and leaf traits, broke buds earlier in spring and set them later in fall; they were more resistant to leaf rust, and had lower photosynthetic rates when exposed to high light levels than clones from the more continental Yakima valley. Most of these differences were as expected and evidently genetic. But the Yakima valley materials were not so uniform. Those from the hotter, drier zone (the lower shrub-steppe) were branchier and more densely covered with smaller and thinner leaves than those from the upper, forested zone. These smaller leaves were also more densely packed with stomates, and this on both leaf surfaces.[10] This is a common adaptation to hot/dry conditions, often found in other tree species,[11] because it allows a plant to maximize gas exchange during the short period of the day (early morning) when conditions are favorable, after which the stomates close down to minimize water loss and photosynthesis ceases for the remainder of the day. All in all, adaptation of these eastern-slope cottonwoods involved a whole suite of characteristics, presumably brought about over time as different mutations of many genes were selected in populations experiencing those divergent environments. Yet beyond genetic differences the

common-garden experiment also showed evidence for short-term acclimation. All materials grown at the hotter Wenatchee site, regardless of
source, showed higher stomatal density (number per unit of leaf area)
and higher photosynthetic rates, when tested at high temperature, than
their "identical twins" grown at Puyallup. In other words, clones were
able to make certain adjustments to current conditions, even if those
exceeded the values of their native source environment—a clear case of
phenotypic plasticity.

The contrasts between black cottonwoods growing east and west of
the Cascades are interesting enough. But equally significant are the genetic differences as one goes from the upper to the lower Yakima Valley,
because these show a dramatic change in populations over a distance
of less than 10 miles. That transition takes place in Bristol Canyon,
between Cle Elum and Ellensburg, and coincides with a change in
the surrounding vegetation from open ponderosa pine stands to xeric
shrub-steppe. Cottonwoods grow along the river throughout that zone
but change both in their appearance and evidently also in their genes.
Apparently, the strong selective pressures exerted by the environment
have been able to counter any gene flow between neighboring populations via pollen and seed, and this even as the river serves as an additional agent of gene flow for seed and asexual propagules. In other
words, any migrants from the upper zone, or any hybrids between the
two zones, would tend to be outcompeted by the fitter local offspring
downriver.

The Dunlap study and its findings have practical implications for
forestry and conservation. One of the current problems in the valleys of
the Washington and Oregon interior is the lack of tree vegetation along
the lower reaches of their rivers. Historical photographs and written
records from the eighteenth and nineteenth centuries describe these
bottomlands as mantled with extensive forests of cottonwoods and willows. It is the spread of settlements, cropland, and grazing land that
has systematically eliminated this vegetation over the years. In current
programs aimed at improving streams and restoring riparian habitat
for fish and wildlife, efforts are under way to bring back native trees
to these bare valley bottoms. The question is, where to get the proper
material. Since black cottonwood still can be found at higher elevations
in these valleys, the temptation is to collect seed or cuttings from those

upper-elevation trees. This would clearly be a mistake, as such clones would do poorly under the hot and droughty conditions downriver (as in fact was shown by some small-scale field tests conducted by the U.S. Forest Service in the interior of Oregon).[12] Any transfer of materials would be better if made from corresponding elevational zones in neighboring valleys, if these are still available. Alternatively, cuttings might even be collected from drought-adapted *P. deltoides* or hybrid stands at lower elevations—especially given the prospect of increased temperatures in the future due to climate warming.

The last four chapters have illustrated what an abundance of variation exists out there in natural populations of trees, and plants in general, and how this diversity reflects the evolutionary forces that have shaped them under the long-term influences of the environment. Some of this variation is evident to the naked eye. Some of it is more cryptic and has to be teased out artificially, as through transplantation studies in common gardens, elaborate provenance tests, greenhouse experiments, or via artificial crosses. And while some of this variation falls into clear patterns that form the basis for taxonomic classification, other aspects of it defy any ordering and may be viewed as evolutionary noise—or at best as a genetic reservoir for future adaptations to new conditions. Thus in all our illustrations so far, as well as in their interpretation, we have described variation in growth, morphology, physiology, and anatomy—in other words, traits that are developmentally removed from the underlying genes by several steps. Yet it is the genes that are the currency of evolution. And if that is the case, even if the above approaches and tools have helped us to get a more accurate idea of the variation that matters, how much closer can we get when we take advantage of the powerful molecular tools that have become available in recent years? This will be the topic of the next chapter. It will take us away from poplars into conifer territory, where so much more has been learned from the early application of these tools in forest trees. And we will soon see why.

12 / GETTING CLOSER TO THE GENES

For years, the link between genotype and phenotype remained an elusive problem for students of evolution in natural populations. If organic evolution was a change in gene frequencies in populations from one generation to the next, as the Evolutionary Synthesis proclaimed, how could this change be quantified if all you could measure were phenotypes? Of course, certain mutant phenotypes had been identified in various organisms and unambiguously pinned to single-gene effects. However, not only were these rare, they were also suspect because of their drastic effects. Albino seedlings, dwarf conifers, columnar oaks, weeping cedars, or corkscrew hazels were hardly representative of the sort of variation that formed the basis of slow, gradual change—the landmark of evolution. As Richard Lewontin, a population geneticist working with fruit flies, phrased the conundrum of that period: what could be measured was by definition uninteresting, and what was of interest was by definition unmeasurable.[1] How to get around this problem?

It turned out that proteins offered a useful access to the underlying genotypes. After all, proteins—or enzymes—were direct gene products, and variation in proteins could be conveniently measured by gel electrophoresis, a laboratory technique that had been used by physiologists for protein analysis for some time. The procedure allowed small variations in enzymes (termed *allozymes*) generated by different alleles (e.g., a_1, a_2, a_3) at a given gene locus to be crisply revealed and identified in the lab as distinct bands on a starch gel. The technique was simple and rapid enough to permit assays of many enzymes from many individuals, as required for calculation of gene frequencies in populations.[2] By the mid-1960s, Lewontin and coworkers decided to apply this technique to the study of fruit-fly populations, a favorite organism of population geneticists. In so doing, they ushered in a new era that defined evolutionary research for the next two decades.

Tree researchers were quick to adopt the new technique. They realized that conifers offered an ideal material to study allozyme variation, namely their seed. Seed was abundant, and could be easily stored, and in addition the bulk of a seed's tissue—the fleshy megagametophyte (endosperm) surrounding the embryo—was haploid (a product of maternal meiosis) and therefore quicker to analyze, having only half the number of genes (see fig. 12.1). Moreover, study of several (diploid) seeds from a tree, resulting from different meiotic products, would reveal whether that tree was homozygous (for example $a_1\,a_1$, or $a_3\,a_3$) or heterozygous ($a_1\,a_3$) at any locus studied. Given these advantages and the hunger for population-genetic information, the conifer allozyme industry was launched and in short order delivered large amounts of data for many different species. Species with extensive distribution ranges figured prominently among the studies, since they promised an abundance of variation to be available for analysis. Lodgepole pine (*Pinus contorta*), one of the most widespread conifers of North America, is a good example, and I will use it here to show the power of this new research approach. The study I describe was initiated in 1980 by Nicholas Wheeler and Ray Guries at the University of Wisconsin. They chose lodgepole pine to investigate the amounts and patterns of genetic

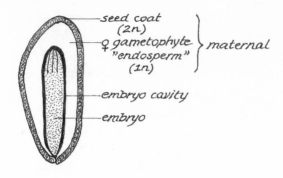

12.1 Longisection through a conifer seed. Note the large amount of nutritive gametophyte tissue surrounding the embryo.

variation discernible by allozyme analysis in the species, but they also wanted to apply these tools to shed light on a fundamental question of biogeography, namely, how did lodgepole pine fare through the last ice age, 10,000 to 14,000 years ago? Since much of its current territory had been glaciated at that time, where had its temporary refuges been, and what migratory routes from those refuges had it followed after deglaciation?

Lodgepole pine, as shown in fig. 11.1 (see chapter 11), is composed of four subspecies, a coastal form, subspecies (ssp.) *contorta,* ranging from northern California to Alaska; a major interior subspecies, ssp. *latifolia,* which extends from southern Colorado throughout the Rockies north into the Yukon Territory, covering all in all 33° of latitude, 35° of longitude, and 3,900 m of elevation; ssp. *murrayana,* reaching from the southern Sierra Nevada into Oregon; and the endemic ssp. *bolanderi,* confined to Mendocino County in California.[3] And wherever lodgepole pine is found, it commonly occurs in dense, extensive forests. For their study, Wheeler and Guries (hereafter referred to as W&G) sampled seeds from approximately 2,000 trees from thirty-six populations throughout the range, and in each tree they assayed and analyzed a total of forty-two loci from twenty-six different enzymes—a real tour de force. In fact, I was interested in finding out how much time it took to carry out the study and was given the following account: Nine weeks for the field sampling, thirteen weeks for the lab work (twenty-six enzymes for each of sixty trees could be assayed on a given day, allowing three populations to be processed per week), and six months for analyzing, interpreting, and writing up the results. Clearly, the lab work took the least amount of time, pointing to the efficiency of gel electrophoresis. Actually, they also had collected morphological data on thirteen traits, including cone size and shape, seed weight, seed-wing size, and more, from cones and seeds of 675 trees, which took twice as long to prepare and measure as running the electrophoresis (Wheeler, personal communication).

The huge dataset gained from grinding up all these thousands of seeds gave three types of statistics. One was an estimate of genetic distance among populations; that is, a measure of how genetically different the many sample populations were from one another. A second described the patterns of distribution of rare alleles among populations and shed light on the duration of occupancy of a given area, as explained below. And a third was an estimate of mean heterozygosity in populations.[4] Just so we understand what these statistics mean, let us remember that the critical unit in all three is the allele, say a_1, that can be distinguished electrophoretically from one or more alleles at the same locus (A), say a_2 and a_3. At another locus (B), there might be only two alleles, b_1 and b_2. At that second locus, the 60 trees sampled in population 1 could have a maximum of 120 b_1 alleles or b_2 alleles if all trees were homozygous for one or the other of the two alleles (remember that trees are diploid). But in reality, population 1 may have had 90 b_1 and 30 b_2 alleles, or a frequency of 0.75 (or 75 percent) for allele b_1 and 0.25 (or 25 percent) for b_2, adding up to 1.0 (or 100 percent) for the two alleles at that locus. At locus A, the same population may have had frequencies of 0.33 for a_1, 0.12 for a_2, and 0.55 for a_3 (again adding up to 1.0). Thus, for each of the 42 loci identified, frequencies could be determined for each allele found in population 1. The same would be done for population 2 and so on. When completed for all populations, comparisons could then be made among pairs of populations at all loci, and the genetic distance could be calculated between them; that is, one would find the cumulative proportion of loci (genes) at which alleles differed in their occurrence. Low values of genetic distance would mean that two populations were very similar; high values, that they were distinct. An inventory of all alleles across all populations would show many of them to be widely occurring, others to be rare. W&G designated as rare alleles those that occurred at frequencies less than 1 percent in most populations, or in fewer than 25 percent of all populations. As for mean heterozygosity for a population, this could be calculated from the frequency of heterozygous individuals (e.g., $a_1 a_3$) at each of the loci examined. (By now, many more sophisticated statistical tools have been developed to refine these estimates, but this will suffice to grasp the essence of what can be learned from allozyme data. And remember that they are estimates, whose accuracy depends on sampling procedures.) Have I lost the reader? If this seems like an accountant's extravagance, just move on to the next section.

When W&G took these collective estimates and compared them with the lodgepole pine distribution map, two patterns stood out. One was expected, and clearly separated the coastal subspecies *contorta* of British Columbia from its interior counterpart, ssp. *latifolia*. The second, perhaps less expected, separated the *latifolia* populations of the Yukon and northern B.C. from those south of there. Apparently, the genetic geography of *latifolia* displayed itself as composed of two subsets, presumably as a result of its history. What this outcome suggested was that the current interior subspecies had come from at least two glacial refugia, one in the south, the other in the north. Further support for this hypothesis was seen in the distribution of rare alleles, groups of which occurred either only in the north, or only in the south. As W&G reasoned, it would be hard to explain how so many rare alleles had arisen (through mutation) in the north in the short time (perhaps one thousand years) since lodgepole pine had arrived there from the south. In other words, the allozyme data seemed to be inconsistent with the hypothesis of refuges persisting strictly in the south and a rapid postglacial migration rate northward. A similar pattern was found for the northern populations of the ssp. *contorta*, again arguing for the persistence of certain source populations up there through the last glaciation. While these patterns were suggestive, historical pollen data would offer additional evidence for the past history of the species.

Another intriguing statistic revealed by the W&G study was the overall breakdown of enzyme variation in lodgepole pine. It showed that of the total allozyme variation measured, as much as 91 percent resided inside populations, whereas only 6 percent was left to account for differences among populations, and even less, 3 percent, for differences among the four subspecies. In other words, this huge distribution range showed that the bulk of enzymatic variation was being shared by populations and that very little genetic variation distinguished them from one another.

How is this explained? Doesn't it run counter to what provenance studies had shown time and again, namely the large amounts of genetic variation among different seed sources, often over even short distances, wherever environmental conditions diverged—let alone among different subspecies? Yes, but those were growth and development traits, subject to strong environmental selection. By contrast, enzymatic variation is more intimately tied to cellular functions and more selectively neutral. Enzymes catalyze the cellular metabolism and the formation of new cells, the building blocks of the developing plant body. Exactly what plant will be built, its shape and size, will depend on how these materials are put together. This process is a function of the plant's genetic recipe and the environment in which it is phenotypically expressed. But the building blocks themselves won't reveal the architecture for which they are intended. Similarly, allozymes themselves and their diversity and frequencies offer little insight into the selective forces under which they occur. On the other hand, their variables tend to be more indicative of such microevolutionary forces as mutation, gene flow, mating pattern, and genetic drift.[5]

Now, wouldn't it be nice if the lodgepole pine study had also included a few morphological traits that would allow us to compare them with the enzymatic variations? It so happens that W&G thought of that too. Recall that in many of their sample trees they also had measured thirteen cone and seed traits, permitting us to ask, How do the two sets of variation patterns compare? If we use the shorthand of 91/6/3 for the allozyme distribution described above, that is, variation within populations, among populations, and among subspecies, the formula for the corresponding morphological variation found would be 44/19/37. In other words, the cone and seed traits showed a much smaller proportion of variation within populations (44 percent) and a greater differentiation among populations (19 percent) that was even larger among subspecies (37 percent). These data would also more directly relate to the effects of natural selection.[6] Thus, the findings from this thorough study make it clear that genetic variation in phenotypic traits at the enzymatic level may significantly differ from that at the morphological level.

Furthermore, the distribution of morphological variation—the tangible characteristics we see in these populations—also more strongly supported the taxonomic assignment of the species into four subspecies. This is not surprising since conventional taxonomy is largely based on visible, morphological traits.

How representative are the lodgepole pine data with respect to the study of other conifers? And, perhaps more broadly, what is the use of allozyme variation when it seems to say little about the type of variation that matters most under natural selection? The first question can be answered with a qualified yes. Most conifers studied, as well as many hardwood trees such as poplars, birches, oaks, and beeches, seem to follow the lodgepole pine model, where most allozyme variation is found within populations, and little among them, although occasionally a latitudinal or longitudinal gradient in allelic frequencies can be seen, as for example when comparing coastal with interior populations. The qualification refers to the total amount of variation found, an amount generally proportionate to the distribution range of a species. As we would expect, isolated or endemic tree species also tend to show little variation at the allozyme level. What about the second part of the question, namely the usefulness of looking at allozyme patterns as opposed to those of morphology or anatomy? For one, gel electrophoresis is very convenient and efficient, and can generate a wealth of data in a relatively short amount of time under highly repeatable conditions. But most importantly, since enzymes are more closely tied to genes, their study allows more direct comparisons among different taxa—and not just among different pines but also among spruces, firs, and larches, even gymnosperms and angiosperms, in fact among plants, animals, and humans. Here, finally, was a currency common to all of life's diversity. It was a foretaste of what later became the genomics revolution.

Given this opportunity for comparison, how did enzymatic variation compare among different groups of plants? Were there any generalities emerging? For example, were there differences in the total amount of variation found between annual and perennial plants, or differences on account of the geographical range, the breeding system, or the seed-dispersal mechanisms? In one of the most recent comprehensive reviews of the seed-plant literature, Hamrick and Godt specifically looked for any correlations between several such life-history traits and the amounts and distribution patterns of allozyme variation. What they found was quite revealing and helps us once again to better understand trees as a life form and how that shapes their biology. It turns out that, in general, outcrossing plant species, to which most forest trees belong, tend to have greater genetic diversity but less population differentiation than selfing (self-pollinating) or mixed-mating plant species. More importantly, woody plants significantly exceed in genetic diversity those herbaceous species that otherwise share the same life-history traits. Apparently, the tall stature of trees greatly helps their abundant pollen and seed to be dispersed over longer distances than is possible for the smaller herbaceous plants. This has two direct consequences: the continual blending of genetic distinctions among populations through gene flow; and second, the greater dispersal of any novel alleles that may arise in any population and, as a result, their lower probability of extinction over time, thereby building up greater genetic diversity. In sum, trees as a group harbor greater levels of allozyme diversity than other plants, both locally and rangewide.[7]

What is the significance of this finding? Here again, but in much more general terms, we see what in earlier chapters manifested itself in the timing of bud burst or leaf fall, and in morphological traits among aspen clones or black cottonwoods: namely, the remarkable variability that can be seen in most natural populations and in fact within local populations. Here too the results confirm what from an evolutionary perspective seems to make eminent sense, namely that long-living organisms that are likely to face changing conditions over time will tend to adopt a strategy of maintaining high levels of genetic diversity among their offspring. Since they have no way of anticipating what specific conditions will prevail a hundred years ahead, individuals that produce many differently equipped seedlings are more likely to leave a genetic legacy in successive generations than those with uniform progenies. The strategy seems doubly rewarding for trees, which as a life form experience the environment on a much larger scale than even long-lived woody shrubs. So just to tie that generalization back to the realm of reproductive biology—and allow the reader a temporary respite from the world of molecules—let me illustrate it with a tangible example of seed variation in ponderosa pine.

Seed characteristics such as size, shape, color, seed-coat thickness, and many more are of vital importance for survival in the face of challenges from the physical (frost, heat, drought) and biological environment (dispersal, predation). These characteristics determine such critical variables as dispersibility, nutrient content, light reflection and heat absorption (dark seeds versus light seeds), moisture uptake and retention, and camouflage, to name a few. As a consequence, this variation is subject to strong but variable selection pressures and therefore under tight genetic control.[8] This also applies to seed of ponderosa pine, a tree that is widespread in western North America.

In part of its extensive range, in the interior of south-central Oregon, ponderosa pine occurs in mixed conifer stands on two distinct soil types. One is a dark residual soil derived from Pliocene basalt flows, the other a light-colored pumice from the Mount Mazama eruption 7,700 years ago. In an undergraduate study at the University of Washington, Alan Ager chose areas in Oregon where he could examine whether there might be correlations of seed morphology with these two substrates. He chose nine populations that bracketed the two soil types, collected seed from eighty-seven trees, and measured a number of variables in these seeds. The results showed remarkable amounts of variation in seed weight (up to threefold), in shape (roundish to elongate), and in color (ranging from black to mottled and all the way to pale tan). The seed from the pumice area tended to be slightly longer and lighter in color than the seed from the dark basalt soils. But the greatest variation, up to 79 percent, was found to reside among trees within populations—following the general rule of variation patterns in forest trees. However, and here is the interesting detail, seed lots of an individual tree were amazingly uniform—as uniform as if cut from the same template. In other words, a typical population was composed of a mosaic of trees, each tree producing seeds of uniform size, color, and shape, but distinct from those of its neighbors.[9] Now, the uniformity of seeds within a tree derives from the fact that in conifers all seed tissues, except the embryo, are strictly maternal (see fig. 12.1). Yet isn't it risky for a tree to produce only a single model of seed, and to do so year after year, putting all its eggs in one basket? Well, that's true, but here comes the insurance policy. As monoecious outcrossers, these trees disperse pollen to the other individuals around them (and even a few farther away), and since those mates produce different types of seeds, the genetic investment via pollen takes full advantage of the existing maternal diversity in the neighborhood. By contrast, the genetic investment via the female route is more conservative. Thus, in trees that have both sexes (as in the majority of temperate tree species), different investments can be made via the male and female routes, the two of them balancing the risks. Further, since in a spatially and temporally heterogeneous environment there is no sure way of predicting where a seed will fall, genotypes that hedge their bets will tend to have higher fitness in the long run. The final outcome will be populations highly polymorphic in seed characteristics. And let us not forget that even the uniform seeds of an individual tree will give rise to genetically diverse seedlings, since the embryos within these seeds are the result of outcrossing and of high parental heterozygosity.

Now back to the enzymatic realm. Here, polymorphic populations seem to be the rule in the world of trees, too, and to a much higher degree than in herbaceous plants. If the measurement of enzymatic diversity helped quantify certain life-form comparisons that were previously impossible to make for lack of comparable terms, it also had its downside—at least in the view of one of the tool's original promoters. In a refreshing recent retrospective on present directions in evolutionary biology, Richard Lewontin laments that

> the introduction of protein gel electrophoresis as a tool to investigate the standing variation within and between species almost totally depauperized evolutionary genetics for 20 years. The immense diversity of research directions was replaced by a massive program of grinding up every species that lay at hand and visualizing their proteins by gel electrophoresis. The rest of the program of evolutionary genetic research became marginalized or totally inactive, and it has yet to recover its diversity.[10]

Science has its fads too, and for a while they are the magnets for the bulk of grant money and for all the promising talents. Lamentable as such imbalance may be, it seems to be a necessary evil for scientific advance. Fortunately, and usually before long, the tilt will go in another direction.

Information about the protein variation existing in populations had one additional limitation: it only gave a hint about the history of that variation. While shedding light on current spatial diversity, it didn't persuasively show how that diversity got there. Once again, genetics alone told only part of the story. It took scientists and their tools from another discipline, paleobotany, to add the historical dimension. Interestingly enough, it was w&g's lodgepole pine study that offered a suitable opportunity for further elaboration. The next chapter will show us how.

13 / MIGRANT TREES

The geographical variation in phenotypic traits we now encounter as we sample natural populations carries the footprint of past history, and no other historical episode has left a larger footprint on temperate-zone vegetation than the last ice age. Glacial and interglacial climates have been major forces in shrinking and expanding the natural distribution ranges of species. Withdrawal into temporary refuges during glacial periods, the experience of population shrinkage, the subsequent rate of migration during interglacials, the role played by the founding of new populations through distant dispersal, and the merging of migratory paths have all shaped the current pattern of genetic variation found in the landscape. Moreover, while it is impossible to accurately reconstruct the detailed history of any species, paleoecologists have been busy in applying a variety of independent tools, from the analysis of pollen records and macrofossils to the use of computer simulation, to come up with plausible approximations. Add genetic data, and a new synergy arises.

Lodgepole Pine

The lodgepole pine data from Wheeler and Guries[1] provided an attractive material on which Les Cwynar and Glen MacDonald, two paleo-ecologists, could test several hypotheses about the likely postglacial history of that species and its genetic consequences. They hypothesized that the range expansion of lodgepole pine happened through successive founding events, in which long-distance seed dispersal established new, small populations ahead of the main body; such a population would then expand and serve as the source for another pioneering group, and so on. But each founding event, owing to the small numbers involved, would also result in some loss in allele diversity because of chance alone, a process termed *genetic drift* (as we saw in chapter 8). If so, one would expect genetic diversity to decrease in the direction of migration. They also hypothesized that since every seed-dispersal event offered a test for dispersibility, repetitive selection at successive founding events would favor traits that improved such dispersal. If so, the most recently established populations should have the most dispersible seeds.[2]

One of the possible, if indirect, tests for these hypotheses was to put the northward expansion of lodgepole pine into a temporal framework. Collections of fossil pollen, combined with carbon dating, made it possible to date the sequential appearance of pine at successive locations along its 2,200 km migratory trek from the south to the Yukon during the 12,000 years of its postglacial history. Fifteen of these locations were close to lodgepole sample populations of the *latifolia* subspecies in the Wheeler and Guries (or W&G) study. When Cwynar and MacDonald plotted data from these populations against the time since their founding, several trends emerged. One such trend showed the mean number of alleles per locus had increased with time since founding; or, conversely, that genetic diversity was lower in the more recently founded northern populations, as predicted. As to the dispersibility of seed, of the thirteen morphological traits of seed and cones measured by W&G,

seed mass and wing length were the only ones showing a relationship to time since founding, and clearly so; the most recently established populations had the smallest seed with comparatively the largest wings, that is, seed that could be transported farthest by lateral winds.[3] Here, too, the data supported the prediction. But how reliable was the assumption that the northernmost populations were really the most recently established? Remember that the allozyme data by w&g were highly suggestive of the persistence of some lodgepole pine in the north through the last glacial maximum. Which data are more informative? Perhaps it may be helpful to briefly familiarize ourselves here with paleoecological methods and their strengths and weaknesses before showing how combining these methods with population-genetic data can strengthen the accuracy of our reconstruction of the past. Such reconstruction of the past need not be viewed merely as an academic exercise; it may give us some clues to the ways biota will respond to future shifts in climate.

Fossils are keys to the past. Just as we trace the evolution of *Homo sapiens* by examining fossil evidence from preserved skulls, teeth, or other skeletal parts, so do paleobotanists benefit from the study of fossilized plant fragments, such as leaves, twigs, wood, and seed. These macrofossils can be found within buried layers in bogs and lake bottoms and often can be reliably linked to a specific genus or even species. The trouble is that they are rare and fragmentary and thus offer insufficient quantitative data for reliably recording the past existence, let alone abundance, of a particular taxon. Fortunately, plants have also left a microfossil record—visible under the microscope—in the form of spore and pollen deposits. Pollen from many species is shed in great quantities, is well preserved and pervasive, can be identified to the genus level (sometimes even to the species), and can be conveniently collected from the stratified deposits in pond or lake bottoms. Tree pollen has additional advantages. Because of its wider dispersal and a tree's longevity, it is likely to settle and get recorded even in sparsely distributed sample sites. Furthermore, as shown by present-day studies, certain tree species (e.g., alders and spruces) are known to closely track retreating glaciers, making their pollen an especially sensitive indicator of postglacial colonization patterns. Over the past century, students of the pollen record—palynologists—have built an impressive database for Europe and North America and have contributed greatly to our understanding of historical vegetations and the way they responded to past climate change.[4]

A common way of compiling such data is in the form of a pollen frequency profile for a given location sampled. It gives the vertical distribution of pollen for each taxon, expressed as a percentage of total pollen at that depth, along with the estimated age of that stratum. Age estimation is based on carbon 14 dating and, whenever possible, calibrated by geochronological signatures, such as deposits from known volcanic eruptions (e.g., Mount Mazama, ~7,700 years ago), or by comparing tree-ring counts with radiocarbon dates on the same wood pieces. In interpreting such profiles, palynologists make appropriate allowance for differences in (1) pollen production by different species (e.g., wind versus insect pollination), (2) dispersal distance (e.g., trees versus shrubs); (3) pollen preservability (e.g., pollen of poplar or larch is much more fragile than that of pines), and other variables that may introduce possible bias. When "cleaned up" (as described below in the discussion of sampling conventions), pollen records for any region have consistently portrayed a picture of continually changing groupings and associations of plant species. In other words, wherever studied, species assemblages have been reshuffled time and again during the postglacial period. In the Pacific Northwest, for example, the now common assemblage of Douglas fir/western hemlock/western red-cedar is a new community of recent vintage that arose only ~6,000 years ago (a relatively short period if you consider a normal lifespan for Douglas fir of about 200–400 years).[5] Similar dynamics have been shown for the vegetation in central and eastern North America, as well as in Europe.[6] In other words, in their postglacial migration plant communities did not move as coherent units. Each species had its own trajectory.

Actually, it would be surprising to find community coherence in migration when we think of the wide range of differences among species in seed production and dispersal, requirements for seedling establishment, maturation time, periodicity of seed crops, and many other life-history variables that affect the successful occupation of newly available habitat. Thus, the paleobotanical findings seem to be consistent with what we know from independent studies of tree biology.

But how accurate is the pollen evidence for the presence of a species?

How closely can boundaries of its past range be determined? If it was a challenge for the U.S. government to conduct a reasonably accurate Year 2000 population census, how much more difficult would it be to do that for past populations, based strictly on sampling of a spotty record, say the analysis of cemeteries? Moreover, once one is in the realm of statistics there is the automatic need to make probability assumptions and adopt reasonable, if arbitrary, conventions. For example, in their efforts to underestimate rather than overestimate a species' existence at a sampling site, paleoecologists required its pollen to make up at least 0.5 percent of all pollen in that stratum in order to count. A single pollen grain in that layer just wouldn't do because it might have flown in from a long distance or even have been misidentified. Interpolations were required to smooth spatial data from individual sampling sites. When combined with carbon 14 dating, a species' expanding pollen footprint could thus be followed across the geography and through time. In this manner, a large number of migratory trajectories were reconstructed during the 1980s and '90s for many tree species on this continent and in Europe.[7] What came as a surprise was how fast some of these migratory fronts seemed to have moved on a continental scale—200 m or more per year—and this for species with such different life histories and seed dispersal capabilities as spruces and beeches. How could such rapid expansion rates be achieved, let alone sustained throughout thousands of years?[8] Were these valid reconstructions, or were they based on faulty premises? As is often the case, combining information from both within and beyond the discipline helped clarify the quandary.

Reexamination of pollen records with lowered minimum requirements indicated that false negatives—that is, underrepresentation—were a common occurrence. A particular species may have actually existed at a given location even though its contribution to the pollen sample was less than the minimum 0.5 percent demanded. This would have been especially true for tree species that occurred at low densities. In fact, in a study that related modern tree distribution to current surface pollen abundance for two such species, American beech and yellow birch, this clearly was the case.[9] Another study reexamining past pollen records made a comprehensive effort to integrate all data (including trace amounts of pollen) of six boreal tree and shrub taxa from 149 arctic sampling sites, covering the period from 21,000 to 6,000 years ago. The resulting synthesis offered strong evidence for the persistence of alders, birches, larches, pines, poplars, and spruces through the last glacial maximum in the nonglaciated portions of Beringia.[10] Evidently, these genera had not vanished in the north but survived in one or more arctic refuges throughout that cold period and were then able to expand again southward after glaciation. This unexpected finding not only speaks for the remarkable adaptability of those trees and shrubs, but it also challenges the paradigm that all postglacial migration happened essentially in a northward direction. This shift in perspective automatically calls for a revision of those high migration rates and helps to bring them within the realm of more plausible estimates. The new evidence also supports the earlier postulate of northern refuges in lodgepole pine made by Wheeler and Guries based on allozyme data.[11] Were those kinds of data perhaps more meaningful after all?

Phylogeography

This brings us back to the molecular world. In the last chapter we stepped away from it during the high period of protein analysis. But that was only a mild foretaste of what was to come when molecular biologists moved from the study of enzymatic variation to that of DNA, the genetic material itself. In the meantime, great strides had already been made in unraveling the information contained in DNA. Elegant molecular techniques had been developed to analyze its diversity and to make use of even minute amounts of it through rapid amplification in vitro. Not only did it speed up the efficiency of analyzing the nuclear DNA, but it also gave access to the much smaller quantities of genes in organelles, namely the DNA of mitochondria and chloroplasts. And that turned out to be especially useful for reconstructing the way present-day genetic diversity among species had come about.

Mitochondria and chloroplasts form part of the cellular apparatus of each plant. Originally independent organisms, they seem to have assumed symbiotic functions and become permanently embedded in the cytoplasm of cells during the early evolution of multicellular organisms called *eukaryotes*.[12] Whereas mitochondria serve critical processes in the energy household of the cell, chloroplasts are the site of photosynthesis, where the energy from sunlight is converted into complex organic molecules. Both of these cytoplasmic organelles still contain part of their own DNA, in haploid form, and keep replicating it faithfully whenever they multiply during the cell cycle. Further, since in all seed plants the cytoplasm of the egg cell and of the subsequent embryo is contributed by the female parent, both mitochondria and chloroplasts are transmitted maternally. The one exception to this occurs in the conifers, in which only the mitochondria are maternally inherited, and where chloroplasts are transmitted paternally, via pollen[13] (as we shall see, in conifers this makes it possible to follow maternal and paternal lineages separately). Also, in contrast to the diploid DNA in the nucleus (nuclear DNA), where recombination continually shuffles the genome, the haploid DNA in mitochondria and chloroplasts maintains its integrity generation after generation, save for the occasional mutational event (which also happens at a lower rate than in nuclear DNA).[14] Thus, organellar DNA typically occurs in a finite number of different forms, called *haplotypes* (since they are haploid), which can be used as convenient tracers of historical lineages. In fact, this novel approach in applying the technology of DNA studies ushered in a new field of research, phylogeography, opening new vistas into the history of organisms.

Phylogeography, as described by Avise, is concerned with "principles and processes governing distributions of genealogical lineages, especially those within closely related species." Aimed at bridging the gap between microevolutionary and macroevolutionary disciplines—studying evolution from short time spans to geologic times—phylogeography attempts to combine population and molecular genetics with paleontology, biogeography, and phylogenetic biology.[15] This is another case where a new tool opens up a new approach to address an old problem and in the process serves to bring a new synthesis of previously separate endeavors. Of special significance is the promise it holds for documenting the continuity of evolutionary forces across different time scales in a seamless process. Still in its infancy, this hybrid field has established itself with common research procedures and protocols, has gained scientific recognition, and has given rise to an expanding literature that already covers the breadth of organisms, from plants to humans. One of its celebrated cases has been the tracing of human lineages from "mitochondrial Eve" through her "seven daughters," as *Homo sapiens* migrated out of Africa and established itself in different regions across

Eurasia.[16] But to us philarborists, there is no less fascination in the many recent phylogeographic accounts that describe the postglacial history of forest tree species in Europe and North America.

Oaks were among the first plant taxa for which cytoplasmic DNA was used to study patterns of geographic variation,[17] and they became the object of a major collaborative investigation in Europe. A truly ambitious undertaking initiated in 1995, the project involved the coordinated work of sixteen laboratories, covered thirty-seven countries, sampled 12,214 individual trees in 2,613 populations from eight white oak species, and serves as an example of how scientific collaboration can transcend national boundaries and help shed light on biodynamic processes on a continental scale.[18] Making use of selected molecular markers, these researchers were able to distinguish thirty-two chloroplast DNA (cpDNA) variants, or haplotypes, in European white oaks, which they then mapped and used in a variety of diversity analyses. What emerged was a strong phylogeographic structure with six major maternal lineages that connected populations along recolonization routes, often involving more than one oak species (see fig. 13.1). Refugial areas identified by earlier pollen data, such as the Iberian and Italian peninsulas, showed higher than average chloroplast diversity, as one would expect, having had a longer time to accumulate mutations. But interestingly enough, regions farther north, at the junction of several migration routes in central Europe, also showed high diversity, presumably from the genetic exchange among maternal lineages, given the well-known propensity of oak species to hybridize. On the other hand, Alpine and northern regions had low diversity but showed greater distinction among populations within lineages, presumably because of greater isolation. At the low end of allelic richness were the British Isles, whose oaks seem to have been recolonized from a single refuge in western Iberia.[19] A host of additional information can be gleaned from this comprehensive dataset, including as well the extent to which human activities such as transporting, planting, and selective management may have influenced the data for individual species. Here may it suffice to point out how well the phylogeographic approach complements information inferred from the fossil record.

In tracing recolonization history in plants via the maternal route (such as cpDNA), one of the key variables involved is the seed and its

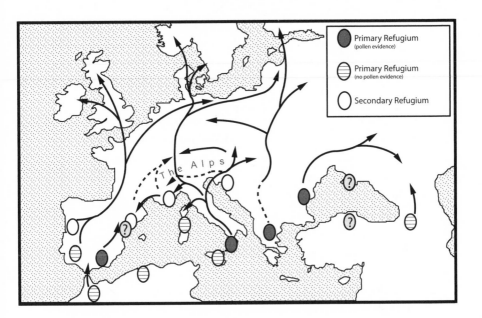

Primary Refugium
(pollen evidence)

Primary Refugium
(no pollen evidence)

Secondary Refugium

13.1   Schematic distribution of primary and secondary oak refuges and postglacial migration routes in Europe. (*Adapted from Petit et al., 2002, with permission from Elsevier Science B.V.*)

type of dispersal. How would oaks with their large acorns, hoarded locally by rodents, compare with smaller-seeded species that are more widely dispersed by wind? In an effort to shed light on such differences, the same group of European researchers (Petit and colleagues) conducted a follow-up study in which they compared oaks with twenty-one other tree and shrub species. Even if based on less-intensive sampling, the data made it possible to estimate the degree of cpDNA diversity among populations within each species. One way to quantify this diversity is to express it as an index of population divergence, termed Gst, ranging from 0 to 1.0, with low numbers indicating little population distinction, high numbers greater distinction. Results from this analysis were in agreement with expectations, and indicated that species with high gene flow through small, fluffy seeds (e.g., willows, poplars) had low Gst values (0.09–0.11), and that those of bird-dispersed species (e.g., hawthorn, ivy, cherry, raspberry, and mountain ash) ranged from 0.24 to 0.60, while those of animal-cached species with more local dispersal (e.g., beech, hazel, and oak) were the highest (0.74–0.89).[20] Evidently, the genetic footprint left by cytoplasmic transmission is strongly influenced by seed dispersal mechanisms. The study also confirmed in these additional species what had been found in the oaks, namely that within-population diversity was highest north of the main European mountain ranges. One explanation for this would be the mixing of several colonization routes in that region and the consequent merging of different haplotypes; another possibility suggested by the authors is that there may have been a systematic selection for greater dispersal ability during migration away from southern refuges, resulting in increased gene flow among populations farther north.

So far, we have looked at tracing historic lineages via the maternal route. Now you will remember that in conifers mitochondrial DNA (mtDNA) is transmitted maternally, but chloroplast DNA (cpDNA) paternally. How comparable would the geographic patterns of each of those two separate lineages be? Such a comparison was precisely the objective of another study conducted by Liepelt and colleagues in Europe, this time focusing on silver fir (*Abies alba*), a species that today covers a broad mountainous zone across central Europe. Sampling 100 populations from the entire distribution range and testing them with both mtDNA and cpDNA markers revealed two sharply contrasting patterns. Both markers confirmed the locations of two Mediterranean Pleistocene refuges (earlier documented by fossil pollen), a western one in the Italian Apennines, and an eastern one in the Balkan Peninsula; both markers also showed evidence of genetic mixing between the postglacial colonization routes from those refuges. But whereas the maternal lineages indicated a fairly low amount of such introgression in a relatively narrow zone, the paternal lineages showed a range-wide gradient of allelic frequencies, interpolating the differences of those at the refugial locations.[21] In other words, while maternal lineages were more distinct over short distances, paternal lineages reflected long-range introgression. Thus, gene flow through pollen far exceeded that through seed. Which, as the authors point out, is even more remarkable, as silver fir has relatively large pollen, long generation times (~40 years) and a long life span (greater than 300 years), all traits that would lower the rates of gene flow. Similar results have been obtained for several conifers in North America, showing greater differences among populations when measured with mitochondrial than with chloroplast

DNA markers.[22] Thus, here again we see further evidence for two different but complementary reproductive strategies at work, namely a conservative one via seed, keeping the genetic legacy in its local context, and an "exploratory" one via pollen, capable of sampling a wider range of genes and environments. In addition it adds the male dimension to what in the last chapter we saw as evidence for the female strategy in ponderosa pine seed variation in chapter 12.

What we have learned from the pollen record and from phylogeographical studies is how the most restrictive recent period, the latest glaciation, has affected the subsequent colonization of emergent habitats—at least in terms of migration from different refuges, in the pathways of different migration routes, and in the sequence and timing of the various genera and species that were present at different stations along these routes. Each species had its own trajectory, and species assemblages kept changing over time. Within a species, the molecular footprint left in organellar and nuclear DNA has also allowed us to make inferences about such historical processes as past hybridization and the gradual accumulation of mutations, as well as population bottlenecks and isolation. But if the molecular variation we measure is largely selectively neutral—meaning it has little to say about past natural selection—what does this mean with regard to the current status of adaptive traits? What are possible and likely consequences from this critical evolutionary period for the way present-day populations are capable of coping with the current environment, let alone with likely environments of the near future? The next chapter will bring us closer to answering these questions.

14 / ADAPTATION AND ITS LIMITS

It would be tempting to imagine that the postglacial environmental change was one of gradual, systematic warming and to see that process as a slow but steady opening up of temporarily inhospitable territory, allowing the expelled plant communities to again reclaim their original turf. However, in reality it seems to have been more complicated. For one thing, the return of a more benign climate to the northern temperate zone didn't occur in a gradual and smooth sequence, but more in fits and starts and with occasional abrupt turnarounds. Also, as we have seen in the last chapter, the migrants were not those previous plant communities marching northward hand in hand, but individual species, each moving at its own pace, constantly forming novel and transitory assemblages. Furthermore and equally important, these species were not inert, immutable entities that merely moved like chess pieces across the landscape but complex ensembles of highly variable populations whose genetic makeup kept changing during the process[1]—a fact that shouldn't surprise us after all we have learned earlier. Putting it more directly, what happened was far more fascinating—not only because it was less predictable, but also because it still continues. Which means that we should examine it more closely. Most importantly, we should ask ourselves, What does this paleoecological history imply about how well individual trees are adapted to their current environment?

First and foremost, we have to accept climate as the key physical agent of ecological change, because it sets the stage for successional dynamics—the sequential phases in ecosystem development—and the evolutionary processes involved therein. Climate is the driver, and the more we grasp its significance and learn about the magnitude and timing of its variation, the better we begin to appreciate how the many facets of biological systems respond to it.[2] Because here, too, variability is the norm. The most obvious of these, diurnal and seasonal cycles, are familiar to all of us. Equally prominent, though less well understood, can be year-to-year changes. Longer periods are noisier and more difficult to scrutinize. In recent years a rapidly evolving climate science has begun shedding light on cycles of climate change that occur at temporal scales of decades to millennia and beyond. What are the tools that offer these new insights, and what is the story they tell us? For empirical evidence, some of the most revealing recent information on past climates comes from the cold-storage vault of polar ice caps.[3] Cores retrieved from them, similar to pollen-sediment cores taken from lake bottoms, contain a serial record of distinct annual layers of preserved gas bubbles that reveal the atmospheric conditions at the time of deposition. Making use of chemical isotopes trapped in these bubbles (e.g., oxygen 18) and an accurate dating technique, scientists have used these proxies to reconstruct a record of past surface air temperatures. For example, a deep core drilled in the Greenland ice sheet has yielded a temperature log for the North Atlantic region for the last 200,000 years.[4] Additional and analogous information can be obtained from buried strata in the ocean floor containing sediments of specific marine organisms, geological deposits, or aerosols—suspensions of fine particles from volcanic activities. Tree-ring records add further information on past temperature and moisture regimes for up to several thousand years back. Finally, in order to integrate these records from different sources and geographical locations around the globe, analyze their variables, relate them to one another, search for repetitive patterns, and develop predictive models, it takes powerful computers that can handle that enormous complexity—in fact, a handful of the most powerful ones currently in existence.[5] All in all, this research has led to new conceptual developments and the revision of previous theories on climate variation.

What has emerged is a picture of a far more variable and complex Quaternary period (the last 2.5 million years) than ever imagined.[6] Simply put, we have to view the climatic record—prior to human influence—as one of cyclic patterns nested within each other, with a hierarchy of periodicities ranging from ~100,000 years (100 ka) down to 20 to 60 years, resulting in a characteristic sawtooth pattern (fig. 14.1). The driving forces behind these cycles are the earth's orbit around the sun, cyclically alternating in the distance to the sun, variation in the sun's intensity, and also changes in ocean circulation patterns. But stochastic events, such as unusually high global volcanic activity, have also been superimposed on these cycles, leaving their own marks.[7] Typically, glacial periods lasted 80 to 90 ka and were followed by 10 to 20°C warmer interglacials of ~10 ka duration. But they were interrupted by occasional reversals, such as the Younger Dryas period that lowered temperatures again for about a thousand years during the early interglacial, 11.5 ka,[8] or the Little Ice Age, a global cold period between AD 1450 and 1920.[9] Importantly too, transitions between climate phases were often abrupt and involved mean temperature changes of 3 to 15°C inside a few years or decades. Short-cycle episodes, such as circulation changes in the South Pacific, called El Niño or La Niña events, have kept adding to the variability and now have been shown to affect climate not only along the Pacific coast but also weather patterns in Europe and Australia.[10]

Thus, a constantly changing climate has kept challenging adaptive norms for plant and animal life, first of all by setting survival thresholds via frost or heat. But what has been equally forceful is the interplay of temperature with moisture—and this along with their combined effect on the type and amount of precipitation, its timing, and the resulting likelihood of droughts, floods, and fire, as well as their periodicity and duration. Further, an influence that may be less appreciated is the

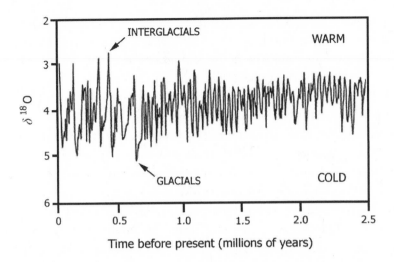

Time before present (millions of years)

14.1 Temperature fluctuations between glacial and interglacial periods of the past 2.5 million years, derived from oxygen-isotope analysis of ice cores from the Greenland ice sheet. High values indicate cold temperatures (glacial periods), low values, interglacials. Our current interglacial period (Holocene) is at the far left, from 0 to 10,000 years ago. (*From Millar and Brubaker, fig. 15.1,* Foundations of Restoration Ecology *by D. Falk, J. Zedler, M. Palmer. © 2006 Island Press. Reproduced by permission of Island Press, Washington, D.C.*)

effect of these physical variables on such vegetation-regulating agents as microorganisms, pathogens, and insects. These symbiotic or parasitic organisms, thanks to their short life cycles and rapid adaptability, must have had a significant impact on the presence and competitiveness of their various host species, thereby helping to shape the temporary composition of ecosystems. As a consequence, there has been perpetual change in vegetation in response to climatic variability through expansion and contraction of species' ranges in latitude, longitude, and elevation. Yet the presence or absence of a particular species at a given location at a given time, as revealed by the fossil record, tells us only part of the story. What would be as important to know is how adapted local populations may have been to the climate at the time, and what evolutionary consequences this may have had for the subsequent fate of the species. How would we go about finding that out?

One way, perhaps the only reliable (if indirect) way, to look for hard evidence is by studying the degree of adaptedness of current populations to the current or immediately past climate—especially where we can rely on natural populations that have seen little human impact. But how would we find out whether a local population, even if now well adapted to its own environment, might not have been performing better in a different environment elsewhere? A clever approach to ascertain this is to take advantage of some of those provenance tests that have been conducted with selected forest tree species. Recall from chapter 11 that these provide a grid of field trials, dispersed over a geographical range, in which trees from different seed sources are grown side by side, so that each source experiences diverse climatic conditions at the different sites and responds to them in its own way. Remember too that some of these tests have been in the field for more than twenty years, thereby concurrently sampling a common spectrum of environmental variables at any location during that period. Remarkably, too, many of these trials have been carefully maintained and periodically remeasured. Here then is a real-time record of the way an individual seed source has fared on its home ground versus at other locations, as well as of how, collectively, the performance of the different sources shows acclimation to prevailing conditions. Thanks to recent work by forestry researchers such records have been carefully scrutinized, and offer new, provocative insights into adaptation and its limits.

A good example of this research is the recent analysis performed by Gerald Rehfeldt, a US Forest Service researcher, and his collaborators.[11] They took advantage of the data collected from the extensive provenance test of lodgepole pine (*Pinus contorta*) established in British Columbia in 1974 by Keith Illingworth[12] and described in chapter 11. Their analysis was based on survival and height measurements taken over twenty years from 118 populations of two subspecies of lodgepole pine grown in common gardens at sixty locations throughout the province—a huge dataset. Here, let us remember that growth in height in an early-successional tree such as lodgepole pine is directly related to the tree's fitness, since it determines an individual's competitive access to light, moisture, and nutrients. Thus, by twenty years, height growth has definitely sorted out the dominant individuals of a stand, while these dominant trees also tend to have the greatest fecundity. In this case, height also reflected a seed source's resistance to breakage caused by snow and its tolerance to several pathogens that differentially affected trees over the years by causing stem rust and needle cast. Thus, height at twenty years seemed to offer a good integrative measure of the degree of adaptedness. These data were then related to seven climate variables taken from 513 weather stations throughout the province, and response functions were calculated for each test site (estimating how the performance of a seed source related to these variables at that site). Transfer functions were then calculated that estimated the performance of each seed source across all test sites, given the seven climate variables at those sites, since each source was grown at multiple but not all sites. Overall, the analysis involved both actual data collected in the field and best estimates calculated according to conventional statistical procedures.[13]

The analysis revealed, as expected, that natural populations of lodgepole pine differ greatly in their climatic optima and, not surprisingly, that individual populations are appropriately aligned with the key climatic variables at their location. However, some less-expected results also showed that these populations tend to occupy suboptimal environments, namely environments generally cooler and slightly drier than their optimum. This discrepancy increases with increasing latitude, so that populations north of latitude 60° are inhabiting climates approximately 7°C colder than their optimum. In other words, given their genetic endowment, populations would actually grow better if they were shifted to generally warmer and moister locations. How can one explain this? The authors suggest that density-dependent selection may be the crux. The way to understand this is to recognize that cold tolerance in a tree does not come free but demands reallocation of the tree's resources away from growth, as shown by the negative correlation between growth potential and cold hardiness documented in earlier studies.[14] As a consequence, in the fierce struggle for height dominance that characterizes stand development in dense populations of lodgepole pine, height growth is at a prime and will favor individuals that are sufficiently, but not optimally, cold hardy. And since these trees will out-reproduce their competitors, their genes will eventually prevail in the gene pools of the next generations. But where did these genes come from to begin with? The answer is, either from mutations or, more likely, from input by more southern populations where cold tolerance is less demanded and height growth is even more superior. In the words of these researchers, "Asymmetric gene flow from the center of distribution toward the periphery is viewed as a primary regulator that provides the fuel for both environmental and density-dependent selection and thereby indirectly perpetuates suboptimality."[15]

In their argument we meet several old friends from previous chapters, such as the concept that your fiercest competitors may be your own kind; that genetic polymorphism is common in forest tree populations, making neighboring plants different from each other; and that gene flow in wind-pollinated species is very effective and not necessarily symmetrical in all directions. A greater abundance of pollen from more central populations may therefore overwhelm those at the periphery and account for the more northern populations being more out of tune with their environment.

Is lodgepole pine an atypical case? As it turns out, similar trends were found in Scots pine (*Pinus sylvestris*), another widespread species, with a range that extends across the northern portions of the entire Eurasian continent.[16] The basis for its study was again a series of provenance tests, in this case drawn from 110 populations and planted at forty-seven different sites in Eurasia and North America—another major effort in experimental field research, much of it conducted in Russia. Analytical procedures followed those from the lodgepole pine study. As determined by thirteen-year heights, these populations also tended to find themselves in cooler than optimal environments, with the discrepancy between occupied and optimal climate similarly becoming greater with increasing climatic severity. In this case, however, longitude was a stronger correlate than latitude, with low temperatures increasing eastward across Siberia.

There are limitations to both studies, such as those inherent in any field experiment based on sampling; for example, how representative were the seeds collected from the local populations? How characteristic were the test sites for the climates of interest? How many trees were grown per field plot? How were soil heterogeneity and its effects on height growth accounted for? How did cultural treatments such as removal of competing vegetation affect the results? How might mortality in field plots remove competition and unduly favor neighboring plots, thereby exaggerating their performance? Were numbers and diversity sufficient to minimize such errors? And perhaps more broadly, how can such artificial experiments with their patchwork quilt of test plots even approach a natural setting in its full complexity? True, we may be looking at sketches, cartoons, rather than at fully elaborated paintings. Perhaps allotting a longer time would have brought out more nuanced portraits. Yet even if these are slightly exaggerated sketches, they are based on hard evidence from real trees growing in real climates in real time. What the evidence from both studies suggests is that while natural populations are adequately adapted to the climate they currently experience, they are not in perfect alignment with it. Is this really surprising? Let's take this opportunity to pause for a moment and reexamine why organisms in general, but trees especially, are unlikely to be in perfect harmony with the environment they inhabit; after that, we will come back and ask what this may mean in the context of prospective climate change.

Adaptation and Its Limits

What, then, are the limits of adaptation? It would be difficult to find a better way to think about adaptation than to see organisms, in the words of Richard Levins, as "systems of environmental tracking, making use of relevant ancestral experience."[17] In this sense, an individual's degree of adaptedness depends on (1) how well it perceives the cues emitted by its environment; (2) how and to what extent it finds relevant past experience in its DNA telling it how to respond to those cues; and (3) how able it is to muster the appropriate responses. Obviously, past history figures in all three components; if cues are new, they may get ignored, and/or there may be no relevant information available in the genetic library on how to respond, and/or there may be no mechanisms available in the cellular machinery for a response, or perhaps those that do exist are ineffective.

To put it in Darwinian terms, natural selection is retrospective, not prospective. It is hooked to the past and cannot anticipate what's coming, unless there are cyclical patterns in the environment that keep repeating themselves (e.g., diurnal, seasonal cycles). Moreover, natural selection is relative, not absolute. Recall that the fitness of an individual refers to its contribution to the gene pool of the next generation, as compared to all others in that population. This means that everything depends on who else happens to be around at that time in that location and under those circumstances. For example, in a genetically impoverished population even a modestly adapted individual may turn out a winner and will unduly perpetuate its mediocre legacy among members of the next generation. In this way, a population bottleneck—with reduced genetic diversity—can cast a long shadow for many generations, and will continue until mutations or gene flow from other populations have restored genetic variation.

Furthermore, there may be long-term developmental constraints embedded in the genetic blueprint, rooted in the ancient history of a species, that act to prevent an organism from responding optimally to a new need. Or, as François Jacob expressed it, evolution is a "tinkerer," not an engineer.[18] By this he meant that evolution, in contrast to targeted engineering design, makes use of whatever is available in an organism at that time, modifying it through random mutations and selection in subsequent generations, but unable to create anything de novo. Thus, if you are a conifer, there are ways to increase the width of your needles to trap more light in the shade, but your basic design won't allow a leap to the broader leaf of a beech. Another hindrance to approaching perfection is that natural selection is of limited efficacy in discarding deleterious genes. Recall that diploidy (or even more so, polyploidy) gives maladaptive mutations a chance to hide as recessive alleles behind their dominant normal counterparts in heterozygous individuals (*Aa*); they will only be detectable and subject to selection when appearing in homozygous offspring. Albinos (*aa*) are a perfect example of this process, and their *a* allele can hang around in natural populations for a long time.

What further slows down a population in its effort to successfully track the environment is that natural selection works on the sum total of all traits, and that the gain per generation in any one trait is inversely proportionate to the number of traits under selection.[19] This becomes evident when breeders work on selecting new wheat varieties. The long list of traits they must cover, from wind firmness to cold tolerance to rust resistance to grain size to protein content to bread quality, and many more, slows down selection progress for any one trait. This is heightened if certain traits, say wind firmness and cold tolerance, are negatively correlated and if the underlying genes happen to be linked on the same chromosome; only when this linkage can be broken through recombination can selection progress be accelerated. Nature has an even longer list of traits to consider and operates even more slowly. Finally, as we have seen earlier, evolution is probabilistic, not deterministic; that is, processes such as mutation, genetic drift, meiosis, and mating are subject to chance and unpredictable.

In sum, adaptation takes time, especially when generations may be anywhere from twenty-five to a hundred years or more apart. As a consequence there is always an adaptive lag through which populations drag their feet in following environmental change—tracking the environment—and it is especially pronounced in trees. Add some of the mixed signals the climate gives from time to time and the message of the "Red Queen hypothesis" comes back to mind: you can only stay in place if you keep running. Is it any wonder, then, that tree populations—and all other organisms too—are hardly in equilibrium with their environment? And why should we be surprised that there is no perfect tree out there? In fact, all organisms are approximations, works in progress.

Climate Warming

So far, we have been looking at adaptation and its limits within the context of natural patterns of climate. Meanwhile, what researchers worldwide are documenting with increasing certainty is that a systematic warming of the climate is under way, in part as a consequence of human activities associated with a steady buildup of greenhouse gases. And the rate of change has picked up, leading to projections of mean temperature increases of about 1.5 to 4.5°C by the end of this century.[20] Symptoms of this global trend are already widely visible and range from the accelerated melting of polar ice caps and mountain glaciers to the thawing of permafrost, to northward shifts in the distribution of certain fish species, to changes in the phenology of plants and migratory birds, and many more. What will this mean for trees? Will their resilience as individuals (phenotypic plasticity), or their high level of population diversity (genetic polymorphism), or their unusual capacity for pollen and seed dispersal suffice to provide for continuity in the face of this new challenge? Will some species reach the limit of their adaptability, and, if so, will other species act as a natural replacement for them? Provided they do, will the replacements adequately fulfill the multiple ecosystem functions of their predecessors?

Here again, provenance tests offer a useful basis for modeling potential responses. And the two pine species investigated by Rehfeldt and his coworkers provide a perfect example. This is because these scientists have attempted to make quantitative predictions of how natural populations of the two species would respond to specific warming scenarios. For lodgepole pine in British Columbia, the two scenarios assumed a rise in mean annual temperature (1) by 3°C, without increased precipitation; and (2) by 5°C, associated with an increase in precipitation of 100 mm per year. As calculated, the expected short-term responses by the current populations to both scenarios would bring increases in productivity in the north, decreased productivity in mid-latitudes, and decimation of forests in the south, with more pronounced effects under option (2). This means that adjusting to the new conditions in the long term, so as to optimize productivity, would require a complete redistribution of genotypes across the province. For example, according to these projections the best potential performers for latitude 60° in northeastern B.C. are now found at mid-elevations at latitude 51°—that is, more than 600 miles away. Since no such move can be made by any tree in one fell swoop the question then becomes, How long would it take the existing populations to make the long-term evolutionary adjustments to match the projected climates at their current locations? Estimates made by these scientists, based on reasonable assumptions on existing variation, heritabilities, gene flow, and selection intensity, foresee requirements of from one to three generations in the north, but as many as six to twelve generations in the south. And with generation time in lodgepole pine averaging ~100 years, this adjustment would take from 200 to 1,200 years.[21] Clearly, climate warming, as currently in progress, will cause major disruptions in this particular species in B.C., not to speak of its more southern distribution range in California, where it is likely to face extinction and possible replacement by other species. Even in the north, there may be additional challenges that have not been included in these projections, such as newly evolving life-cycle changes in parasitic insects, as already observed in Alaska and British

Columbia, or the emergence of more virulent pathogens that would weaken or decimate local populations.

As for Scots pine, the projected impacts of global warming are very similar to those in lodgepole pine.[22] Short-term effects would be favorable for populations in the cold climates of eastern Siberia but negative for those in the warmest climates of southwestern Russia. Again, realignment of populations would require transfer over long distances or, if left to the natural processes of evolutionary adjustment, would involve periods of ~100 to 1,500 years. In both cases, the more pronounced mortality in the warmer end of the current distribution would also shrink the source of warm-adapted genes for gene flow to more northern populations, a change ultimately reverberating through the entire distribution range.[23]

These factors explain why adaptive opportunities under directional selection in such a climate gradient would differ between the leading edge and the trailing edge of the distribution range.[24] At the migrating front, populations could draw on preadapted genes from more southern populations, whereas that would not be possible at the retreating edge; adaptation there would depend largely on mutational changes—a slower process that might not keep pace with environmental change.

These pine studies thus offer a glimpse into the ways one can approach the tricky business of making forecasts on population changes within a species in response to climate warming. Their strength is that they are based on actual data from large-scale, long-term field experiments during which detailed weather records have been kept. Not surprisingly, they have received new attention from the global-change research community and have served as a template for other studies of their kind.[25] They complement the large number of studies that have tracked changes in distribution at the species level and have used that information to speculate on the likely fate of vegetation under anticipated climate scenarios. The emergent consensus is that major changes in species representation, species composition, population density, health, and productivity are to be expected or already underway, and that such changes in such keystone species as trees will have cascading effects throughout entire ecosystems.[26]

But we cannot remain passive bystanders in watching that process.

As creators of the problem we are responsible for seeking solutions. Thus, apart from supporting the obvious need for energy reform, we must mobilize a major effort in monitoring the changing planet and find out how best to intervene where needed. In the realm of tree biology, experiments combined with modeling will have to play an important role in this effort, and the work here will need to include silvicultural experiments, experimental plantings, transfer of provenances, introduction of non-native species, releasing cryptic genetic variation by challenging native materials with new environments, and testing hybrid and selectively bred material. All in all, this will require establishing networks of instrumented field trials that engage the full complement of multidisciplinary scientific expertise. Let imagination reign and reason be the guide.

This discussion brings us to the fourth part of the book, which will be devoted to the role of trees in human society—or, more broadly, to the interdependence of trees and humans. Here again, our angle of vision will continue to come from an evolutionary and genetic direction. And the first chapter in that section will bring us back to the world of cottonwoods.

PART IV

Trees and Society

Up to this point we have stayed safely in the natural world, where we have tried to find out, through observation and experiments, how trees function as individuals, populations, and species within their constraints. Here in the final part of the book we will be dealing with the real world, dominated by humans and inescapably shaped by their activity. People have worshiped trees, treated them as symbols, used them for shelter and transport, tapped them for resin, burned them as fuel, milled them into lumber, cleared entire forests, planted and tended them, restored their habitats, and conserved them in parks and reserves. Wherever trees have grown on this planet, no known community or society has failed to relate to them. But of course wherever people deal with natural systems they have conflicting perceptions of the services they expect from them. The final section of this book will look at several episodes in this long relationship and consider some of the bonuses derived from it as well as the dilemmas it has posed. Poplars will again be in the foreground as we examine the history of plant and tree domestication, learn more about new methods in genetic manipulation and their benefits and risks, and consider ways in which we may arrive at compatible combinations of production and conservation functions in our landscapes of the future.

15 / CHANGING RIVERS—
CHANGING LANDSCAPES

R ivers figure prominently in human history. Rivers and the riparian environment have also provided the major venue in which
we familiarized ourselves with the dynamic life of cottonwoods.
This chapter brings us back to that world—in fact, to a geographic area
we visited earlier in our discussion of natural hybridization.

A River Story

The St. Mary River originates in the Rocky Mountains of northern
Montana and flows northeasterly across the border into the prairie land
of Alberta where, near the city of Lethbridge, it joins the Oldman River.
In 1951, a dam was built near Cardston, forming the St. Mary Reservoir
for the purpose of regulating the river's flow for irrigation agriculture

and hydroelectric power. What then happened in subsequent years was a gradual decline of riparian woodlands downstream, an effect commonly observed along dammed rivers in semiarid regions of western North America. It drew the attention of Stewart Rood and his co-workers at the University of Lethbridge, several among them kayakers familiar with the streams of the region.

Riparian woodlands in general, and even more so in the semiarid West, are corridors of unusually high biodiversity. In those regions they often are the only zones where arboreal vegetation can be sustained. Apart from supporting fish and other aquatic organisms, they harbor a rich flora of trees, shrubs, and herbaceous plants as well as offering habitat for a host of mammals, amphibians, birds, and insects.[1] Cottonwoods and willows play an especially significant role in these communities. While obviously important ecologically, they nonetheless seem to be vulnerable to human activity, especially the management of stream flow. It was in this context, given the widespread practice of river damming, that the St. Mary seemed to provide a perfect case study for research aimed at finding out which variables in the water regime were crucial for tree regeneration and survival, and how they could be managed to stem the woodland decline. What followed was a series of studies that eventually led to revised water management procedures for the river and the revival of the threatened vegetation. In fact, the approach became a model for riparian restoration elsewhere.

What Rood and his colleagues found was that traditional flow regulation at the St. Mary dam increased the mortality of existing trees and prevented the recruitment of new trees, resulting in a collapse of woodlands downstream; they also noted that these phenomena were not observed in reaches above the dam, nor along the undammed Belly River nearby.[2] The culprit was the interference with normal river dynamics. Specifically, the St. Mary Reservoir had a relatively small capacity and allowed high water flows to persist during major spring floods. But after the crest, spillway gates would be shut, resulting in a sudden reduction of downstream flow. This would cause an abrupt recession of the riparian water table and would deprive young seedlings of a sustainable water supply, eventually killing them. The lowered water table would also subject older trees to increased stress during the dry summer months and increase their mortality.[3]

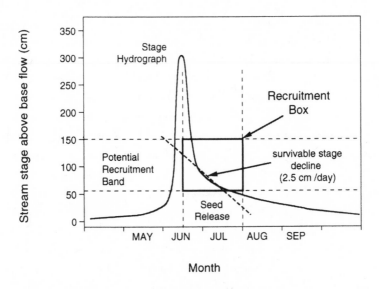

15.1 Application of the riparian Recruitment Box model to the lower St. Mary River. The box frames the critical period (seed release) within which the rate of water recession after the spring high should not exceed the rate of root growth (2.5 cm/day) by cottonwood seedlings to ensure their survival. (*Rood and Mahoney, 2000*). *Reprinted from* Rivers *Vol. 7 (2), p. 113 (2000), with permission from S.E.L. & Associates.*

In an effort to arrive at possible remedies, the scientists studied cross-sections of the river's floodplain at different reaches, related them to the history of water-flow records (based on gage data), and related those to demographic data on the major woodland species found at those locations—mainly cottonwoods and willows. In the greenhouse, they then simulated water withdrawal on seedlings that grew in deep tubes on sand and gravel. What they found was that as long as the water table was lowered at a rate of 2 inches or less per day, root growth of seedlings could keep up with the receding water. Based on those data, they developed the "Recruitment Box" model (fig. 15.1)[4] and calculated the required post-flood ramping of stream flow (the rate of gradual flow reduction) below the dam that would allow seedling regeneration. Lastly, they determined the appropriate timing of flow reduction so that it would coincide with the seed release from the still remaining old cottonwoods.

As might be expected, knowing the desired water regime was one thing, implementing it another. Fortunately, they found the water-resource managers to be responsive to their proposed changes and the dam engineers prepared to try them out. Thus, when a fortuitous rainstorm in June of 1995 caused a fifty-year flood, filling the reservoir to the brim, a favorable stage was set for a first test and the spillway was regulated within the parameters specified by the study. By the end of that year, and to everyone's delight, most river reaches close to seed sources were covered with an abundance of new cottonwood seedlings, confirming the model's predictions. And as if to bolster the case, dams of the Oldman River, operated in that year on the same schedule, resulted in similarly successful cottonwood regeneration downriver.[5]

This almost too-good success story has received considerable attention from the riparian conservation community and has since led to additional restoration projects in other parts of the West.[6] What is significant about it is the way the problem was approached: how the critical variables were identified, how experiments were conducted to quantify the variables, how these values were applied to the actual conditions in the field, and—most importantly—how the key agencies and their personnel were engaged in implementing the desired changes. That didn't happen overnight and required political savvy, social sensitivity, and a progressive mentality among all parties involved. Obviously, irrigation needs had to be duly incorporated, and it became clear that only in years with high snowpacks could such modified water regimes be considered. But since cottonwood regeneration along free-flowing rivers tends to occur only at five- to fifteen-year intervals even under natural conditions, the normal periodicity of high snowpacks would suffice to sustain regeneration of woodlands on dammed rivers.

What adds a genetic and evolutionary dimension to this case—which was not lost on the Lethbridge scientists—is that the St. Mary and its neighboring rivers traverse that famous introgression zone where four species of cottonwoods hybridize (as described in chapter 9). Thus, these rivers' floristic and faunal diversity is even richer than elsewhere, serves as an important conduit of gene flow, and deserves all the more to be restored and maintained.

Restoration and Rehabilitation

The St. Mary project is but one example of the numerous river restoration and rehabilitation efforts now under way in North America and worldwide. Over the last twenty years, streams, rivers, and the riparian environment have systematically moved to center stage on the environmental agenda. This has come about for the simple reason that human heavy-handedness has failed to successfully coordinate the multiple and conflicting services that rivers were supposed to deliver to society: clean water, navigation, fisheries, wildlife, sand and gravel, power, irrigation, waste disposal, recreation, scenery, inspiration—and every one of these in the right amount and at the right time. But rivers have their own dynamics, and periodic floods are a basic part of that. In fact, in the United States, floods—along with wildfires and hurricanes—are among the most common and costliest natural disturbances affecting the national economy. According to data from the US Federal Emergency Management Agency, about nine out of ten presidential disaster declarations are associated with floods, and flood-damage costs for the years 1990 through 1997 amounted to close to $34 billion.[7] Floods also cost lives. As a consequence, ever since a major flood event in the lower Mississippi in 1850, flood control has been one of the key mandates of the Army Corps of Engineers. While the initial emphasis was on building protective levees, later floods revealed their inadequacy, resulting in a call for additional engineering measures such as spillover reservoirs, floodways, and channel improvements.[8] Yet even these were incapable of containing the century floods of the Missouri and Mississippi in 1993. More unusual flooding happened again in 1995 and 1996. In 2002, similar catastrophic floods of several large rivers in Europe, such as the Elbe, Oder, and others, caused enormous losses of life and property, including priceless cultural treasures in art collections and museums. Altogether, these events seemed to call into question the long history of containing these rivers. Apparently, turning rivers into sterile canals is not the solution, even for safety alone, not to speak of all the other beneficial functions we expect from them.

Rivers, more tangibly than any other component of the physical world, embody the central conundrum in our relationship with the environment. Oceans in their immensity seem immutable and timeless in their tidal pulse; mountains are lasting formations in the crust of the earth, comforting symbols of permanence. But rivers are the ever-changing fluid that connects all parts of the landscape and touches every one of us, whether we are city dwellers or farmers. Moreover, because of their dynamic nature, rivers visibly convey to us their immanent process. This may explain why our interference in changing their shape and form not only affects that very process with all its ramifications, but also reveals itself at a perceptible scale and over periods short enough to draw our attention. In addition, cause-effect relationships tend to become evident more rapidly than does our impact on the oceans, the geology of the terrain, or the climate. Yet since river processes touch so many of us in so many different ways, resolutions about how to best deal with their functions are by necessity contentious and will always reflect the social priorities of the period. Science will keep providing the latest information on the underlying mechanisms, but decisions about what changes to make and how to implement them are in the political arena and will ultimately rest with an enlightened public.

The emerging systematic revision in the ways we view and value river functions stems largely from the shortcomings of past approaches to their control and has gained added momentum from the many studies in which free-flowing rivers have been compared with their tamed counterparts. These studies have offered deeper insight into the functioning of riparian ecosystems and have shown floods to be disturbances essential to the maintenance of their health. Seasonal flooding, through erosion and accretion of sediment and organic material, provides habitat for fish, waterfowl, and wildlife. It also increases the connection between the river and the floodplain and its wetlands, thereby augmenting the biodiversity and productivity in the aquatic-terrestrial transition zone. Flooding also helps in maintaining natural succession, controls the distribution and age structure of plant communities, and may stem the invasion of exotic species.[9] If all of these are desirable goods and services, then the emerging paradox is—as aptly stated by Haeuber and Michener—that "people have spent, and continue to spend, tremendous sums of money to alter ecosystems on which they depend for vital ecological services, only to subsequently pour more money into efforts to restore some approximation of the natural disturbance regime to these same ecosystems."[10]

From Control to Management

The change in perspective, in a nutshell, is the change from river control to river management—meaning the adaptive management of processes as a function of time and scale. Many examples now show how this change is gaining wider acceptance, ranging from the selective removal of existing dams, to the careful management of periodic floods, to the reopening of former side channels in major rivers, to bank stabilization via "green engineering," and on to reconfiguring meanders in formerly channelized streams.[11] Clearly, since this is as much a social and political process as it is one of science and engineering, documentation and publicity are essential, in both informing and educating the public. To this end, I can hardly think of a more appealing and compelling publication than *The Flooded Forest*, a brochure recently published by a European working group, FLOBAR2, under the leadership of Keith Richards and Francine Hughes at Cambridge University in the United Kingdom. Compiled by seven researchers and beautifully illustrated, it guides the reader through a sequence of five basic questions: (1) Why have floodplain forests? (2) How do floodplain forests work? (3) How can floodplain forests be restored? (4) What are the prospects for restoration? (5) What are the principal challenges? Combining basic background information with specific case studies, it persuasively shows how real situations can be addressed in efforts to remedy the damage of past river "remedies."[12]

When I say that I see rivers as the examples par excellence through which to portray our changing views concerning the natural environment, I mean that they link our concept of wilderness with that of the human environment; or, in Michael Pollan's term, second nature.[13] To glorify paradise lost is a lost cause, because we are here to stay. Nevertheless, there are lessons to be learned from first nature, where it still exists, and they may well guide us in the ways we manage our human environment. There are two corollaries to this assertion: First, the modest number of remaining pristine river ecosystems deserve special attention. Close study and long-term monitoring of a suitable subset of these deserves high priority. Second, equal attention must be given to a range of rivers that are vital arteries in our inhabited landscapes. We might call them domesticated rivers, and coordinating their monitoring with that of their wild relatives will provide important data on variables that can be manipulated according to need and opportunity. As described above for the St. Mary, this parallel approach is well under way but needs more public recognition and political support.

The changes we see in the paradigms that govern river restoration have their parallels in the broader arena of conservation biology. Increasingly it is recognized that the study of pristine ecosystems is only one part of the agenda—though needless to say it is an exciting part, as anyone who has tasted the wilderness will tell you. But what is equally important is the other part: our better understanding of the far more common environments occupied by humans. In a recent resolution, the Ecological Society of America has declared that it intends to shift its primary focus from the study of undisturbed ecosystems to that of human-influenced systems, so as to better contribute to the improvement of human societies.[14] A similar decision by the Association for Tropical Biology and Conservation pleaded for an "interdisciplinary, participatory, and socially relevant research agenda to study and conserve human-impacted as well as pristine tropical ecosystems."[15] Clearly, there is a continuum out there—not merely a quilt of stitched-together patches—governed by the same underlying processes that function everywhere in a continually changing orchestration. Focusing on the processes that link them all will be the most productive approach toward long-term environmental solutions.

In this broader context, it has been suggested that the term *restoration* is misleading, as it conveys the false notion that the wheel of time can be turned back. We must understand that there is no way that truly pristine conditions can be recreated anywhere on the planet, as humans by now have exerted their influence everywhere. One paleo-ecologist has gone so far as to name the last 8,000 years of the current Holocene the "Anthropocene," suggesting that the spread of agriculture, with its attendant increases in wetlands and the burning and clearing of forests, has had a global effect on climate.[16] For these reasons, to be realistic, the goals of restoration biology, in the view of Millar and Brubaker, have to be reset "to focus less on the dream of restoring apparent 'natural' ecological structures, which turn out to be anthropogenic after all, and more on enabling natural macro-dynamics, which have persisted for multi-millennia prior to and throughout the time of human invasions."[17] Accordingly, these scientists see a need to shift the focus to the mechanisms that underlie biological flexibility and resilience to changing conditions. Rather than emphasizing historical ranges and pre-disturbance species assemblages, they suggest it would be wiser to

> embrace instead landscape macro-dynamics that have characterized populations and species over deep time: the ability to shift locations significantly, fragment into refugia, expand or contract in range, coalesce with formerly disjunct populations, alter dominance relations, foster non-equilibrium genetic diversities, and accommodate population extirpations and colonizations—all in response to changing external conditions.[18]

What that means in practical terms—focusing on mechanisms and processes in the real landscapes of today—will concern us again in a later chapter. First, however, let us examine more closely a category of organisms that more than any other carry the stamp of human interference, a category that over the past 8,000 or more years has systematically spread across the globe and now makes up a significant part of the existing flora and fauna—in fact one without which our cultural landscapes would be unimaginable. I am thinking of the plants and animals that helped lay the foundation for our civilizations of today, namely the domesticated species. What distinguishes them from their wild counterparts and how do they figure in the overall dynamics of human-influenced ecosystems? Here again, we will stick to the bias of our past deliberations and will focus exclusively on plants, with special emphasis on trees. As it turns out, while forest trees were latecomers among domesticates, poplars received some favored treatment early on.

16 / THE DAWN OF AGRICULTURE

The Euphrates River rises in the mountains of eastern Turkey, crosses through the foothills of the Güneydogutaurus Range before heading south into Syria, then makes a major turn east of Aleppo, traverses the wide plains of Syria, and heads in southeasterly direction toward the Persian Gulf. It is at the big bend in its middle course that a prehistoric village, Abu Hureyra, was founded 11,500 years ago. Located on a terrace above the river safe from floods, the settlement relied on a dependable source of water and offered food and shelter for a succession of inhabitants over a period of more than 4,000 years. One of the larger treasure troves of archeological research, it has yielded a great deal of information on one of the most seminal periods in human evolution, namely the transition from a hunting and gathering mode of existence to that of an agricultural society. Embedded in the Fertile Crescent, one of the cradles of modern civilization, the rich vestiges of the village document some of the earliest traces of plant and animal domestication. Paradoxically, its discovery was triggered by a development that would also cause its demise. In early 1971, plans had been completed for the building of a dam to generate a large reservoir in that vicinity. The prospect of irreversibly losing possible sites of historical significance alerted the authorities in charge of antiquities and museums in Syria to invite archeologists from abroad to scour the area before it would be permanently flooded. Responding to the call, Andrew Moore from Oxford University assembled a team of English, American, and Australian archeologists, paleobotanists, and anthropologists who, over the next two years, were able to carry out a major dig under the pressure of time. As it turned out, the ample harvest of research that their work provided belied the haste in which it had to be conducted, and examples have been prominently showcased in many publications and books.[1]

Actually, the site revealed two settlements, one atop the other. The earlier one (at the bottom) was smaller and more primitive and dated back into the twelfth millennium BP (before the present). The later one had its beginnings around 10,400 years ago and eventually developed into a complex village, covering an area as large as 11.5 ha (28.5 acres) and providing permanent residence to a substantial population. Thanks to the abundance and diversity of materials contained in the remains of these settlements, scientists were able to learn more about the original inhabitants, their changing tools, working methods, and diet throughout a time span of several thousand years. Few sites have been so informative about the transformations that accompanied the emergence of agriculture, particularly in a single location at such an early stage. Notably, many of the insights gained derived from the power of modern analytical techniques provided by multidisciplinary science. For example, careful sorting of the soil, layer by layer, and subsequent separation of its components by floating, helped in the recovery of charred plant remains, such as individual seeds, husks, and their fragments from ancient fireplaces. With current radiocarbon accelerator dating techniques such individual grains could be dated to an accuracy of +/- 200 years, thus allowing comparisons of grains from 10,500 years ago with their counterparts from 2,000 years (and generations) later.

Further anatomical and histochemical techniques—employed in examining specific tissues—permitted seed identification and comparison with wild relatives still existing in the region today, thereby offering insight into whether these grains came from wild or domestic origins.

What Gordon Hillman and his botanical coworkers from the Abu Hureyra team were able to synthesize from their twenty-five-year painstaking analysis of the excavations was a sequence of changing scenarios that can be summarized as follows. The occupants of the earlier settlement were hunters and gatherers and used a wide diversity of wild plants, among which were several used as caloric staples. This diversity shrank rapidly during the onset of the dry, cool climate of the Younger Dryas period, which lasted about a thousand years. That climate change led to a decline in wild cereals that in turn triggered the initiation of cultivation practices and the first appearance of domestic rye, either a variety domesticated locally or one introduced as a domestic variety from other settlements nearby. By 9,860 years ago, cultivation had expanded to include domestic einkorn, bread wheat, and lentils, which by ~8,000 years ago were joined by domestic barley, chickpeas, and broad beans. Around 8,500 years ago, these villagers—with their plant-based energy needs—seem to have become entirely dependent on domestic plants. Altogether, the shift from the reliance on caloric staples gathered from the wild to their complete replacement by domesticates took 2,500 years. Changing climatic conditions and a reservoir of suitable crop candidates played key roles in the process. In human terms, the original hunter-gatherers either died out or were driven out by the deteriorating climate, eventually to be replaced by a second wave of settlers as more benign climatic conditions resumed. These long-term inhabitants then cultivated the site with domesticated plants they had brought along, or with plants they domesticated from the vicinity.[2]

Beyond shedding light on crop plants, remains dug up at the site also revealed specifics about the use of wood. Microscopic analysis of charcoal deposits dating back 10 to 11.5 millennia showed that for their fuel wood the villagers relied largely on the gallery forests along the river, which were composed of poplars (*P. euphratica*), willows, tamarisk, and ash. Among these, the quantity of poplar and willow deposits far exceeded those of the other species.[3] This concentration may reflect the relative abundance of (or preference for) species with soft wood that is easy to harvest, dries quickly, and—importantly—regrows again from the stump. Poplars also were believed to have been used as posts in the construction of the earlier dwellings.[4]

Accelerated Plant Evolution

Abu Hureyra is one of a number of archeological sites that helped frame the critical period during which humans have taken plant evolution literally into their own hands. Four aspects in this process deserve special attention, namely (1) the remarkable simplicity of the underlying genetics; (2) the rapidity of change under domestication; (3) the assemblage of different domesticates; and (4) the role of human migration in the spread of domesticates. In the following section, we will briefly address each of these aspects, and then see how the synergy of the four sped the spread of agriculture. After that we will be in a better position to appreciate similarities and differences between crop plants and trees, and the taming of the latter.

When genetic differences between crop plants and their wild relatives are examined, a few domestication traits—characteristics selected for either deliberately or inadvertently—stand out and have been identified as the initiators of the domestication process. Interestingly, almost all of these traits are caused by the strong influence of one or few genes. Probably the earliest ones were mutations that prevented the free shedding of seed. In cereals, this meant a change from ears that shattered when ripe to nonshattering types that had either blocked or weakened abscission mechanisms.[5] If gatherers harvested cereals in the wild with crude sickles (as evidence at Abu Hureyra and other places indicates), they would have brought home a greater proportion of plants that held onto their seed, thereby inadvertently selecting against those that had done their shedding in the wild. Unintentional spillage of these seeds after threshing at the settlement would then form the starter crop of the first domesticates. Subsequent cultivation practices would further favor these mutants and would rapidly spread their genes through the follow-up generations. And then another mechanism came into play that sped up the process: Not only were these plants annuals, but wheat, barley, and several others of these cereals are predominate self-fertilizers (selfers). This means that even recessive mutations could quickly get established in successive generations under selection, year after year, leading to inbred lines of the desired quality. Importantly, too, selfing in these incipient lines would protect them from being genetically contaminated by the surrounding wild forms. By keeping some seed after harvest for the next sowing, the farmers would thus be assured of quality control in their crop. Among neighbors, comparisons between their different lines would further help to identify promising varieties, gradually refining the emergent domesticates. And since these plants were predominate (but not absolute) selfers, occasional cross-pollination among inbred lines would increase the rate of evolution and set domestication on a fast course.[6]

Another important lead-trait under domestication was the loss of seed dormancy. Grasses in Mediterranean-type climates characterized by extremely dry periods have carefully controlled germination patterns. These include inhibition of early germination after seed maturation until the onset of the rainy season in autumn. Also, only some of the seed germinate in the first year while another subset stays dormant into the second year as an insurance policy against the occasional drought year. Needless to say, such protective mechanisms lost their value under cultivation, and in fact were counterproductive. Farmers must have rapidly selected for lines that germinated in synchrony. Additional traits that found early favor in domesticated cereals included erect plants with synchronous flowering, larger numbers of larger seeds through increased size of ears, and the reduction of awns and seed coats.[7] Ultimately, a few strategic mutations, and their accumulation in selected genomes, were what launched the onset of the first Green Revolution.[8] What is even more remarkable, as has recently been demonstrated through comparable DNA analyses, is that some of these mutations not only affected identical traits in such diverse crops as sorghum and rice, but in fact involved corresponding genes in their genomes—and this in plants having been independently domesticated on different continents.[9]

Now, let us be clear that these key mutations didn't happen because early farmers were impatiently waiting for them and favoring their incidence. Presumably those same genes had mutated before over millions of years, along with mutations in other genes, whenever errors occurred during cell division or meiosis. However, out in the wild—in free competition with normal siblings and other species—they succumbed to natural selection and were discarded. Not to shed your seed, not to protect it with a thick coat against drought, not to delay its germination until the time was right, was to ask for trouble in an unforgiving environment—at least until you were able to hitch your fate to a willing biped. And from that moment on, this creature increasingly assumed the necessary protective functions to restore the lost fitness—and in fact enhanced it way beyond its original value under a new set of rules. In this new world, if you stuck to the old rules you were suddenly a weed. In essentially turning evolutionary strategies on their head, domesticates gained on their wild relatives by using humans as their new fitness agent. Similarly, because of more intense and more directional selection, the pace of evolutionary change in these new plants picked up.

Early centers of plant domestication in the Near East, such as Abu Hureyra, and others in the Jordan Valley and central Anatolia, all have one additional feature in common. And it is evidence for the joint existence of several domesticated species in those locations, in fact, a characteristic *assemblage* of domesticates. This assemblage typically included einkorn wheat (*Triticum monococcum*), emmer wheat (*T. turgidum*), barley (*Hordeum vulgare*), chickpea (*Cicer arietinum*), lentil (*Lens culinaris*), and pea (*Pisum sativum*), and also occasionally broad bean (*Vicia faba*), bitter vetch (*V. ervilia*), and flax (*Linum usitatissimum*). What this indicates is that once cultivation began it soon reached out to embrace a whole suite of plants that had favorable agronomic characteristics to begin with. In these candidates, too, traits became selected that rapidly set the domesticates apart from their wild relatives. Evidence thus suggests that each of these crop plants, rather than having had its own independent pathway of domestication, shared trajectories that show a definite clustering in time and space.[10]

When people adopted a sedentary existence through the concentrated use of domesticated crops and animals, the stage was set for the emergence of more elaborate societies. More efficient farming increased harvests and raised survival rates and family size. Excess grains could be stored or made available to others, opening the door to barter. Specialized skills became an asset and led to the emergence of crafts. And with that, society became more complex and structured.[11] At the same time, as villages turned into more sophisticated towns with larger and more differentiated populations of inhabitants, they also became more dependent on a sustained production from their fields and grazing grounds. If harvests declined or even failed, the impact would affect the entire settlement. In other words, if the nomadic way of life had allowed humans to opportunistically track plants and animals to where they thrived, the sedentary lifestyle, with its physical and social structures, robbed people of that flexibility. Thus, the development of a system of raising, harvesting, and storing a complementary range of crops for normal, recurrent conditions was no guarantee of permanent benefit if those conditions changed.

Such a period seems to have happened 8,200 years ago, as another global climate change, the Mini Ice Age, brought a cold and dry spell to that part of the world. It lasted a full 400 years—sixteen human generations—and its effect is reflected in a sudden and simultaneous gap in archeological records at many locations in the Near East. Evidently, it resulted in the abandonment of settlements throughout the region, from the Jordan Valley to the heights of the Anatolian plateau.[12] Forced by the harsh conditions, people apparently left their towns in search of more hospitable places to settle. And in all likelihood, as farmers do whenever they have to move elsewhere, they took their crops and animals along. An attractive oasis during that period must have been the mild shores of the Euxine Lake (later the Black Sea), then a freshwater body fed by the Danube, Dniester, Bug, Dnieper, and Don rivers. As suggested by recent geologic and archaeological evidence, that basin served as a refuge for the early agronomists and their domesticates for a short period, although they were once again driven away. What precipitated the exodus this time was a cataclysmic flood through the Bosporus. That signal event has been dated to 7,600 years ago and is attributed to the systematic warming occurring after the Mini Ice Age, causing glaciers to melt and sea levels to rise. What happened at the critical moment was that the Mediterranean spilled over into the 105 meter lower Euxine Lake. A landmark in the history of the human race and possibly related to the biblical flood, the event has been graphically described in a fascinating book by two of the scientists who reconstructed it in detail, William Ryan and Walter Pitman from Columbia University.[13] The changes it brought about happened at breathtaking speeds, uncommon with most geological processes. At that crucial time, the waters rushing through the disintegrating dam at the Bosporus must have turned into a mighty waterfall, gouging out a flume below and developing into a torrential river that raised the level of this enormous freshwater lake at a rate of one foot a day! Inside two years, Euxine Lake was transformed into the Black Sea. And what once had been fertile fields and thriving villages were now buried below 300 feet of salt water.

It is hard to visualize the immediacy and scale of the cataclysm, let alone imagine its impact on those who happened to be caught in its vicinity. Untold numbers must have perished, while others barely survived by sheer luck. But there may have been enough people in more favorable locations that allowed them to move away from the advancing waters in a more organized fashion, even permitting them to carry away some of their most precious assets. Undoubtedly these would have included the basic tools and seeds that were the basis of their livelihood, as well as their domestic animals. It seems likely too that the exodus must have taken several different directions away from the Black Sea basin, ranging from the west toward the Mediterranean, to the northwest up the Danube Valley, to the north into the Ukraine, and east toward central Asia. Artifacts recovered in many studies of these different routes have helped to trace the migratory process and its timing. What has been found suggests that the Black Sea flood may well have helped to accelerate the spread of agriculture from its origin in the Fertile Crescent.[14] The repeated findings of the original founder crops in successive locations suggest that the migrants held on to their proven bundle of domesticates and established them anew at their new domiciles.[15] Finally, as persuasively explained by Jared Diamond, the similarity of climatic conditions in the Mediterranean basin to those of the original source region allowed these crops to be instantly successful in their new locations so that no new physiological adjustments were required to new weather regimes. In fact this genetic readiness may have strongly contributed in giving the Mediterranean a head start in the evolution of advanced societies compared to other regions of the world.[16]

It would be tempting to stay with the development of crop plants for the remainder of the book, as they are so rich in genetic and evolutionary detail and so intimately tied to geography and human culture. All of us who have traveled to different corners of the world and off the beaten track have been fascinated by the diversity of farming practices, the color of regional produce in local markets, and the food derived from these sources. But farming also involves woody plants—if it didn't, we wouldn't have apples and walnuts, let alone wine. In the next chapter we will remain in the cradle of agriculture, but this time to get a feel for the role played by trees in these early times.

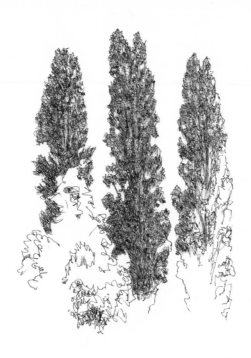

17 / THE FARMER'S TREES

If annual crops allowed early farmers in the Near East to take advantage of nutritious plants with short life cycles, reaping the benefits of culture within months and thereafter adding successive improvements year after year, this was not as easily accomplished with the trees growing in their surroundings. As a consequence the shift from collecting nuts and fruit from dry woodlands to actually planting and tending these trees near settlements happened much later, only around 6,000 years ago. Several factors contributed to this delay. First and foremost, trees take three to eight or more years before they bear any fruit. This means that a stable sedentary existence is a precondition for starting even the mere beginnings of an orchard. Another problem has to do with the genetics of trees—by now no longer a secret to the reader. In contrast to the selfing habits of crop plants, trees are predominately outcrossers, requiring cross-pollination to set any fruit. And as a consequence they are highly *heterozygous*, giving rise to highly varied progenies, most of which would be unsuitable for cultivation. In turn, that means that it takes at least two trees with desirable fruit or seed characteristics to get fruit production going, that only a small fraction of their progeny will inherit those traits, and that these characteristics will only reveal themselves once the seedlings have reached maturity. Therefore, selection gains via sexual reproduction are slow and late in coming, requiring major up-front investments with few early returns. These factors explain why what occurred almost as a free by-product with cereals and other annuals, thanks to their genetic makeup, presented a major obstacle with trees.

No wonder that the earliest evidence for tree cultivation in the Near East is from trees such as olives, figs, and date palms—species in which vegetative propagation allowed the grower to bypass sexual reproduction. In fact, a recent discovery in the Jordan Valley suggests that fig cultivation may have been initiated as early as 11,400 years ago—even before the domestication of cereals and legumes.[1] Vegetative propagation worked well by taking cuttings in figs, by the rooting of basal knobs in olive, and by transplanting offshoots in date palms.[2] Grapevine cultivation via the use of cuttings began about the same time. Vegetative propagules were passed on from one generation of farmers to the next and migrated with them. In fact, some of these clones may still be in cultivation today, as suggested by the comparable fingerprint of certain current date pits with well-preserved ancient specimens from the same region (Daniel Zohary, personal communication). Only much later, during the first millennium B.C., did apple, pear, plum, and other fruit trees appear in the ranks of domesticates, and this strictly by the use of grafting—a technique possibly introduced from China that provided another method of bypassing sexual reproduction. Thus, the capture of suitable cultivars was a question of identifying rare deviants among wild types that held promise as desirable individuals, and then making more copies of them through cloning. However, since among these rare deviants even fewer were governed by a dominant mutation, subsequent breeding brought little reward. One such exception was almond, in which a single, dominant gene changed the bitter, toxic seed into a sweet one.[3] Almond culture could therefore be pursued through collecting non-bitter seed, planting them again, and later culling the fraction of bitter trees among their progeny.[4]

Apart from fruit trees, other trees were clearly of use to the early farmers, among them those that we have already encountered in the earliest remains of Abu Hureyra, 11,500 years ago—namely poplars and willows. Both grew close to fresh water, where humans liked to settle, and both had properties that made them useful in many ways. Their low-density wood dried relatively quickly for use as fuel, while their foliage was an excellent forage for goats. Goats, the notorious browsers around the perimeter of a settlement, probably revealed to their keepers a most essential trait about poplars and willows, which is their propensity to regrow by root suckers and sprout shoots. Nothing would have been more welcome than a perpetual supplier of twigs and leaves near one's abode, especially if it exhibited a growth rate far superior to that of other trees. Impervious to the annual floods, these trees were able to take advantage of water when it was abundant and then stretch it out into the dry season thanks to their deep rooting. Most importantly, poplars grew in forms and dimensions that made them uniquely suitable in house construction. Their straight trunks, strong but not heavy, were especially good as rafters, thus not unduly weighing down the mud-brick walls. By contrast, it was the supple, flexible nature of their shoots and branches that made willows useful for binding and tying, for making baskets, and for anchoring reed nets in a stream. Also, knowledge about the medicinal value of willow leaves and bark, which contain salicylic acid, must have been transmitted to these early farmers from their ancestral hunters and gatherers.

Unfortunately, the ephemeral nature of poplars and willows—with light wood that doesn't preserve well, and tiny, quickly degraded seeds that disperse widely—left meager identifiable traces in archeological digs aside from charred remains. Occasionally, the favorable combination of extreme aridity and high average temperature allowed the preservation of wood in buildings to modern days. Such a find was made in the Ein Bokek region in today's Israel, an excavation that brought to light a castle from the Limes Romanum line dating back to the fourth century AD. Its roof logs were preserved in their original position and identified from microscopic specimens to belong to poplars and tamarisks.[5] Another carefully investigated site, the St. Catherine Monastery in Southern Sinai, originating in the sixth century AD, showed the wide use of poplars as roof timbers, along with Mediterranean cypress and date palm.[6] In both cases, poplar timbers would have come from Euphrates poplar (*P. euphratica*), commonly growing in that region, or else from black poplar (*P. nigra*), a species widely occurring throughout Anatolia and spread by humans beyond its natural range.

Columnar Poplar Cultivars

What would make black poplar especially desirable, and why would migrating farmers have included it among the live possessions they carried along to their next destination? Here, I will stick my neck out and argue that it wasn't just any black poplar they kept with them—it was a columnar cultivar of that species. Let me say up front that this is speculative, strictly a hypothesis that still waits to be tested by hard evidence, and let me develop my argument and its plausibility.

What first needs repeating is that the current columnar cultivars of *P. nigra* (e.g., 'Italica,' 'Thevestina,' 'Plantierensis,' and others) are deviant forms of the normally broad-canopy wild type. Similar columnar forms have spontaneously arisen in other poplar species (*P. alba*, *P. tremula*) and in many other genera, such as beech, cypress, maple, oak, pine, tulip tree, yew, and more. In other words, it is not uncommon to find this aberrant columnar form cropping up among normal cohorts whenever large numbers of seedlings are raised in nurseries. Apparently, all it takes is for one or two genes governing branch angle to mutate, and pronto you have a skinny tree. (It may well be that some of these "sports" from diverse genera share exactly the same mutation.) In *P. nigra*, such an individual can be easily propagated from cuttings and thus multiplied and perpetuated at will.

Let me then enumerate the key reasons why early farmers would have been particularly keen to take advantage of such a mutant. (1) The columnar type manifests itself early, in the first or second year, and allows easy quality control. (2) The form is predictable and stable; environmental influences may affect the growth rate but won't change the form of the crown. (3) Narrow crowns demand less space and allow tight plantings, especially in single or double rows; more production of wood, branches, and leaves can be obtained in less space. (4) Narrow crowns, when grown in the open, maintain a long live crown, often extending to the base of the tree. (5) Narrow crowns allow easier branch harvest; lopping of branches for fuel and fodder is easier than on wide-crowned trees. (6) The propensity of these cultivars to regrow epicormic branches anywhere along the stem allows continual harvests, year after year, while the tree maintains an expanding root system. (7) Row plantings make excellent windbreaks and serve to delineate property boundaries; the flexibility of the long, thin, upward-angled branches, combined with the small leaves, gives the trees high wind stability. (8) Row plantings minimize the length of irrigation ditches where these are needed to sustain trees in an arid climate. (9) Upon final harvest, the tree's straight stem makes for good building material. (10) Once harvested, one or several sprout shoots may allow regrowth of a tree while drawing from the existing root system, and the tendency for those roots to seek and find even fleeting sources of moisture is an added bonus. In sum, columnar *P. nigra* must have been a farm wife's dream of a multipurpose tree—except for the absence of edible fruits.

What further strengthens the case is that, to this day, the columnar poplar is among the ubiquitous trees seen around farms and villages in Anatolia and the Near East. And it is not a mere vestige of the past, a historical remnant of earlier times. When visiting a state research institute in Izmit, Turkey, back in 1989, I was intrigued to see a vigorous program in place aimed at expanding the germ plasm collection of columnar *P. nigra* for the country. It was considered a priority in the selective breeding of poplar for extensive use, and the research was considered just as valuable as the development of fast-growing poplar hybrids for more intensive plantation culture. I could see the justification for it on later visits to local sawmills in Anatolia, where the bulk of the lumber and roundwood was derived from these trees. So if the widespread presence of columnar poplars in arid regions of subsistence agriculture in the temperate zone is any indication—I'm thinking of Uzbekistan, Afghanistan, Pakistan, Northern India, and the continental regions of western China—it is hard to dismiss the notion that these cultivars must have been actively dispersed by early migrants from an original source in the Fertile Crescent and later perhaps by travelers along the Silk Road.

In fact, branch harvesting, or lopping, is still widely practiced today on poplars and other trees in that part of the world. I had a chance to see it up close on a trek in the mountainous region of Nepal. What first drew my attention as I was approaching one of those remote hamlets along the path were a number of columnar silhouettes against the horizon. My poplar receptor hastened the pace, but what became increasingly darker green as I came closer eventually turned out to be a group of evergreen oaks that had been trimmed by machete. I then learned that *Quercus semecarpifolia* is one of several native trees eminently suited to repeated lopping, since it keeps regrowing new branches and thus provides a long-term source of fuel, fodder, and bedding for domestic animals. Remarkably, the task of climbing these trees and harvesting the branches was largely delegated to young girls, since they were lighter and caused less breakage than boys—at least that was the explanation given. Knowing how the task of collecting fuel wood, often requiring a full day on those steep, deforested hillsides, fell to women and children, made the explanation more plausible. Nonetheless, having been in the top of trees myself many times, I had to admire the courage and skill of these girls hacking away at tough branches, often on trees growing precariously over some steep precipice. In India, the tradition of tree lopping was considered highly undesirable among forestry officials because it downgraded the quality of timber. But here in the meager existence economy of villagers in the Himalayas it made good sense, especially because it maintained live trees on the ground and kept the soil in place in this erosion-prone region of seasonal monsoon rains.

Now we may ask, If the columnar form was an asset to poplars in a new domestication environment, why would it have been a disadvantage before? Why don't we see more columnar individuals in the wild, in natural populations of cottonwoods, balsam poplars, aspen, or other poplar species growing off the beaten track, far from civilization? Indeed, we may ask the same question for all other tree genera mentioned above in which columnar cultivars have been found and propagated—Why do they occur only in nurseries? Interestingly, the person who has helped shed light on these questions is not a botanist or forest scientist, but the river geomorphologist whom we met in chapter 2. Luna Leopold's interest in branching patterns in river drainages once led him to compare them with those in trees. Having studied many cases of drainage nets and their hierarchies of tributaries, he recognized that they shared similarities with branch orders in trees. Assuming that principles of economy would constrain the probable outcomes in both types of systems, he analyzed a number of conifers and hardwoods and compared the numbers and lengths of the different branch orders with those commonly found in river drainages. The quantitative comparison—another example of physical laws optimizing efficiency in both physical and biological systems—showed remarkable parallels.[7]

One detail in Leopold's study specifically relates to the columnar form. He found that for tall, narrow trees the most efficient crown geometry is one with a central stem and successive tiers of short, horizontal branches (see the cartoon trees in fig. 17.1). By efficient he meant that this form minimizes the total amount of branch length—or plumbing—needed to feed the leaves at the periphery of the crown.[8] Indeed, that is the crown geometry we typically see in most tall conifers, perhaps in its most extreme form in the slim spires of subalpine fir or black spruce. However, the same crown space could be filled with other branching types, for example by the tree on the right in fig. 17.1. Here, more branch length is needed to reach the periphery, and mutual shading limits the light that reaches the inner portions of the crown. In other words, the angled branching, as found in columnar cultivars of poplars and other species, wastes too much assimilates (nourishment) on branch wood in relation to the corresponding gains in photosynthetic surface. In competition with other crown forms in a stand, this inefficiency would become a liability. In addition, columnar trees cast a narrower pattern of shade and allow closer root competition from other vegetation, thereby diminishing their own growth. In sum, trees that achieve a narrow crown by means of narrow branch angles are at a competitive disadvantage and tend to succumb to natural selection in the wild. Angled branching is more efficient for shorter, broader, umbrella-like crowns. But if you want a tall, narrow tree with lots of branch wood that can even sustain itself via resprouting, a columnar poplar is hard to beat. Besides, if planted in the open, some mutual shading by branches may actually not be a bad thing for some of the inner leaves, especially in arid climates where high heat load on the outside leaves makes them less efficient in photosynthesis.

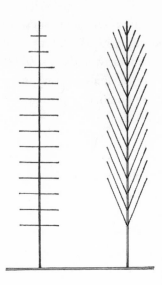

17.1 Comparison of two different branching patterns that fill the same crown space with an equal number of branches. The pattern on the left minimizes branch length and mutual shading. Note that on the tree to the right each branch is more than twice as long as its counterpart to the left.

Poplar Varieties and History

Today, we can travel the five continents and will run into columnar poplars in the remotest corners of the globe. In fact, ask anybody anywhere about poplar, *peuplier, pioppo, populieren, alamo, topola*—and they'll draw a fingerlike form in the air. How many different clones are there, and how old are they? Who dispersed them, and when did they first appear in a given region? These are all questions that beg to be answered. Perhaps the most notable form of all is still the Lombardy poplar, *P. nigra* 'Italica,' a male clone probably stemming from the Levant and which saw wide propagation in the Mediterranean region during the eighteenth century. It became the signature tree of Napoleon I, who—during his expansive campaigns—had it planted systematically along major routes to mark them for easy orientation, especially in winter. Its counterpart in the hotter, drier regions of the Balkans, the Near East, North Africa, and central Asia is the female *P. nigra* 'Thevestina,' conspicuous by its pale, smooth trunk and small leaves. An equally pale trunk, but a slightly broader crown characterize the columnar *P. alba* 'Bolleana' (or cv. 'Pyramidalis'), which has shown its mettle in some of the most extreme continental climates in Asia. I am thinking, for example, of Tulufan (or Turpan), an ancient town along the old Silk Road in northwestern China. Lying in a depression of 150 m below sea level, it experiences temperature differentials between summer and winter of close to 100°F, receives zero precipitation, and derives its water supply strictly from its *Karezs*, an underground irrigation system fed from the nearby Heavenly Mountains. This is an area famous for its melons and raisins, grown in irrigated orchards, and every one of these orchards is surrounded by a lush screen of columnar white poplars—testimony to their remarkable hardiness. Indeed, it may be in their aggregate plantings as windscreens where columnar poplars find their greatest commercial use today. And nowhere will you see that on a larger scale than in the aggressive program adopted by the Chinese government to stop desertification in the country's interior northwest.

If columnar poplars may have given farmers the initial impetus to propagate these trees for multiple uses, did these proto-domesticates, or other poplar cultivars transported along with them, gradually spread their genes into the gene pools of resident native populations of poplar? An obvious region to receive such gene flow would have been Europe, the destination of much early migration, and its native black poplar. What do we know about that species and its genetic diversity? That question was raised in 1990, and the answer then was, precious little. Actually, the question had come up in a much broader context, when general concerns about the European forests and their genetic resources had called for action by the European Union (EU). This attention resulted in the establishment of a European Forest Genetic Resources Program (EUFORGEN), and black poplar was designated as one of the species to be given high priority.[9] This riparian poplar had experienced a systematic erosion of its populations over the centuries as a consequence of the full array of human pressures and had persisted only in fragmented pockets of its original distribution range. Preservation was urgently called for, and an inventory of existing genetic diversity seemed to be a logical beginning. To this end, a coordinated study was launched, involving researchers from eleven different laboratories in Europe. They chose to focus on six river systems ranging from Spain to Hungary, and ended up analyzing material from 615 native trees in twenty-three different populations for selected morphological and biochemical markers. As in the other species described earlier, chloroplast DNA (cpDNA) offered a sensible probe for the purpose (remember that cpDNA is maternally transmitted and haploid, and so is especially suited to identify historical lineages and their migratory paths). Results showed that the total of 615 sample trees broke down into eighty-one different haplotypes (or haploid genotypes) that could be divided into two major groups, a western and an eastern group. Spain harbored the greatest diversity, with forty-one haplotypes occurring in the Ebro Valley alone, thus supporting palynological evidence that the Iberian Peninsula served as a refuge during the last glaciation.[10] Other clusters of variation were in Austria, Hungary, and Italy. At the same time, certain haplotypes could be found widely dispersed throughout the many regions sampled. For example, the most common one was in as many as 46 percent of all trees and absent only in Hungary. The way these results were interpreted was that the Pyrenees and the Alps were major impediments to the postglacial migration from the refuges, thus acting to conserve major pools of diversity south of their ranges. The few haplotypes that made it across or around them in the East then rapidly colonized the more northern habitats in the absence of much competition, thereby systematically expanding their own numbers. And the ever-changing conditions along river courses kept favoring the rapid colonizers afterwards.[11]

But as the authors of the study rightly observed, human influence in shaping the current distribution pattern of black poplar cannot be ignored, especially since vegetative propagation greatly facilitated the dispersal of select genotypes at the expense of others.[12] Here we are back to the original question, namely, How important may also have been historical gene flow from domesticated cultivars of black poplar, such as the columnar types, that were introduced by farmers from the Near East? A current study at the University of Gent, Belgium, is under way to shed light on this question (Wout Boerjan, personal communication).

Chestnuts

Among the trees mentioned earlier for their value as fruit trees, I omitted one that may have been important to early farmers as much for its fruit as for the multiple products of its vegetative growth—a true multiple-use tree, the European chestnut, *Castanea sativa*. Member of a genus that during the Tertiary spread to both the west and the east from its center in Asia, its distribution range now covers the southern part of Europe and northern Turkey. Well known for its sweet, starchy fruit, chestnut also produces valuable timber, and its decay-resistant wood has long been utilized for fence posts and stakes for orchards and vineyards. In addition, thanks to its high tannic acid content, the bark has been widely used in tanning. Today we can find the European chestnut in two distinct types of stands: in extensive mixed hardwood forests covering mid-elevation hillsides, and in carefully tended groves or orchards around settlements. The latter are managed for their fruit and represent cultivars selected for edible quality that have been grafted onto wild rootstock. Forest stands, by contrast, are managed for fuel wood, timber, and wildlife habitat, and have much smaller-seeded fruit.

How did chestnut fare during the last ice age? Was it able to survive in southern Europe, or did it suffer extirpation and then remigrate from northern Turkey? The species seems to be missing in pollen records of the Mediterranean peninsulas from that glacial period, although it does show up in profiles 9,000 years ago in Spain and Greece and about 5,500 years ago in Italy.[13] What is beyond doubt is that its major expansion happened during the Roman Empire and thereafter, resulting in its current distribution about 1,000 years ago. Evidently, humans played a major role in its spread, eventually bringing the tree as far north as the British Isles. The question has even been raised as to whether it was the selected fruit cultivars that arrived first, then giving rise to descendants that became feral thereafter, like those now populating the Mediterranean hillside forests, rather than the other way around—an interesting idea.[14] Further light has been shed on the species by a recent phylogeographical study that analyzed amounts and patterns of variation in cpDNA sampled from thirty-eight Mediterranean forest populations located between Portugal and northeastern Turkey. The results confirmed the importance of Turkey as a source region after the last glaciation, but also pointed to the Iberian Peninsula as a likely refuge during that period. The overall diversity measured was moderate, showing eleven haplotypes—and the most frequent haplotype could be found almost everywhere. Also, in comparison with other members of the European Fagaceae, cpDNA differentiation among populations of chestnut was much lower (Gstc = 0.433; a quantitative measure ranging from 0 to 1) than that of beech (Gstc = 0.902) and European white oak (Gstc = 0.782). Given this overarching similarity throughout the present range, with its corresponding low level of geographical structure, little insight could be gained into the likely patterns of postglacial migration. However, this itself is consistent with the notion that humans have been the major agent of distribution of the species, largely blurring any regional differences that might have arisen through natural dispersal and colonization. Clearly, the European chestnut today carries the genetic imprint of the last thousand years of human interference.[15]

This chapter has offered a brief overview of the emergence of trees as domesticated crops. Here, given trees' longer life cycle and the presence of a mating system (cross-pollination) less favorable for rapid domestication, vegetative propagation of favored cultivars has played a significant role in the process. As in annual crops, mutant forms with desirable characteristics provided the raw material for selective cultivation. Poplars and chestnuts are good examples and to this day form a link between farms and forests, and between domesticates and wild relatives that coexist in close proximity. In the next chapter we will follow poplar on its pathway from a farmer's tree to one of the most intensively cultivated trees, first in Europe, and eventually in other parts of the world.

18 / FROM FARMERS' TREES
TO TREE FARMS

On New Year's Day 2005, the *New York Times* carried an article on "Techniques That Might Smile upon Mona Lisa." It described work by a Smithsonian Institution materials expert who had examined the conditions under which typical paintings from the classical period between the thirteenth and sixteenth centuries would undergo physical change and develop cracks. Since most of this art had been painted on wood, much depended on how different types of wood responded to variations in temperature and humidity. Having conducted careful tests under a range of conditions, the expert came to the conclusion that some museum practices did more harm than good to paintings and could be improved in specific ways.[1] Since curators at the Louvre had recently found new warping in Leonardo's *Mona Lisa*, an icon of the museum that had been painted on poplar wood, the expert's studies on cottonwood were considered especially relevant. To say this caught my eye is an understatement. Mona Lisa issuing her mysterious smile from a poplar panel! What nobler purpose for this humble wood!

It turns out that poplar wood was a common substrate for paintings in the Mediterranean region from the Middle Ages forward. This was the finding of a comprehensive study of wood-based paintings conducted by Jacqueline Marette, a scientist associated with the Louvre.[2] Her research involved a painstaking analysis of hundreds of paintings from a wide range of museums and was carried out with the aid of all available macro- and microscopic techniques. What she found was that Cimabue, Giotto, Fra Angelico, Botticelli, Ghirlandaio, Leonardo, Fra Filippo Lippi, Raphael, and other luminaries from that period, all seemed to have had a special affinity to poplar. In fact, of 345 Italian paintings studied, a full 90 percent had poplar as a base. Why this preference? Was poplar wood the ideal substrate, singled out through a careful selection based on comparative tests? Or was it merely common practice, the accepted tradition that reliably gave good results? A geographic comparison helped to shed further light on the question. What Marette found was that in Spain the bias for paintings on panels in fact moved in favor of Scots pine, with poplar down to 36 percent, followed by walnut and oak; those last two woods, on the other hand, were preferred in France, where poplar was left with a mere 11 percent. In Germany, from a total of 219 paintings examined only a single one was on poplar, whereas spruce, silver fir, linden, and oak shared the majority of other panels in almost equal proportions. Marette concluded that the wood chosen by painters largely reflected whatever lumber was commonly available in the different regions at the time, which in turn mirrored the composition of timber species in the local forests.

The Marette study did more than identify the type of wood under the paintings; it also gave their dimensions, the number of panels used, and further details on wood condition, support structures, visible damage, and the like. These details help us to get some idea of the dimensions of the original trees from which the lumber was cut. For example, the Mona Lisa's modest size fits on a single panel of 80.0 x 53.4 cm that is 1.5 cm thick. But some paintings, such as a portrait of Seneca from the Italian School of 1464–1476, had panels as wide as 77.7 cm (31 inches), calling for a good-size tree. The largest artwork described, a representation of the Madonna and Child surrounded by saints (Venetian School, fourteenth century), now hanging in the Vatican library, is 2.0 m tall and 9.55 m wide and is made up of six panels. These panels had to be on average 1.6 m (5.3 feet) wide, and if they came from the same tree (quite likely since lumber was then typically stacked for drying, tree by tree) that would have been a colossal specimen. Did poplars grow that big? Only exceptionally, and most likely not around farms. Quite possibly the source of that lumber may have been one of the residual white poplars, *P. alba*, left over in a remote river valley.

Now, isn't it stretching it a bit to extrapolate from data on wood-backed paintings to the lumber market in general? How could poplar have played such a dominant role in Italy, a country with one of the richest arborifloras of Europe and with a seafaring tradition actively bringing home many exotic woods? Recall that this was a feudal society with a powerful church that had long supported a sophisticated artisan culture. Would the discriminating cabinetmakers of Florence or Venice have preferred poplar to the readily available walnut, maple, oak, cherry, rosewood, mahogany, or ebony? Indeed, as other studies have shown, those woods figured prominently in post-Renaissance furniture, and poplar was largely relegated to use in framing and inlay.[3] Thus, it seems more plausible that the adoption of poplar as the preferred substrate for paintings must have been more deliberate than incidental. Considering such favorable properties of this wood as its light weight, low tendency to split when nailed or to warp when dry, the absence of resin and other inclusions, and its uniform capacity to bind with paint or gesso, the choice seems quite appropriate.

Poplar in the Padana

The role of poplar wood in the history of Italian art offers only one glimpse of the tree's multiple uses in that country. A more comprehensive look at its changing significance in Italy may well focus on the *Padana,* the Po Valley, the place where, over time, poplar culture has been most prominent on the Italian peninsula. In fact, that region turned into a hot spot for poplar culture worldwide. Now, when we think of European rivers, the Po hardly comes to mind, given such heavyweights as the Danube and the Rhine. Yet in terms of annual discharge into the Mediterranean it ranks only behind the Nile and the Rhone.[4] Originating in the Piedmont Mountains close to the French border, the Po threads its course eastward, and along its 400 miles through Lombardy, Emilia-Romagna, and Veneto collects the major tributaries descending from the Alps and the Apennines. As do all large rivers, it has a long history of recurrent floods and changes in its meandering course, being both a provider and a threat to the communities in its vast basin. Natural forests along the river used to be chiefly composed of poplar, willow, and alder in close proximity to the stream, and of elm, ash, maple, and oak at safe sites on higher terraces. Some of these forests served as hunting grounds for the nobility, some were part of large farms (*Cascine* or *Casale*), and others belonged to monasteries. Records show that the abbeys of Lucedio near Vercelli and of San Benedetto di Muleggio planted poplars on the banks of watercourses as early as the thirteenth century.[5] Goethe, in his *Italian Journey* (1786–87), wrote that on arriving in Cento on October 17 he climbed the church tower (as was his habit), so as to have a view of the countryside, and that he saw "a sea of poplars" extending into the distance.[6] Over the years, as the population in the Po valley increased— and with it the hunger for agricultural land—forests were shrinking, just as some of the wetlands were systematically diked and canalized. The development of irrigation helped expand the culture of rice, which had been introduced to the Piedmont and Lombardy in the early fifteenth century. Those forest stands remaining tended to be left in the major hazard zones of the river, giving the resilient poplars and willows an extended lease on life. These trees, then, served the household needs of the local people who learned to use them through coppicing and pollarding—cutting the trees back to resprout either at the base or at 6 or 7 feet above the ground, out of the reach of cattle—in a quasi-sustainable fashion.

Industrialization during the 1800s brought new demands for energy. Here, let us step back for a moment and look at the Padana in a broader context. Its geographical location in the north of the peninsula puts it within the cross-cultural influences of France to the west, the Germanic peoples to the north, Roman traditions in the south, and Venetian mercantilism in the east. This allowed for a potent mix of creativity, innovation, and solid craftsmanship that, when combined with entrepreneurial savvy, would allow new industries to spring up and flourish in a short time (the analogy with natural hybridization zones will not be lost on genetically minded readers). The region soon became the center of a thriving metallurgy industry, which later gave rise to Fiats, Alfa Romeos, and Ferraris. The introduction of the silkworm led to mass propagation of mulberries in the Po valley and formed the basis for the silk and fashion industry in Milan. The shift in papermaking from a rag base to wood, introduced from Germany, contributed to the development of a local pulp and paper industry, which in turn stimulated the mass propagation of poplar and the nursery industry. Not to be forgotten is rice culture, with the French influence of the *cuisine piémontaise* helping to develop new varieties of the grain, such as Arborio and Carnaroli, which created a new niche market that can hold its own to this day (to the delight of us risotto lovers). Of course, all these riches came at a political price. The turbulent history of the House of Savoy, monarchs of Savoy and Piedmont for nine centuries, and their ever-changing alliances with the rulers of France, Burgundy, Spain, and the Hapsburgs, has left a telling record of the continual tensions and warfare also experienced in the region.

Yet it was also the political savvy of a son of the Piedmont, Count Camillo Benso di Cavour, that in 1860 helped Italy to its nationhood. Cavour possessed an interesting blend of views; influenced by the July 1830 revolution in France (and perhaps his Calvinist mother), he was also a conservative monarchist with a liberal mind, and became the first prime minister of the new kingdom of Italy. Considered one of the cleverest and most successful statesmen in nineteenth-century Europe, and known for both his duplicity and charisma, his ministerial reign was sadly of short duration, as he died one year after his ascendancy at the age of fifty.[7] Nevertheless, and of particular interest to us, Cavour and his ancestors also left a legacy of some consequence for the role of poplar in the *Padana*. Here, as in other parts of Europe, the large estates of the aristocracy were often true centers of progress, trial grounds for novel agricultural practices, new machinery, new crop plants, and new cattle breeds. That was the case at Leri, one of the Cavour estates near Vercelli and long managed by Camillo himself in highly innovative ways, inspired by his travels abroad. He had also been instrumental in founding an Agricultural Society in Turin to establish a forum for new ideas in more productive land use. At another family estate nearby, in Santena, an earlier Cavour back in the 1770s had been pathbreaking in another way, planting some of the first—maybe *the* first—"Canadian poplars" in Italy, introduced from a French nursery in Chambéry, the old capital of Savoy.[8] These "gigantic" poplars, as they were later described, combined with the newly modernized cultural practices, were to revolutionize poplar culture in the region for years to come.

Where in Canada had these giants come from, and what made them grow to such dimensions? Isn't it a bit surprising that northern poplars would outperform the southern natives on their home ground? In truth, these trees had nothing to do with Canada, although they definitely had exotic blood—from the American eastern cottonwood, *P. deltoides*, a species that had been introduced into France by the end of the seventeenth century.[9] The New World and its abundance of diverse tree species had become an ideal source from which to obtain plants and trees to enrich the much sparser flora of the European continent, and any large landowner of that time prided himself in surrounding his villa with exotics and unusual tree forms. Genetic contamination of native germ plasm was no issue at that time; in fact, if anything, it was welcomed. And it happened. As mentioned in chapter 9, spontaneous matings between eastern cottonwood and the local black poplar, *P. nigra*, gave rise to some unusually good growers, and it turned out that they could be easily propagated by stem cuttings. Probably the earliest of these hybrids was identified and described in 1755 by Duhamel du Monceau and later named *P. serotina* Hartig.[10] Of course, given the ease with which these matings occurred, additional hybrids entered the stream of nursery propagation under a variety of designations. These included, for example, Carolina poplar, Swiss poplar, and Euramerican hybrid poplar, although today's nomenclature includes all such *P. deltoides* × *P. nigra* hybrids under the name of *P. × canadensis* Moench.[11] What all of them seemed to have in common was superiority in growth and stem form over the native parent species; they soon became the poplar of choice in France—and, thanks to the French connection, the favored material in the Piedmont.

Thus, three key factors contributed to a rapidly expanding poplar culture in the Po Valley by the end of the nineteenth century: the emergent pulp and paper industry's hunger for a suitable raw material; the promising new hybrid material from France; and a nursery industry capable of propagating this material in sufficient quantities—and of such quality—to guarantee its successful growth in a plantation environment. Agronomists and academics did their part in coming up with recommended plantation regimes in terms of tree spacing and rotation length for estimated economic returns. Before long, other industries became interested in this new raw material and saw its potential for use in the fabrication of matches, boxes, furniture, plywood, wooden clogs, excelsior for packaging, and even scaffolding in mining and tunnel excavations.[12] Poplar plantations became part of the Padana landscape, vertical blocks of dark green interspersed in the horizontal geometry of rice fields, sucking water from the alluvial plain and transpiring it into the morning fog.

But plants are not inert commodities. Biology can be sobering—or, as an old vintner at Martini Bros. in the Napa valley once told me, "*Madre Natura* always has something up her sleeve!" Some plantations with the so-called Canadian poplars began suffering from a loss of leaves in spring, apparently affected by a fungus. Others remained healthy. Did the trees come from the same material? How could you tell different hybrids apart? How reliable was clonal identification in commercial nurseries? What happened when you kept vegetatively propagating one and the same clone year after year? How might diseases spread from one nursery to another? On the other hand, did plantation setbacks have to do with soil differences, or inappropriate site preparation, or with the spacing of trees, creating different microclimates? It soon became apparent that, promising as they were, these hybrids were not miracle trees, able to solve all problems. Experimentation was called for to better understand the material as well as the conditions under which it could reach its potential. In the early 1930s, an institution for the improvement of poplar was founded in Turin; by 1937 it had resulted in the establishment of the first research institute exclusively dedicated to the study of poplar culture. Since then, the Istituto di Sperimentazione per la Pioppicoltura in Casale Monferrato has been the center of an active research program on poplar that has continued to this day. It is in good measure to the credit of this institute that, over the years, poplar production in Italy systematically increased to eventually reach a level where, at 1.3 percent of the total forest area, poplar stands generated 45 percent of all the roundwood harvested annually in the country.[13]

Wider Potentials of Poplar

Italy was not alone in recognizing the potential of poplar. After all, it was in France where the fast growth of Euramerican hybrids had been discovered. As more hybrid material was being planted, interest spread to England, Germany, Belgium, Holland, and Scandinavia. At the same time, active breeding began to generate more hybrids from new cross combinations. In 1924, such a program was established on the North American continent, at the Oxford Paper Company in Rumford, Maine.[14] Some of its hybrids are still planted today. With the systematic proliferation of poplar material and the expansion of plantation acreage, the same concerns that had beset poplar growers in Italy became more widely recognized, calling for some cooperation across national boundaries. After World War II the time seemed ripe, and in 1947 the International Poplar Commission was founded to serve this purpose. Later placed under the aegis of the Food and Agriculture Organization (FAO) of the United Nations, the commission has helped, through its regular meetings, to set policies on testing and registration of clonal materials, to coordinate collection and conservation of germ plasm, and to exchange information on diseases and insects and their control. Together with a Working Group on Poplar and Willow of the International Union of Forest Research Organizations (IUFRO), it has served as a forum for both researchers and practitioners, acting to guide poplar culture through the ever-changing challenges of the twentieth century and on into the twenty-first.[15]

In the year 2000, the International Poplar Commission chose Portland, Oregon, as the venue for its annual meeting. Oregon, of all places, the heart of conifer country, the state that sports a Douglas fir on its license plate. But, perhaps surprisingly, during the preceding twenty years the Pacific Northwest had become another hot spot on the poplar map.

When you drive east from Portland through the Columbia Gorge on Oregon Highway 84, you traverse one of those striking environmental gradients that even a seasoned truck driver won't fail to register. As you emerge from the deep green of coastal conifers you soon have to reach for your sunglasses as the hills gradually change to yellow, the vegetation becomes short and scrubby, and the air turns hot and dry. Where lush vegetation had dominated the view before, now it is the geology that takes center stage. Basalt cliffs from ancient lava flows, terrace lines from the catastrophic Bretz Floods at the end of the last Ice Age, and undulating hills formed by aeolian forces now fill the picture. Vegetation has been reduced to a flimsy mantle, barely covering the prominent contours left by the physical processes of the past. As you keep driving, every mile seems to add to the bleakness as the horizon widens and a dry wind picks up. Then, all of a sudden, east of Boardman, a dark green line appears like a mirage in the far distance. Gradually the line becomes more defined and climbs up from the road, ascending a gentle hill to the right and turning into a dense cover that morphs into a solid wall of trees. Before you know it, you are driving by an extensive stand of hardwoods, blocks of plantation trees with branchless trunks that are too tall for fruit crops and too big for nursery stock. Indeed, so many travelers are puzzled by this unexpected forest in the middle of nowhere that they take the next exit and follow the signs directing them to a group of small office buildings to find out what this is all about. There they learn that they are in the midst of the GreenWoodResources Inc., Boardman, and Sand Lake Tree Farms, a contiguous block of managed plantations, totaling some 25,000 acres. In fact, the total acreage dedicated to this novel tree crop in this region is close to 45,000 acres (18,000 ha), making it one of the largest of its kind in the country.

A tour of the plantations with Jake Eaton, the company's managing director of resource planning and acquisitions, offers a glimpse into the modern technology of this new type of forestry. What first strikes the visitor is the size of the trees, a full 80 feet tall at eight years, after having started from almost zero as cuttings planted flush in the ground. At their rotation (harvest) age of fifteen years they will have a breast-height diameter of 15 inches. A Douglas fir would take twice as long to reach that size.

The factors that explain this remarkable growth are what brought about the Green Revolution in agriculture, namely combining superior genetic material with intensive culture. Add the many clear days during the growing season in this region, with sunlight during the day and cool temperatures at night, and you have a winning combination for high productivity. However, it comes at a price. With annual precipitation as low as 6 to 7 inches, irrigation is a must to grow any crop here. Under agricultural use, water is commonly provided from a center pivot via a rotating sprinkler system, accounting for those green disks you see in the midst of a desert landscape when you're flying over the west. Here, water is delivered less wastefully—namely by a network of drip lines with an emitter at each tree, thus limiting the evaporative loss. After the fifth year, the lines are moved to the center of the rows so as to ensure a greater spread of the root system, critical for wind firmness as the trees get taller. Soil quality, moisture, and nutrients are carefully monitored on every acre, and a central computer system continually regulates the allocation of water and nutrients to achieve optimum growth at the lowest possible cost. Carefully timed pruning aims at maximizing the volume of clear wood while minimizing reductions in growth. The poplars are highly selected hybrids from controlled crosses made mainly among three species: the native black cottonwood, eastern cottonwood, and European black poplar. Typically, four to six different hybrids are deployed at any one time, and an active breeding and selection program provides for genetic diversity and periodic renewal of the planting stock.

The conversion from center-pivot irrigation to drip irrigation began in 1993, and plantations were developed sequentially over the following years under the previous ownership of Potlatch Corporation. This has led to a staggered distribution of age classes that now permits sustainable harvests every year. And thanks to the well-drained loess soils, mechanized operations can be conducted year-round. Before harvest, all drip lines are rolled up, to be used again for a second rotation. A feller-buncher then drives down the rows and shears off the trees at ground level. After this the trees are transported to a central processing site where they are mechanically delimbed, debarked, and cut into logs. Log size and quality determine the subsequent steps. End use of the wood ranges from furniture framing to moldings, veneer, door skins, cabinets, and bookcases. The biomass from chipped bark, limbs, and leaves is combined with agricultural processing waste and composted, then taken back to the harvest site, spread, and then rototilled into the ground to build the soil. Then the site is replanted, typically with new hybrid material, and another generation is on its way. Under Oregon law, tree plantations operated on rotations up to twelve years can be managed under agricultural regulations (allowing use of certain herbicides and pesticides). Extending rotations to fifteen years, as allowed in neighboring Washington, will permit growing the trees to a size where quality veneer and clear lumber would make up an even larger portion of the harvest. The farms are managed sustainably under strict environmental, social, and economic standards, and have been accredited by the North American Forest Stewardship Council to market their products as FSC-certified hardwood.

But every crop comes with its own headaches, and the Boardman operation is no exception. To provide each tree on 17,000 acres with its life-sustaining water most days of the growing season calls for a flawless functioning of pumps, manifolds, thousands of miles of drip lines, and more than 20 million emitters. And as in our arteries, clots and leaks can be fatal if not instantly spotted and repaired. Apart from mechanical malfunctions, it turns out that rabbits and coyotes too love a cool drink on a hot day and find that chewable drip lines offer just what they were looking for. This is where the computerized monitoring system kicks in, locating and flagging a pressure change and helping direct a repairman via radio to the problem area. This troubleshooter is busy all day, roaming around the plantations on his four-wheeler and keeping the vital network from breaking down. Strong winds, common in this region, present another challenge. On many days, especially in spring, they swirl the light loess into a sandstorm, turning day into dusk. The problem is exacerbated by common practices in agriculture such as annual tilling. In fact, one of the plus points of tree plantations in this area is the way they conserve the soil and keep building it up for a dozen years or so via annual litter fall. But these trees better be wind resistant. Experience with some fast-growing hybrids showed them vulnerable to having their large leaves ripped and shredded, while others suffered from breakage and uprooting. Field testing of new material may reveal such deficiencies only after a number of years.

And then there are the pests. Pack 6 million trees into a solid block of timber and you generate a breeding ground for insects and diseases, especially when the trees are composed of only a handful of genotypes. Many diseases are clone specific, which means that an active breeding program is a key step in continually generating new crop diversity. Early testing in the nursery makes it possible to identify disease-tolerant production material with which to replace past clones. Staying one step ahead of the disease is a common strategy here, just as it is practiced in agriculture. Of course, there is no guarantee that a new, virulent strain may not arise during a twelve-year rotation.[16] Having the plantations designed as a mosaic of diverse monoclonal blocks—an array of blocks, each with a different clone—means that such an affected unit can be treated individually—perhaps by thinning it, or harvesting it prematurely. Insects, such as defoliators or borers, tend to have broader, less selective tastes and often require sprays or systemics for their control. Occasionally, biological control methods work too. At Boardman, a recent infestation of the clearwing poplar moth, a stem-boring insect, was approached in this manner. Thanks to collaboration with entomologists from Washington State University, a pheromone was developed that confused the male moths in their search for females. Monthly flights by a crop duster spraying minute amounts of the chemical sufficed to prevent a population buildup of the borer, and since the pheromone was specific for the clearwing moth, no other insects were affected.[17]

Moving into the Market

Not the least challenge in this process is marketing the wood produced. The traditional conifer culture of the Pacific Northwest has not exactly been waiting eagerly for a new competitor. Yet even back in the 1970s there were some in that industry who began worrying about the cyclic nature of the pulp fiber market and its dependence on the ups and downs of the construction industry. Since fiber was typically derived from residual chips and sawdust from lumber mills, the fluctuating demand for lumber had a direct effect on the supply of raw material for pulp and paper. One way of disconnecting the two and providing for a more even supply was to establish short-rotation plantations near pulp mills. In 1982 that actually led Crown Zellerbach Corporation to begin planting hybrid poplar on former grazing land in the lower Columbia River floodplain close to its Wauna mill at Westport, Oregon. Over the following years these plantations expanded to 11,000 acres and established a precedent for a new tree crop in the region. Benefiting from the earlier genetic and silvicultural work of the University of Washington/ Washington State University Poplar Research Program, the company rapidly developed a complete system of poplar farming on an industrial scale, from breeding all the way to the finished paper product.[18] Where earlier farmers had removed the extensive stands of native black cottonwood to gain grazing lands, the company now returned trees to their original habitat—although these were new, selected hybrids grown under intensive culture. The mild coastal climate provided for a long growing season and allowed these hybrid plantations to reach unprecedented levels of productivity. At 600 trees per acre, a harvest at eight years would yield 28 to 45 dry tons of clean pulp chips and an additional 10 to 15 tons of fuel. And with the plantation close to the pulp mill, the chips were usually processed the same day the trees were cut, thus retaining the inherent brightness of poplar wood so desirable for papermaking. Even the wood debris was used as an energy source in the plant. And beyond its own acreage, the company advised interested farmers on how to convert their unprofitable pasture land to poplar on a smaller scale.

Yet markets too never remain predictable. Increasing competition from the Southern Hemisphere during the 1990s, offering hardwood supplies from eucalyptus and acacia plantations at much lower prices, forced the industry to consider other product options. A shift to extending rotations to 12 to 15 years seemed advisable, as it would offer opportunities for poplar in both the solid-wood and chip market. This was the moment when companies on both sides of the Cascades began thinning some of their plantations and planting new ones at a wider spacing for longer rotations. With veneer and lumber as target products, stem quality became more important. Pruning schedules had to be developed, and breeding too shifted toward model trees with clearer and straighter boles. Results from this strategic change are encouraging, especially as some sawmills and wood-manufacturing plants are beginning to appreciate some of the inherent features of hybrid poplar and are including it in their product lines. However, as with any new raw material, there first has to be a critical mass and a predictable supply before a converter will commit to its adoption. This means that only industries with longer vision tend to accept the economic risks in the development of this new product. At this point it is too early to say that plantation-grown poplar has firmly established itself in the forest-product market of the Pacific Northwest. But as a new wood resource with many desirable characteristics, it certainly shows great promise of finding a solid niche there.

Finally, perhaps the best indicator of the effect of continually changing markets is the recent interest several companies have expressed in hybrid poplar raw material from the Boardman plantations for potential use in cellulosic ethanol plants at the nearby Port of Morrow, in Oregon (Brian Stanton, personal communication). This development reflects the growing concern about carbon sequestration in the context of global climate change as well as the potential role poplar plantations may play as a source of biofuels.[19]

Will poplar plantations become a permanent feature in our landscapes? Or, to ask a more general question, What is the future of plantation forestry in our world, both in the forms we see today and in the future? This is a topic of broader significance, not without controversial issues and deserving a chapter of its own, and we will return to it in chapter 21. Before that, however, let us find out more about the tool kit we have available and ready to influence poplar to grow optimally toward desirable goals under plantation conditions. As we will see, all the answers depend on how well we understand the basics of growth and development in this eminently useful tree.

19 / POPLAR—A MODEL TREE

So far, we've found that poplars are among the fastest growing trees, that hybrids are even better in putting on height and diameter than their parent species, and that growing these hybrids in large plantations may be an efficient way of producing raw material for shelter, fiber, and energy. Actually, all these elements differ little from exploiting what nature is already doing for us, although we have chosen to put them to work in a favorable setting—just as we have done with crops for thousands of years. But if we want to be more deliberate about it, if we want to understand which way to push the system and how to recognize what may be its limits, as well as the specific trade-offs among growth, hardiness, and tolerance of pests, we have to peek at the machinery behind the bark—ideally all the way to its DNA. This would also help us to better understand the intricate system of adaptations the tree uses in tracking its environment. As it turns out, one could hardly find a more suitable tree for this purpose than poplar, and by now we should have an inkling of some of its favorable features. Let us enumerate the most significant ones.

1. Poplar's fast growth allows for the discovery, observation, and measurement of many traits in a short time (the downside is that a plant may quickly outgrow its space in a growth chamber, greenhouse, or field plot).

2. The tree's easy clonability permits replication of experiments in space and time.

3. Early sexual maturation (in 3–5 years) means rapid progress through generations.

4. Use of detached floral branches in the greenhouse permits convenient breeding that can produce thousands of seeds in limited space in four to six weeks.

5. Nearly instant germination of seed allows diagnostic studies of seedling properties within a few weeks.

6. A wide-ranging array of about thirty species, adapted to diverse environments, offers abundant variation for the study of many traits.

7. Because all these species share the same chromosome number (2n = 38), crossability is enhanced among them, with crosses resulting in fertile hybrids in many combinations.

8. The tree's small genome (480 megabases, or Mb) facilitates molecular analysis.

9. The plant material is amenable to cell and tissue culture as well as genetic transformation, opening the door to genetic engineering.

10. The broad array of uses for poplar in production and conservation makes for a rapid transfer of research results to practical application.

In combination, these features have made poplar the study tree of choice. By now, it has become widely accepted as a model tree, joining such model systems as the fruit fly and the annual crucifer, *Arabidopsis*.[1]

What turns an organism into a model system? No other field can link its history as closely to the sequential choice of model organisms as genetics. From Gregor Mendel to recent Nobel laureates, their key discoveries have hinged on choosing the right system at the right time. Mendel's peas had to meet several explicit requirements to be accepted as experimental plants. "The selection of the plant group which shall serve for experiments of this kind must be made with all possible care if it be desired to avoid from the outset every risk of questionable results."[2] In fact, had he chosen the hawkweed (*Hieracium* sp.), favored plant of Karl von Nägeli, his revered botany professor in Munich, the outcome would have been disastrous. (As shown by later experiments, hawkweed has a tendency to produce some asexual seeds, thereby defying the Mendelian laws of inheritance.) The sea urchin, thanks to its large eggs, helped Theodor Boveri discover the individuality of chromosomes, thereby giving critical support to the chromosome theory of inheritance.[3] Soon thereafter, thanks to its short and lab-friendly life cycle, the fruit fly helped T. H. Morgan and his coworkers discover the linkage of genes on chromosomes, which later could even be seen under the microscope thanks to the large salivary gland chromosomes of the fly.[4] And so the parade of genetic favorites continued with yeast, a bread mold, a gut bacterium, a phage, a roundworm—each associated with a breakthrough, each offering a shortcut to a significant new insight. Model organisms have provided the steppingstones in our quest to understand nature—and ourselves.

What all these organisms have in common is a short life cycle, convenient handling, and easy association of phenotypic with genotypic variation, combined with qualities permitting accurate tracking of genetic lineages, and easy storage and shipment, thus allowing exchange of materials among researchers and repetition of experiments. After all, repeatability is one of the critical dictates in science. Sharing of materials also means that new experiments can be systematically built on previous ones in an iterative process. This way, every bit of new information can be added to the existing fund of knowledge on a given organism, gradually filling in gaps while at the same time enhancing the value of every new observation. Altogether, that means the more people who study a particular system, collaborating and coordinating their work through joint publications, symposia, and shared resources, the more useful the system becomes and the more it justifies funding. Yet helpful as these model systems are, each has its limitations. In the end, their ultimate value lies in the way they mutually complement each other in their collective ensemble revealing both commonalities and idiosyncrasies. Within this universe of systems it may be easier to understand why such an awkward, slow-paced, bulky, long-lived organism as poplar may add something new to the anointed guild of existing models.

Among favored plant systems, crop plants such as wheat, corn, rice, and tomato have held a prominent position in genetic research, and this for obvious reasons. But since the 1980s, the small wall cress, *Arabidopsis*, has gathered much of the limelight and by now has become the model plant par excellence. And no wonder, when you consider its biological profile: short life cycle (five weeks), small size (15–20 cm, can be grown in test tubes), obligate self-pollinator (rapid generator of inbred lines), producing thousands of seeds per plant, amenable to cloning and genetic transformation, and having a small genome (120 megabases) comparable to that of the fruit fly *Drosophila*. It was the first plant to have its complete genome sequenced and by now offers hundreds of mutants that shed light on basic processes in plant growth, development, and stress response.[5] It also figures as a basic supply house for many of the modern molecular tools used by current plant researchers. However, while it supports other plant systems, it doesn't replace them. As recently voiced by Mandoli and Olmstead,

> [P]lants—from green algae to angiosperms—represent the most diverse biochemistry, architecture, life history (including alternation of generations), reproductive biology (sexual and asexual), and body plans on Earth. Flowering plants have an estimated 300,000 species, compared with only 4,500 for our closest relatives, the mammals, a group approximately the same age. No one plant, not even *Arabidopsis thaliana*, can encompass this enormous diversity at the whole plant, physiologic, chemical, genetic, or molecular level.[6]

What can poplar deliver that the wall cress can't? Poplar, as a perennial plant, can shed light on the complex sequence of steps involved in tracking seasonal change from spring growth through winter dormancy, in its responses to cues of day length and temperature, and in its cyclic changes in nutrient transport, storage, and mobilization. As a large plant, it can elucidate the long-distance pathways over which signals have to be transmitted, received, and responded to in prioritizing the allocation of resources to growing tissues both above and below ground, and in maintaining the elaborate architecture of a complex canopy. As a woody plant, it can reveal how wood is formed and how that tissue responds to the physical forces of pressure, tension, and torsion. As a long-living plant, it offers insight into phase changes from the juvenile to the mature state, and into the cyclic trade-offs between growth and reproduction. As a large and long-living plant—the ideal host for insects, fungi, and microbial organisms—it can also tell us about its strategies of engaging in long-term mutualistic or symbiotic relationships while successfully warding off the intrusion of highly flexible parasites. Together, all of this information will illuminate a keystone species that significantly influences an entire forest ecosystem and also serves as a proxy for other such species.[7] *Arabidopsis* simply cannot deliver these goods. Nevertheless, as we will see, it can be of great use in providing access to specific genes in poplar's genome.

Insights Gained in Poplar Hybrid Research

How has recent research contributed to our better understanding of poplar biology, and what next steps are likely to provide further advances? Here let us remember again that when we say poplar, we mean an entire genus of approximately thirty different species, and that while they all share the critical features enumerated above, they also bring many intriguing variations to the table, reflecting the different environments they hail from. Combining some of these variations through hybridization has been a favorite experimental approach, because hybridizing offers an analytical tool that is useful in the study of individual traits, as well as of their joint expression in hybrids. What have we learned from them? To get closer to that question, let us distinguish two types of experiments, namely (1) comparing parental species first with their F_1 hybrids, and then (2) with their F_2 hybrids.

If two parents differ in many traits and their F_1 hybrid progeny outgrow them, the question is, how do they do that—or, more precisely, what trait combinations are responsible for the superior performance in the offspring? This question came up in the early 1980s when experimental hybrids between *P. trichocarpa* (T) and *P. deltoides* (D) clearly exceeded their parents' growth in field trials in the Pacific Northwest (for convenience, I will resort to the shorthand of referring to T and D parents, and to TD hybrids). Of course hybrid vigor, or heterosis, was not a new thing in poplar; it had already been noticed and exploited in the *P. × canadensis* hybrids in France and Italy—even if not understood. There was also much precedent for the phenomenon in agricultural crops. Plant breeders had long realized that in many crops favorable results could be obtained from making crosses among inbred lines. Perhaps the best example was hybrid corn, the epitome of a high-yielding modern crop.[8] And just as crop physiologists and geneticists had elucidated the mechanisms behind hybrid vigor in corn, a similar group of scientists now went to work on the new poplar hybrids in the Pacific Northwest. Their quest became one of the most in-depth studies of poplar ever conducted and involved the coordinated research of dozens of scientists from academia, public agencies, and industry. Moreover, what helped their study was the priceless capability of their research material, which allowed clonal copies of parents and progenies to be grown side by side in replicated field trials where they could be compared over several years. It also permitted parallel studies in which a more intense focus on specific traits could be conducted with exactly the same material in the greenhouse and in growth chambers under highly controlled conditions, and that could be repeated at will. Not surprisingly, the results rewarded the effort.[9] What follows is a brief extract from these studies.

It turned out that the vigorous F_1 hybrids profited from a whole series of favorable trait combinations. While D leaves were made up of many small cells, and T leaves of fewer large cells, TD leaves were composed of many large cells and accordingly greater in size; yet these leaves were produced at the same rate as in the parents, meaning that more leaf area was generated per unit of time in the hybrids. Since leaves are the basic engine of growth, the hybrids gained volume more rapidly. Hybrid leaves also adopted the greater drought-responsiveness of stomata from their D parent. Whereas T plants were slow in responding to drought stress, losing water through prolonged transpiration, hybrids were quicker in closing their stomates and minimizing water loss. In fact they were even better than their D parent in sensing the coming of drought stress, maintaining a favorable water balance throughout the drought, and resuming growth earlier when it was over, a definite plus in the dry Northwest summers. Hybrids also maintained this larger and more responsive leaf canopy longer into the fall than the local T parent, thereby adding another boost to F_1 productivity. This came from choosing D parents from more southern latitudes (Mississippi or Texas) for hybridization, taking advantage of their already existing adaptation to longer photoperiods. In this manner, active photosynthesis could be extended into November in the mild autumns of the Pacific coast. The list goes on—but in brief one can say that, overall, these comparative studies gave detailed insights into the machinery that drove the F_1 hybrids to higher performance and revealed the specific components and processes responsible for it.

However, not all the F_1 hybrids were superior to their parents. As explained in chapter 8 on genetic passwords and crossability, T × D crosses gave only about half as many viable seed as normal matings, and those that germinated showed considerable variability within each seed lot. Actually, this is not surprising when you think about the high levels of heterozygosity in the parental species. But it is in sharp contrast with hybrid corn, for example, where the parental lines used in crossing are highly inbred (essentially homozygous) and as a consequence give a uniform F_1 progeny. In poplar, the internal genetic diversity in each parent will generate even more diversity among their offspring. Fortunately, this variability is no problem, and is in fact an asset since it offers choices from which the very best F_1 performers can be picked and thereafter cloned. Thus, the combination of hybridization and vegetative propagation offers a powerful way to (1) expand variation beyond the constraints of a species and then (2) freeze it in the most desirable form.

What about the underlying genetics? Could specific genes be identified that accounted for the parental differences and how they were expressed in the hybrids? These were the next questions, and they called for another round of crosses and a new set of field experiments. Remember that Mendel had already realized that he had to go to the F_2 generation (through matings among F_1 individuals) to find out whether any specific genes were responsible for a given trait difference in his peas—which he then found. Such crosses were carried out with the poplar hybrids (i.e., TD × TD) and gave rise to F_2 hybrids. These were then clonally replicated and planted in the field. What were the results?

If ever one dreamed of a showy field trial that put the power of genetics on full display, here it was. Try to imagine 375 different pairs of identical twins (here cloned individuals) standing on a large field side by side, always paired, together with their cloned parents and grandparents at the same juvenile stage (possible in plants), and replicated three times across the field so that each pair has different neighbors in the three locations. In the case of these F_2 hybrids, tall pairs stood next to bushy ones, large-leaved next to willow-leaved, broad-crowned next to semicolumnar, slim trunks next to stocky ones. It was an explosion of diversity, yet always patterned in strikingly similar pairs that showed the degree to which the diversity was due to their unique combinations of genes expressing themselves in a common environment (see fig. 19.1). Moreover, this enormous variation didn't merely range between the grandparental values (the original P generation), but—thanks to meiotic segregation and recombination—it mixed values from different traits in new combinations. To further amplify this genetic mosaic and to allow its expression in more than one environment, copies of exactly the same material were grown simultaneously at two contrasting locations, west and east of the Cascade Range. Needless to say, these two large plantations not only became premier research sites but were also showpieces for many field tours. When I once took a visiting swine breeder from Switzerland to one of the sites, he was overwhelmed by this spectacular display of tree genetics and shook his head, saying, "Why am I working with stinky pigs?!" (He had much better funding.)

Here let us pause for a moment and see these plantations in a broader context. From the research viewpoint, they were examples of an approach that is commonly used in biological analysis, namely stacking the deck. When we try to figure out how plants adapt to cold, we first pick individuals from low and high elevations and expose them to two or three temperature regimes that bracket the extremes, high to low. Once we detect differences between the plants under these exaggerated conditions, we know what to look for and what to measure and can then move on to more subtle experiments. Similarly, if we want to test for disease resistance, we first do an overkill application with a heavy-duty inoculum before moving on to a more natural simulation of infection. The same applies in trials of fertilizer, irrigation schedules, and so on. In genetics, stacking the deck means crossing parents that differ sharply

19.1 Clonal pairs of four-year-old members of a hybrid F_2 family, grown at Clatskanie, Washington, showing contrasts in size, crown architecture, and autumnal leaf shedding.

in one or many traits (this is what Mendel did) and then studying their offspring in successive generations to investigate how these traits are transmitted and expressed. In the case of the above poplar hybrids, the two parental species (T and D) differ strikingly in many morphological, anatomical, physiological, and biochemical traits; and since they have evolved separately for a good long period, we can assume that the genetic underpinnings for these traits are likely different, too. Thus, if we correlate the genetic with the phenotypic trait variation in these hybrid offspring it should get us closer to the genes that matter in explaining the differences. Once we know those genes and their extreme alleles (say for a given trait $A_D A_D$ in the D parent vs. $A_T A_T$ in T), we can move on to look for more subtle variation among different alleles within each species (say A_{D1} vs. A_{D2}, or A_{T3} vs. A_{T4}).

In order to accurately correlate phenotypic with genotypic variation in the trees in these plantations, all traits of interest had to be measured in all individuals of the three generations, and each tree had to be genotyped at the DNA level—no minor task. What were the results? Contrary to the Mendelian experiments, in which key trait differences (e.g., round vs. wrinkled peas) could be attributed to single genes, no such simply inherited trait differences could be found in the F_2 poplar hybrids. This didn't come as a total surprise because such complex traits as tree height or volume are the cumulative result of many contributing processes, each under the control of one or more genes. What was more surprising was that in several traits a few genes seemed to have a disproportionately large effect on trait variations. In other words, neither the single-gene model nor the polygenic model (many genes with small effects) seemed to apply, but instead one involving a small number of critical genes, called *quantitative trait loci* (QTLs). Interestingly too, the small set of critical genes from the two parent species had complementary effects: those from the T-parent pushed height growth, whereas those from the D-parent, diameter growth. It was this combination that accounted for the high tree volume in the hybrids. Equally significant, some of the critical QTLs for diameter growth coincided with those for leaf area on *sylleptic branches*.[10] These are the branches that are added and develop during the growing season and that keep on placing more leaves into the growing crown. Earlier physiological studies had shown these branches to be largely exporters of photosynthates and important contributors to stem volume.[11] Thus the genetic information obtained not only helped explain how the overall volume increase came about but also confirmed the importance of a specific growth component that was critically involved.

The Limits of Hybrid Analysis

Now, as extensive and revealing as these plantations were in their visually striking display of genetic diversity, they ultimately lacked the needed resolution to pinpoint the individual genes responsible for the trees' growth and development. How can we explain this? Perhaps a comparison with maps will help. Large-scale maps will reveal major landscape features and indicate locations of major towns, but won't accurately show you how to find an individual house. Using a magnifying glass won't help, either! Similarly it would be futile to measure the phenotypic variation in these plantations more accurately, down to the micron. The resolution of the underlying genes would still be inadequate, and that has to do with the limited number of offspring in this F_2 generation. Remember that each of these offspring is a different meiotic product, the result of segregation and recombination, in which chromosomal segments were exchanged among corresponding chromosomes of the two parental species. Every individual recombination breaks up the chromosomes into different chunks, which each contain many genes—perhaps hundreds, not just one. This is why the more offspring we can compare, the greater the likelihood that a given chunk gets broken up in so many ways that individual genes become identifiable via their manifestation. However, for this to happen, we would need thousands of offspring from such a cross. And for them to fully display their genetic differences they would have to be planted in dozens of field trials in many different environments, replicated in time, and this for a good part of their life cycle—a program easily accomplished with agricultural crops but virtually impossible with trees because of space and time constraints. This also means that the QTLs identified in those two trials above, based on 375 genotypes, are still only coarse indicators of specific chromosomal segments, constituting genetic neighborhoods that may harbor quite a number of genes, only some of them directly associated with a measurable phenotypic effect. In other words, the limitations are inherent in the experimental approach. While it is sufficient to reveal the genetic basis of qualitative traits (say, rust resistance vs. rust susceptibility), it won't quite do for quantitative traits such as height, volume, leaf mass, growth period, and the like. And these are the traits of greatest interest for understanding growth and adaptation in a tree.

If these elaborate field trials didn't fully deliver the goods, they still offered important insights. They revealed the complementary contribution of the two species to volume growth, identified critical QTLs related to growth components, and also showed that few of the many F_2 recombinants approached the growth performance of the F_1 hybrids. They also gave important clues for the direction of future breeding. To physiologists, the trials offered a plethora of diversity for the study of tree architecture, and this in two contrasting environments in which the remarkable phenotypic plasticity of poplar could express itself. And pathologists were able to identify patterns of disease incidence within a well-defined hybrid pedigree.[12]

But how to get to those elusive genes? How can poplar live up to its promise as a model tree and more fully reveal its inner machinery? Here is where molecular genetics offers the key to the inner sanctum. Two approaches in particular—the physical sequencing of the genome, and the process of genetic engineering—have been instrumental in giving access to that remarkable domain. And recent work with poplar has shown that it easily yields to analysis by these powerful new tools. The next chapter will help us understand how they work.

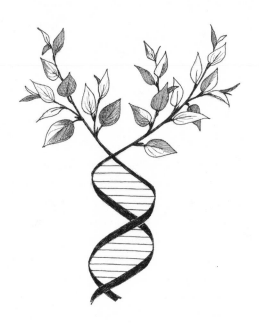

20 / TREE GENOMICS AND BEYOND

In a White House ceremony on June 26, 2000, President Clinton announced to the world the completion of the draft sequence of the human genome. A ten-year international effort to sequence the 3.2 billion units of our DNA had reached its culmination. This momentous achievement, compared by some to the successful landing of man on the moon, would usher in a new era in medicine and, in a broader sense, pave the way to a better understanding of human nature. At the announcement the president was flanked by the two scientists who had been most instrumental in driving the ambitious undertaking, Francis Collins from the National Human Genome Research Institute, and Craig Venter from the private company Celera Genomics. What gave the event an added human touch (and welcome press coverage) was that the two scientists had been embroiled in a competitive race to the finish, pitting private enterprise against governmental research. To the satisfaction of the research community at large, the two had agreed to call it a tie.[1]

Why the excitement? Here, finally, was the complete deciphering of the human genetic code, the blueprint—or, as Richard Dawkins more succinctly stated, the recipe for what turns a fertilized egg cell into a fully functional human. Embedded in this linear sequence was a wealth of information, from the basics of cellular function to the causes of disease, from the basic measures of human identity to the potential of individually tailored medicine, and from illuminating the evolutionary past to shedding light on biodiversity. Here, for example, was a way to quantify in tangible terms the similarity with other sequenced organisms. That humans share 99 percent of their genes with their closest primate relative, the chimpanzee, may have been surprising enough. But perhaps even more fascinating were the genetic overlaps with other organisms, such as the mouse (89 percent), the fruit fly (45 percent), baker's yeast (28 percent), the roundworm (26 percent), *Arabidopsis* (21 percent), rice (11 percent), and even *E. coli* (9 percent).[2] Evidently evolution has been far more conservative than ever imagined, preserving genes that had worked in the past and using them in new contexts across emergent lineages, tinkering with what was available—in François Jacob's terms—rather than engineering de novo.[3] What more powerful testimony to the continuity of life on earth than this overarching commonality among organisms as diverse as primates, plants, insects, and bacteria?

Sequencing a genome means deciphering the linear arrangement of the DNA carried in an organism's genetic complement. It is the linear arrangement of *nucleotides,* or base pairs, that confers meaning to a stretch of DNA. Four nucleotides—adenine, thymine, guanine, and cytosine, abbreviated A, T, G, and C—are the available building blocks, and the specific sequence of any three of them, say GCA, or AGT, is what contains information in the genetic code. These triplet codons can spell out any one of twenty amino acids (the sequence of which in turn defines a protein), or, alternatively, code for the beginning or the end of a gene. Thus, simply put, the sequence of a stretch of DNA offers information on the number of genes contained therein, their physical arrangement, and the arrangement of amino acids in the proteins they code for. Well, not quite. What complicates the picture is that some stretches of nucleotides between genes (as well as within genes) do not code for amino acids; these are termed non-coding sequences. Nevertheless, they may play an important role in regulating gene expression, that is, in regulating which genes are turned on and when.

DNA sequencing is thus a physical approximation to the biological recipe of an organism. Its success is based on the assumption that any random arrangement of fewer than 100 nucleotides will result in a unique sequence which, much like a bar code or fingerprint, has no counterpart anywhere else in the genome. Sequencing is a laborious process that in the late 1980s was only proceeding at a pace of 50,000 nucleotides a year even in a well-equipped lab. Ingenious improvements in analytical procedures, such as speeding up replication of DNA through the DNA polymerase chain reaction (a method by which DNA in successive cycles can be exponentially amplified), and the development of automated sequencers stepped up the process to one million nucleotides per day. Today, what in 1990 was a bold and highly contested initiative at the onset of the Human Genome Project has turned into a routine procedure in chemical engineering.[4] As a result, the number of organisms being sequenced has dramatically increased and now includes poplar.

As in the case of the human genome and other sequencing initiatives, the poplar project was a truly international effort, combining the work of 109 scientists and their coworkers in thirty-nine laboratories located in eight countries in North America and Europe.[5] Coordinated by Gerald Tuskan from the Oak Ridge National Laboratory of the US Department of Energy, the analysis focused on the genome of a black cottonwood tree from a natural population along the Nisqually River in western Washington. Why that species, and why that tree? While for the human genome Craig Venter had analyzed his own genetic endowment, the choice could here be made with some greater detachment. Black cottonwood was an obvious candidate because a great deal was known about its basic biology, and the Nisqually tree was a member of a population that had figured in several previous genetic studies and was also easily accessible (H. D. Bradshaw, personal communication). In the genome analysis, several different and complementary approaches were used that allowed the identified sequences to be assigned to the nineteen pairs of chromosomes of the poplar genome. On completion, most of the findings were consistent with expectations but gave them a new molecular underpinning. Among the first was the large total number of genes identified in the poplar genome, estimated at 45 to 50,000 — the largest among all sequenced organisms (for humans, the estimate is 30,000, for *Arabidopsis* 26,000). A plausible reason for this large number is that during their evolution all modern taxa of the Willow Family (Salicaceae) had undergone several genome duplications, bringing their chromosome sets to the polyploid level. That finding came as no surprise, since chromosome counts of 2n > 20 (such as in poplar, 2n = 38) are generally assumed to have arisen through duplication from lower numbers. More interesting was a second insight. A common evolutionary consequence of such polyploidization is that the resulting genetic redundancy allows some genes to mutate and assume a new function without impairing the original one (since the unaltered "twin" continues to perform it). This *neofunctionalization*, as it is called, involves minor nucleotide changes and can be quantified in the genomic analysis. Assuming conventional mutation rates, one can then estimate how long ago the last duplication may have taken place. In the case of poplar, the estimate was 10 to 12 million years ago. However, independent evidence from the fossil record indicates that the modern genus has existed at least since the extinction of the nonavian dinosaurs, some 60 to 65 million years ago.[6] How to account for this discrepancy? The authors suggest that the explanation may well lie in a slower evolutionary rate in poplar than in other organisms. Several factors would contribute to a slowing down of genetic change per unit of time: poplar's long life cycle, its outbreeding habit, its propensity to hybridize, and the long persistence of old genets (through asexual propagation), allowing them to keep making gametic inputs to later generations of descendants. Recall how old some clones can get through successive cycles of vegetative propagation. Even in their advanced age they can contribute "outdated" pollen or seed to the younger generations that surround them, slowing down their change.

Also of much interest were the comparisons with *Arabidopsis*, the versatile model plant we got to know in the last chapter. Here it should be pointed out that in the current classification of the plant kingdom, *Arabidopsis* and *Populus* are found together in the Eurosid I clade, and are thus more closely related than to other dicotyledon taxa, including those of other trees.[7] In the genomic analysis, these two genera were found to share as many as 13,000 genes—half of the annual's genome—with an average sequence alignment of 93 percent, a remarkable degree of congruence. As we will see, this makes the little crucifer a powerful source of software and hardware for the genomic analysis and genetic engineering of poplar. Equally important, if they are to serve as complementary model systems, are the differences between the two. Poplar has significantly more genes and gene domains associated with disease resistance, meristem development, metabolite transport, and carbon allocation to cellulose, lignin, and flavonoid biosynthesis—all traits that have helped it to develop the upright habit of a long-lived woody perennial. Poplar also has a higher number of non-coding RNA, indicating a more complicated gene-regulation system.

Finally, and further supporting earlier data from isozyme analysis (described in chapter 12), the Nisqually tree displayed very high levels of allelic variation, or heterozygosity (individual genetic diversity). In fact, to compare it with human variability, the diversity between the two haplotypes in this single tree—that is, the two chromosome sets handed down by its two parents—would exceed the genetic diversity commonly found among human individuals from unrelated populations.[8] Here once again, at the molecular level, is evidence giving further substance to the claim that genetic diversity in forest trees is in a class by itself.

From Sequencing to Function

Now, we might ask, How do we know that poplar has more genes associated with cellulose and lignin production than *Arabidopsis*? In other words, how do we get from the actual sequencing, or structural genomics, to functional genomics? Here, we have to go back to one of the basic tenets of molecular genetics or to what has been termed the Central Dogma. It stipulates that gene expression proceeds through two steps and involves an intermediary, as the DNA code is first transcribed to a complementary code of RNA, which then is translated into the amino acid code of a protein.[9] And since in the cellular machinery RNA serves as a messenger to the site where proteins are assembled, it is called *messenger RNA*, or mRNA. This mRNA may then be a good indicator of functional gene activity in an organism. In fact, what it reveals is that at any one time only a small fraction of an organism's genes is being transcribed and translated, or actually expressed, while all others remain silent. This means that the mere inventory of all genes existing in a genome (as revealed by sequencing) won't tell us much about their collective effect on the organism. What matters is how many of these genes are expressed in which tissue, at what time, in which combination, and in which sequence.

Just as the total number of different instruments in an orchestra won't tell us what music will be played, it is the score—the orchestration—that determines whether it will be a Mozart symphony or a Sousa march. This is why we can use mRNA to find the score for gene expression for specific tissues in the tree. For example, to screen for genes involved in wood formation, mRNA can be extracted from the cambium tissue (which builds xylem) and then used as a template for a reverse process that synthesizes a complementary DNA strand. Once a second complementary strand has been attached to it, you have a complementary double-stranded DNA (cDNA) that contains only the expressed genes of the cambium. Comparison with cDNA derived from epidermis or floral tissue then allows identification of expressed gene groups that differ between the tissues. In this manner whole "libraries" of cDNA can be built of the different tissues in poplar at different stages of development, and they can then be compared with those of other plants, where the responsible genes already have been identified.

Here is where another inventive technique, the microarray or gene chip, has revolutionized the study of gene expression. To describe it briefly, a microarray is a matrix of hundreds of tiny spots arranged on a small chip into which a robot places a selection of DNA sequences of different genes from the whole genome, each gene going into a predesignated spot. The mRNA from a tissue of interest, equipped with a fluorescent tag, is then washed over the chip and will bind wherever it finds a complementary stretch of DNA. A laser detector will then read the fluorescent dots from the whole array and reveal the critical ensemble of genes that are expressed in that tissue. The dots light up in different colors—wavelengths—and intensities, and will be quantified accordingly by the detector. Common microchips today can accommodate 300,000 or more dots on a 1 x 1 cm chip.[10] As generally found, it is the interaction of a whole number of genes that form the expression profile of a given tissue at a certain stage of development, or of the response of that tissue to a signal. Further, this interaction of genes tends to be non-random, often revealing an orchestrated pattern. In fact, regulatory DNA and RNA sequences can be identified that seem to direct which genes will express themselves and in which cascading sequence. Thus, much about understanding the functioning of an organism—and its difference from other organisms—has to do with how it regulates the activity of its genetic machinery in response to environmental cues. What facilitates the analytical approach to its study is the fundamental capacity of DNA to replicate itself and/or to find complementary sequences in other DNA or RNA with great precision. With appropriate methods, this property can be dramatically enhanced and made visible. And since it works the same way in plants as in humans, plant researchers can profit from the rapid methodological advances made in chemical engineering and informatics, driven by the interest in human disease and its cure (and the economic incentives associated with that). Several poplar research groups in Sweden, Belgium, and Canada have been especially active in this area and have compiled an impressive amount of data on the tree's gene-expression profiles. Similar information is becoming available for other tree species such as birch, black locust, the eucalypts, oak, and pine.

Genetic Engineering

Another tool on the workbench of functional genomics is the transformation of DNA via genetic engineering. One way of doing this is to enlist a natural agent such as *Agrobacterium*. This soil bacterium has the habit of infecting a wide variety of plants in which it stably integrates its DNA into the host's genome, causing the formation of tumors. Carefully studied in the laboratory and further refined through the work of Milton Gordon and Eugene Nester at the University of Washington, and many others elsewhere, *Agrobacterium* has become one of the favored vectors for generating transgenic plants.[11] In essence, the procedure involves disarming the bacterium, so it won't cause a tumor, and then attaching to its DNA the desired gene(s) it is to deliver. Once these genes have been incorporated into the recipient's genome, tissue-culture methods are used to grow the transformed cells into transgenic plants for study of the phenotypic effects of their altered genome. In this manner, for example, it is possible to insert a gene sequence of unknown function that has been equipped with a strong enhancer or "promoter" (an activating sequence that turns on any gene to which it gets attached), causing it to be overexpressed. The resulting exaggerated phenotypic manifestation will then help in unraveling the functions underlying the change, ideally all the way down to the responsible genes. In a similar way but in the opposite direction, a "silencer" can be added to the gene sequence, thereby suppressing its expression and allowing genetic inferences to be made from the absence of a specific function. Both of these approaches have become powerful tools in elucidating gene function in poplar and shedding light on the genomics of its development and its mechanisms of adaptation.[12]

In this way, genetic engineering allows us to manipulate the genetic constitution of a plant with much greater precision than has ever been possible through breeding and selection. It permits introducing into the recipient host a single gene instead of a whole gamete. And the gene may come from an unrelated plant, say *Arabidopsis*, and may be one of the 13,000 that share 93 percent sequence alignment with the corresponding gene in poplar. The gene may also be in an allelic form unavailable or rare in poplar, yet of potential value either in illuminating the internal workings of the tree or enhancing its genetic endowment.

If genetic engineering is used for improving commercial traits, poplar again offers an important advantage over many other tree species: its suitability for propagation via both cell and tissue culture. Since only a small fraction of targeted cultures tend to be successfully transformed and will manifest the desired alteration, their reliable cloning—in vitro and through subsequent perpetuation via cuttings—is key to applying this approach on a larger scale. And with poplar culture being almost exclusively practiced in clonal plantations, this approach to genetic improvement has much to be said for itself, especially when compared to conventional breeding. Apart from being more precise, as explained above, genetic engineering can save a great deal of time. For example, when trying to introduce a desirable gene—perhaps one that confers resistance to a new rust—into an elite tree by traditionally crossing it with an unimproved (but resistant) donor, the result is that along with the resistance gene comes half a genome of other traits of lower quality. It then takes repeated backcrossing to the elite tree, while always selecting for the resistant offspring, to gradually get rid of this unwanted baggage. In fact, some of it may still be hanging on after many backcrosses because of tight linkage between the wanted gene and some undesirable neighbor. Add to this the time it takes for such a cleansing to be carried out in an organism with a breeding cycle of five to seven years per generation, and you can see why genetic engineering has some strong advocates among tree breeders.[13] They point to the comparative efficiency of transferring an isolated gene or two into a recipient genome in one fell swoop. In Jesse Ausubel's view, genetic engineering can be seen as a process of "editing a genetic text" by systematically fine-tuning the genome with pinpoint precision for the purposes it is to serve.[14] Of course, there is no way of targeting the insertion gene to a specific chromosomal location, and so multiple insertions must be conducted, resulting in various expression profiles. Subsequent testing is then needed to sort out the desirable transformants from the undesirable ones.

Thinking about poplar in this context, what desirable domestication genes might be introduced? In an effort to maximize productivity in plantations, the priority will be on genes that steer the tree to preferentially allocate its photosynthates to stem wood rather than to roots, branches, and reproductive organs. For example, a simple allometric shift that increases the diameter-to-height proportion—in effect making a "barrel-tree"—would instantly bring multiple improvements, namely an increase in the harvest index (the relative fraction of harvestable tree mass), a reduction in water stress (by shortening vascular transport distance), and a reduction in wind susceptibility. The latter would also bring a further reduction in the formation of undesirable tension wood, and consequently would allow selection for reduced lignin content, which in turn would lower the cost of chemical refinement of wood fiber. Interestingly, it turns out that short, squat poplars actually exist in nature, if only in extreme environments such as the arid Junggar Basin of northwestern China (fig. 20.1). Members of the Euphrates poplar (*P. euphratica*), they demonstrate that with a restricted water supply this species is capable of redirecting its carbon to diameter

20.1 Euphrates poplar (*Populus euphratica*) growing in the Junggar Basin of northwestern China under highly arid conditions. (*From a photo by the author.*)

growth, where the added capacity to store water and nutrients—along with their easier subsequent reallocation—has evidently paid off in increased fitness in the past. In more favorable locations, trees from the same species reach heights of 90 feet or more. Apparently, these trees don't just simply arrest height and radial growth in a proportionate fashion when water becomes limited, but respond by strategically shifting sink strength toward their cambium, thus favoring radial growth—they track the environment, making use of relevant past experience. Conceivably, there are few regulatory genes at work that orchestrate this reaction or overexpress a key function; if so, they would be desirable candidates for a swap with other poplars. The same species is of great interest as a possible donor of genes for elevated salt tolerance. Another factor high on the list of desiderata for plantation-grown poplars is reproductive sterility, both to channel carbon to harvestable products and to minimize the risk of transgene spread in the environment. Here, the many floral mutations from *Arabidopsis* and their corresponding loci in poplar are promising sources for directed gene transfer.[15] Plantation-culture traits such as tolerance of selective herbicides, useful in early weed control in plantations, have already been experimentally incorporated in hybrid poplars and have shown persistent expression in field tests over several years.

A new area in which poplars are proving to be of value is in the rapidly expanding field of phytoremediation, in which plants are used to clean up contaminated environments.[16] Deep rooting, rapid growth, and high use of water are attributes that rank high in this context. No wonder there are many examples where poplars have been successfully put to work, such as in aiding the disposal of municipal wastewater, re-mediation of sites spoiled by industrial processes, and filtration of agri-cultural runoff. Here, too, genetic engineering offers ways to specifi-cally tailor cultivars for the intended purpose. This may involve genes for increased root growth and enhanced root absorption, as well as for elevated expression of genes active in the translocation, sequestration, or breakdown of heavy metals and other pollutants. For example, re-cent research by Sharon Doty and collaborators on the remediation of trichloroethylene (TCE), a common industrial pollutant, has focused on a specific enzyme, cytochrome P450 2E1, which is critically involved in the metabolism of TCE. By overexpressing a mammalian P450 2E1 gene that was introduced into poplar, these researchers were able to develop transgenic plants that showed a 45-fold greater metabolism of the pollutant. The same poplars were also able to remove three common volatile pollutants from the air at greatly increased rates, compared to nontransgenic controls.[17] In a similar way, genetic engineering may be enlisted to optimize poplar and willow cultivars that now have become prime arboreal contenders for short-rotation biofuel production. Given the complex pathways in which cellulose and hemicelluloses can be converted to ethanol, small qualitative or quantitative changes in the original wood chemistry could greatly enhance the conversion process. This would offer another option in piecing together the puzzle, which type of biomass in which region may offer a sensible and efficient solu-tion toward the energy demands of the future.[18]

The Importance of Field Testing

Whether genetic engineering is used for commercial purposes, for improvement of the environment, or strictly for research toward a better understanding of tree physiology and adaptation, the engineered plants need to undergo careful scrutiny under rigorous testing before being put to use. Some of this testing can be conducted in the confinement of growth chambers and greenhouses. Eventually, however, especially with a tree that grows 6 feet a year, you have to go outside. Besides, it is in the field environment, with its high radiation, wind, and other physical and biotic challenges, where a tree shows its mettle. Field testing is especially important in the case of complex traits that have to do with growth, wood formation, timing of vegetative and reproductive development, and the like—as opposed to, say, rust tolerance, which can be tested on seedlings in the greenhouse. Even if the initial procedure of inserting a gene or two offers a shortcut over breeding, the necessary progeny testing takes just as long as it would in conventional tree improvement. And it is here, owing to the need to conduct such tests in the field, where strong opposition has been voiced. What are these concerns and how can they be met? One is rooted in the view that such genetic manipulation is against the laws of nature and violates some basic principle that keeps species pure. This view is perhaps even more strongly held where forest trees are concerned than with agricultural crops. Aren't trees the last holdovers of an untamed nature? Now, as to natural processes, we have learned that nature has been generous in allowing genetic exchange among species for millions of years, that about half of our modern plant species have arisen as hybrids, and that molecular data today show that many genes are being shared among unrelated plants as far apart as poplars and rice—some even among plants and humans. Nature is also full of bacteria and viruses that regularly introduce genes of their own or from other plants into new hosts. And with regard to keeping our hands off trees and preserving untamed nature, it can be argued that concentrating forest-production functions on intensive plantations will in fact remove pressure from old-growth forests and help to keep them as protected ecosystems. This is especially relevant in a world in which a burgeoning population will keep demanding more wood products for some time to come.

Another concern about field testing of genetically engineered (GE) trees is the potential risk of their spreading unwanted genes into the environment, and especially of contaminating their native wild relatives. That risk is indeed there and deserves attention, especially with wind-pollinated forest trees that spread their pollen far and wide. The key question, therefore, is how the engineered gene(s) would affect the unintended hosts. Here we must remember that many domestication transgenes are aimed at improving the quality and value of crop trees in their plantation environment, not in a natural setting. Just as crop plants are tailored to a pampered cultural setting, plantation trees will increasingly become dependent on such regimes too. They or their offspring would have a hard time competing with wild types in a more natural environment, which would limit or prevent their genes from spreading. Imagine a barrel-tree having to fight wild neighbors that will already be shading it out in its first few years. Further, in the case of poplar, preferred GE cultivars also tend to be the better-growing F_1 hybrids, which means that their unwanted offspring would be either F_2 hybrids or backcrosses to the native wild types, both of which have proven to be generally inferior in growth to their parents. In other words, while the potential for gene flow is there, effective gene flow is likely to be negligible.[19] This will be especially true where native populations exceed plantation acreage, as in the case of small-scale field trials. The problem is more acute when the shift is made to large-scale commercial plantations, in which case mitigation measures to minimize the impact are called for. These include rendering GE trees sterile, or regulating their reproductive phenology (genetically or culturally) to reduce the overlap with that of wild trees, or surrounding them with isolation strips, or planting them at some distance from wild populations, or using preferentially female cultivars with shorter-distance dispersal than pollen-bearing trees.

Overall, environmental concerns about GE plantings have a lot to do with their scale. Small-scale field tests are one thing, but commercialization may create large artificial environments that are hostile to insects and microorganisms and that thereby affect neighboring ecosystems by limiting food sources, symbionts, and other services. Extensive monocultures with GE trees, especially those carrying transgenic insect resistance, may hasten the evolution of new pest races (through mutation) that become immune to the existing control. These new races may then become an economic nuisance to neighboring unrelated crops.[20] (Of course, normal plantations with exotics would present the same risks.) Scale also has a temporal dimension. Unlike annual crops, tree plantations stay in place for ten to fifteen or more years and can exert their influence on neighboring ecosystems for a longer period. How can you adequately anticipate complex interactions and their consequences for such time spans? Cumulative effects may not be discernible in a three-year trial. And computer modeling may lack scientific credibility unless it is based on some hard data from local experiments. With this uncertainty, risk-averse ecologists will tend to adopt the precautionary principle and delay any GE plantings even on a small scale, whereas biotechnologists will want to see hard evidence for the functioning of new cultivars in the real world rather than a virtual one.

Scale is also influenced by economic considerations. Not only is it costly to develop transgenic trees, but federal and state environmental laws in the United States further raise the ante when it comes to commercializing such trees. This typically involves premarket licensing, often in a cumbersome way, separately for different transgenes, and an assessment of potential environmental impacts. It also provides governmental agencies and the public with instruments for legal action against actual or perceived violators.[21] Small companies are less inclined to accept such economic hurdles. Large corporations that already have a stake in agricultural biotechnology are more likely to risk investments in tree-oriented genetic engineering and will also want to protect their intellectual property therein. Academic researchers looking for financial support in an increasingly competitive grant world may welcome collaborative arrangements with such companies in furthering their GE studies. In this way, research and development of GE biotechnology tend to end up in the influence sphere of a finite set of corporations, whose opaque agendas don't exactly invite public trust. Some of the skepticism or outright hostility to this new technology may then be directed more against its social context than its inherent promise.[22]

In its advisory capacity to the government, the US National Research Council has issued several guiding reports on GE plants in which it emphasized that the critical variables involved in their production are (1) the trait, and (2) the weediness of the recipient—but not the method of production.[23] This guideline sets a favorable stage for the genetic engineering of non-weedy forest trees, especially those involving complex traits of growth, development, and adaptation. As genomics research progresses, expanding into more species and genera and shining more light into the rich diversity of forest trees, there will be increasing opportunities to recruit transgenes from within species or from close relatives, thus reducing actual and perceived risks associated with genetic engineering. In this way GE technology may become a valuable addendum to the conventional tool kit of breeding and selection in the domestication of forest trees for some of the specialized functions for which they can be grown. At the same time, economic disincentives, environmental concerns, and lack of public acceptance may limit the application of these tools in the near future. This will likely keep the mainstream forest tree improvement programs within the traditional domain of selective breeding, although they will be increasingly sharpened by molecular information. Systematic screening of natural populations for favorable alleles in genes that are associated with commercially important traits (the field of *association genetics*) will render breeding and selection procedures more efficient.[24] Programs along that line are already well under way.

I trust this chapter will have given a sufficient inkling of the controversial climate surrounding GE technology and its application to forest trees. Much has been written on this topic and special symposia have been dedicated to its deliberation. A meeting convened in 2001 by Steven Strauss from Oregon State University and Toby Bradshaw from the University of Washington to review the many relevant issues of forest biotechnology provides a good example of these discussions. The conference was attended by more than 200 people from twenty-three countries. A well-balanced distillate from the meeting has been published under the title *The Bioengineered Forest: Challenges for Science and Society.*[25] Its breadth reflects the diversity of speakers, ranging from biotechnologists to legal experts to environmental ethicists and beyond. It equally speaks for the broad vision of the two organizers, who—through their own research and guidance of numerous co-workers—have significantly helped to shape this emergent field during the past twenty years.

In concluding this chapter, let me emphasize what a remarkable enrichment genomics and its parent discipline, molecular biology, have brought to the world of tree biology. Questions that used to be of interest strictly to biologically inclined foresters, tree physiologists, and forest geneticists have drawn in a whole new population of researchers with entirely different backgrounds, new tools, a new language, and refreshing visions. Just as the application of more rigorous ecological principles in the 1970s and of computer simulation in the 1980s have introduced more quantification and prediction to forestry, biotechnology and molecular genetics will bring a new magnifying glass through which to look at many of the inherent regulatory mechanisms behind much of forest biology and community ecology.[26] The secret for success will be to keep a dynamic balance between laboratory and field research in the future and to educate young scientists accordingly.

Having acquainted ourselves with these momentous developments in genetics, let us step back and look at the broader issues of tomorrow's forests. After all, there are many different types of forests that serve a wide range of purposes, from the preservation of old-growth ecosystems to protection forests, recreation forests, and plantations for the most efficient production of pulp and paper. How can their different functions be integrated into environmentally sound and socially acceptable landscapes?

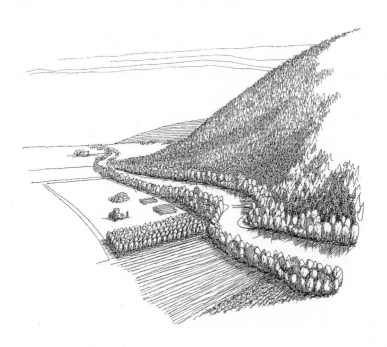

21 / BETWEEN OLD GROWTH
AND PLANTATIONS

Genetics is not context free. Even if genes—as Richard Dawkins argues—should be viewed simply as replicators having the sole purpose of making more copies of themselves, they are tied to an organism, at least temporarily. And even if DNA is the grand connector of the living world, from microbes to redwoods to humans, most of us geneticists have our favorite carrier of that molecule. After all, one has to focus on some creature with which to carry out experiments and with which to peek behind the curtain. That this favorite in my case happened to be poplar has filled most of the chapters in this book. But there are many more trees out there, and what drew me to genetics in the first place were trees in the aggregate, the vast forests of the Northern Temperate Zone, and the unexplored inner mechanisms that shaped their populations. Forest trees still held secrets. Perhaps they were unwieldy, raw, and complicated—but they had the taste of nature.

So let me broaden the perspective and use this chapter to reflect on a number of issues related to the wider world of forests and the way society deals with them. And when I say world of forests I might as well say Nature. Forests, of course, have intrinsic values that long predate the appearance of humans and their social drivers. Forest ecosystems in all their wonderful complexity and multiple functions didn't wait for humans to invest them with content. But once humans took over the situation changed, and this irreversibly. Remember the suggestion by a paleoecologist that the past 8,000 years of the Holocene be called the Anthropocene.[1] Today, forests are at the mercy of man, to the extent that it would be unrealistic to view forests in the abstract rather than through the human prism. In fact, we have to see them in a world in which true nature is no more. As aptly observed by Peter Kareiva and several other ecologists in a recent review, our world is one of a domesticated nature, in which landscapes and ecosystems have been gradually and systematically shaped for human welfare. From the early removal of large mammals and the setting of wildfires and deforestation for agriculture, to the domestication of plants and animals, to the development of trade and its associated spread of invasive species and diseases, humans have shifted natural ecosystem services to maximize productivity, reduce natural risks—such as fires, floods, and predators—and promote commerce.[2] It is in this context that I will consider in the sections below a number of forest types that fit on the continuum from the most artificial to the most natural, and touch on such questions as how I see their role, their management, and their functional relationships, and then go on to consider how we can integrate them into a coherent landscape.

Plantation forestry has received considerable impetus through the recent developments in molecular genetics, as described in the last chapter. There is the hope that these developments will make forestry more effective, scientifically more justifiable, ecologically more beneficial, and that it will do so in different contexts, from generating useful information to allowing targeted intervention. Advocates for a more widespread application of the new tools argue, for example, that they could dramatically increase productivity and thereby reduce pressure on natural forests. In the words of Jesse Ausubel and coauthors, "Forests do an admirable job of collecting solar energy and storing it in stable chemical form. The problem is spatial. The collected energy of trees is spatially dilute and in forms awkward to handle. Harvesting requires lots of manpower and sophisticated machinery. Further, harvesting is only the beginning." Thus, concentrating production on rapidly growing trees of desirable form in intensively managed plantations would significantly reduce the space needed for the target outputs of the future and at the same time make the forest-products industry more competitive. The land spared by higher yields could lead to a great restoration of nature.[3]

Forest plantations now occupy an estimated area of 185 million hectares worldwide, 60 percent of them in the temperate area, 40 percent in the tropics. In Europe, they make up over 50 percent of all forests.[4] In the southern United States, pine plantations have almost doubled during the past 50 years and now cover 14 million hectares, while during that same time their yields have been raised sixfold.[5] Evidently, the move toward plantation forestry is well under way. At that rate, half the world's volume of industrial wood, one billion cubic meters, could come from plantations by the year 2050.[6] The attraction of this option is that it makes it possible to choose where trees should be grown in the first place—not just by default. Sites on abandoned farmland with higher fertility, better access for machinery, and closer proximity to conversion plants are especially attractive. Where they replace annual crops, tree plantations are environmentally more benign; they root more deeply, build up the soil, and require less fertilizer, fewer pesticides, and less use of machinery. That is not to say that plantation management is free from cultural improvements. Here too gains in yield can be obtained from judiciously tailored weed control, fertilizer application, and—if needed—irrigation. Also, with the interest in maximizing productivity, the tendency will be to gradually select planting stock that is especially responsive to such treatments. Typical plantation rotations (harvest cycles) range from two-year coppice plantings of willows for fuel, to forty years for pine for solid-wood products. Most plantations use single species, and—in species that allow vegetative propagation—a few production clones. Backup material from ongoing breeding is in the wings to replace inadequate performers or failures due to physical or biotic stress. Short rotations allow flexibility in targeting markets and in revising treatment schedules. Yields of 20 cubic meters per hectare per year are commonly obtained with selected *radiata* pine in Chile and New Zealand, 50 cubic meters with hybrid poplars in the Pacific Northwest; and with eucalypts in industrial plantations in Brazil, numbers as high as 70 cubic meters per hectare per year have been recorded.[7] Further gains in yield and quality of planting stock can be expected from using trees that have been even more carefully fine-tuned to deliver the raw material desired by modern society. New, unusual images of tree crops will appear in the landscape—uniform rows of barrel-shaped trunks— and we will have to get used to them, just as we did when extensive fields of dwarfed sunflowers with their downturned black heads came to dominate stretches of the Midwest. Harvesting machines that slowly mow down row after row of trees may become as common a landscape feature as combines moving across the wheat fields.

But plantation forestry comes with its own set of problems. Typically, it involves monocultures, and often a small number of clones of nonnative material, which means a local reduction in biodiversity unless in an area where it replaces agricultural land use. It packs this material into even-aged, single-story, uniform stands that are perfect breeding grounds for insects and diseases. It depends on biocides, petroleum products (including fertilizer), and the use of heavy machinery for cultural maintenance, harvest, and transport. Each of these negative aspects can be addressed and in some way mitigated but not entirely eliminated. Then there is public perception. While miles and miles of wheat fields and the way their surface waves in the wind have become part of our cultural scenery, even celebrated in poetry, tree plantations have yet to gain their acceptance in landscape aesthetics. Again, scale has a lot to do with it. You can look over fields of grain to a distant horizon—but trees block your view. And their uniform spacing in straight rows and unvarying form seem to violate all we know and feel about natural patterns. But size has its plus side too. In an agricultural landscape, tree stands can be a relief from the horizontal monotony; they also can significantly enrich wildlife habitat for birds and ungulates.

Perhaps the most significant variable with plantation forestry is ownership. There is an economy of scale, pushing operations toward greater uniformity on larger acreages. It goes hand in hand with globalization, drives ownership toward fewer and larger corporations, and tends to subject strategic decisions to short-term profits. In the end, a small number of corporate decision-makers may determine the fate of an ever-increasing fraction of private forestland. With no allegiance to the land, they may decide to sell the property from one day to another and jeopardize the personnel who have diligently managed the land for years—forcing a loss of continuity in stewardship and of what was learned over time.

In spite of its flaws, intensive plantation forestry is here to stay and will expand, and its necessity has also been recognized by vocal advocates of the environment. Thus, in his concluding recommendations in *The Future of Life*, E. O. Wilson not only calls for the cessation of all logging in old-growth forests but links it to his endorsement of tree farming. "The time has come—rich opportunity shines forth—for the timber-extraction industry to shift to tree farming on already converted land. The cultivation of lumber and pulp should be conducted like the agribusiness it is, using high-quality, fast-growing species and strains for higher productivity and profit."[8]

By comparison, multipurpose forests are perhaps the oldest form in which forestland has been purposely managed. In contrast to forest plantations, and as the name implies, they serve a broader spectrum of functions, if at a lower level of productivity than plantations.[9] They represent the bulk of managed forestland and, together with the shrinking acreage of natural forests, make up the majority of the world's forest cover. These forests tend to be relegated to less fertile land, steeper terrain, and are exposed to less favorable microclimates, such as are common at higher elevations, or in frost- or drought-prone areas. This is a natural consequence of the long history of allocating the best land to agricultural fields and orchards. In fact, in some parts of the world today we see an expansion of forests back onto land that had previously been cleared but eventually proved to be only marginally productive for grazing or crops. Thus, in Europe, forest area has increased by 10 percent between 1960 and 1990 alone and now covers 140 million hectares within the twenty-five European Union countries, or about 36 percent of the land.[10] Typical forms of ownership range from predominantly national and state or provincial forests (as in Canada and the United States) to community and cooperative forests, and in the private sector have tended toward smaller properties (such as farm woodlots) rather than corporate land. These forests have a long history of providing wood for shelter, fiber, and energy while at the same time offering wildlife habitat and serving to protect water and air quality. More recently they have also become recognized as an important repository of carbon. In their totality they constitute a vast reservoir of biological diversity at all levels, even if past use in individual locations has been exploitive or subject to "high-grading"—where desirable species and crop trees have been removed, leaving commercially inferior stock to regenerate. Genetically too, these tree populations have experienced only a few generations of directed human intervention and therefore still harbor a diversity that largely reflects the breadth of long-term natural selection. In fact, studies have shown that even more intensive management practices, such as replanting with seedlings from seed orchards composed of highly selected crop trees, seem to perpetuate a broad diversity of genetic variation. This is the boon of having high levels of genetic diversity to begin with, which—as discussed earlier—is a fundamental attribute of most kinds of forest trees.[11]

Social considerations too argue for the continuity of a broadly oriented management of these forests. Their rural base is an effective counterforce to the pervasive process of urbanization. This can work in various ways. Jobs in the forest keep people from migrating to cities. Such jobs may be associated with traditional forestry (logging, transport, planting, etc.) or with the marketing of secondary forest products (berries, mushrooms, honey, medicinal plants, ornamentals, and the like), or with such recent developments as ecotourism or the training and employment of paraprofessionals in forest and wildlife conservation. Tying forests and their management to local communities and providing new economic incentives to their inhabitants increases a sense of ownership and favors a long-term interest in the stewardship of their resources. New, fairer arrangements by pharmaceutical corporations should allow economic gains to also benefit the source communities from which medicinal plants were obtained. There is also a broader interest today in seeing that cultural diversity in language, social traditions, and crafts of local regions are recognized and perpetuated. Various nongovernmental organizations and private foundations (such as

Pew, the Rockefeller and Ford Foundations, and The Nature Conservancy) support these developments internationally.

But the pace of urbanization and industrialization can at best be slowed down, not halted, and this has intensified the demand for recreation forests in the vicinity of the rapidly expanding urban centers. Increased leisure time, extended by the longer life expectancy of humans today, has placed strong emphasis on the recreational role of woodlands. As a result, production functions have taken a back seat behind accessibility, aesthetic value, experiential diversity, and the development of interpretive centers, nature paths, picnic sites, and the like. New technology and marketing have brought mountain-bikes, off-road motorcycles, snowmobiles, and all-terrain vehicles into the woods, and a new segment of society now enjoys the forest environment in a different way, as a playground for their machines. New lobbies raise their voices and make claims that are in conflict with those from hikers, birders, and other nature-lovers. At the same time, parks in and around the cities have lost their formerly isolated function as green patches on the city map and have become recognized as coherent components of an urban ecosystem. Their management too calls for new professionals in urban forestry, people capable of integrating the ecological and social functions of these natural resources. Moreover, such resources increasingly reflect the pressures of the urban environment, which in turn inevitably leads to selection of a vegetation tolerant of elevated pollution, heat, drought, and physical damage. Here, the pragmatic has to be matched with the creative in promoting diversity within given constraints. But if there are biological checks to an urban manager, they are more than compensated for by the social opportunities. Where else can you find a more responsive and educated public than in an urban setting, where visitors are eager to learn more about the role of trees and forests in our environment?

And so it may well be the urban dweller who—more than anybody else—dreams of old-growth forests, and who may do the most to see them preserved. Such terms as primeval, pristine, and *Urwald* seem by their very definition to ban the heavy hand of man. To say that the most pristine reserves among them deserve the utmost protection as continual shrines of biological conservation for study and inspiration is only to repeat what should be obvious. Their value far exceeds the short-term utilitarian purposes for which they have often been sacrificed, and their increasing scarcity calls for stringent conservation. But with the exception of a few regions in the tropics and the northern taiga, they are relatively small and disconnected. This is especially true for those located in North America and Europe. Here is a case where leaving them entirely to the vagaries of nature and to the scale at which nature tends to operate may often jeopardize their continuity and their critical functions. Fires, windstorms, insect outbreaks, and other calamities generated in their midst, or transferred from neighboring managed land, may threaten their existence or transform them to long-term, treeless scrub land. The current infestation of millions of hectares of pine forests by the mountain pine beetle in western North America offers a good example of the problem. Alternatively, the very absence of disturbances may stagnate forests in a senescent state and systematically eliminate early-successional species, leading to a loss of biodiversity. Such developments are even more problematic in the case of designated protection forests. These are forests that serve a protective function for settlements both as watersheds and as barriers against avalanches, mudslides, and erosion. There, a persistent tree cover is imperative for the continuity of human life and shelter as well as for the conservation of soil and water. Putting a fence around these forests and letting nature run its course would precisely deny the functions for which they were set aside in the first place. Careful monitoring and appropriately timed silvicultural treatments will be the best recipe to guarantee their vital role in long-term landscape management. Of course, human intervention has been commonplace in national parks too, where the development of trails and campgrounds, predator and fire control, and even the protection of meadows against natural encroachment by the forest have controlled the ecosystem for the benefit of visitors. The questions there are, How accessible should nature be to how many, and what is the right mix of wilderness functions to be sustained?

New Forest Partnerships

As functionally diverse as these different types of forests are, we should view them not as separate entities but as interconnected parts of a continuum. In their different combinations they are fulfilling the counter-vailing functions of protection and production. At one end, old growth and forest reserves maximize protection and conservation, have high biological diversity, and are managed as needed to serve as long-term ecosystems. At the other, intensively managed plantations maximize production with a minimum of biodiversity and are grown in short ro-tations with frequent cultural treatments. Protection forests, multiple-use forests, and recreation forests line up in between with appropri-ate trade-offs. As should be clear, these categories are arbitrary and their boundaries fuzzy. Moreover, these forests form part of a wider landscape with other natural resources, transportation networks, rural settlements, and urban agglomerations. In total, we are looking at a wide array of public and private ownerships, operating on a range of spatial and temporal scales, driven by divergent and often conflicting objectives, and subject to different jurisdictions. To complicate matters, they each come with a historical legacy, both in evolutionary and social terms, representing temporary local endpoints of a cumulative past. To integrate such diversity into a coherent whole seems improbable, to say the least. Yet there are recent examples that meet that challenge and have arrived at workable solutions, each in a different way, but collec-tively offering proof that the impossible is in fact approachable. Let me briefly mention two of them in the Pacific Northwest that are now in their second decade of operation and have become permanent fixtures, embedded in the region.

One of them, the Applegate Partnership, located in the 500,000 acre Applegate watershed of southwestern Oregon and northern California, arose in 1992 out of public concerns about conflicting land-use priorities and the decline of environmental quality in the watershed. Focusing on three core principles, ecosystem health, economic stability, and com-munity involvement, the partnership has managed to engage thirteen public agencies at the federal, state, and county level, ten communities, a host of nonprofit organizations and interest groups, and many pri-vate landowners. In joint projects, participants work to restore wildlife habitat, improve water quality, develop forestry practices for sustained stewardship, reduce fire hazard, and take advantage of educational op-portunities and volunteer efforts. Distribution of a regular newsletter to all Applegate households helps to inform the public about ongoing projects and maintain its support.[12] Two of the partners in the Applegate, the USDA Forest Service and the USDI Bureau of Land Management, are managing their forests in the area according to principles of "adaptive management" (a catchy term for learning from doing) and have added them to the international model forest network.[13]

The second example has a similar structure but is in the Puget Sound region, in the vicinity of a major metropolitan area. Born in 1991, the Mountains to Sound Greenway Trust was initiated out of concern about unchecked urban sprawl eating its way into the forested hills of the Cascade range. Here the potential target was a 100 mile stretch along the Interstate 90 corridor across the mountains, the highway linking Seattle's waterfront with the grasslands of Central Washington. In the ensuing years the nonprofit Greenway Trust has systematically worked toward public purchase of private lands within the corridor as well as by exchanges for equal-value land beyond it. Although not owning any land, the Greenway today encompasses 700,000 acres of public farm, forest, and park land, administered by different agencies, from the federal to the community level. It also has secured a conservation easement on some 90,000 acres of a privately owned working forest. Serving an agglomeration of 3 million people, the Greenway is not only to be conserved but also made accessible through an expanding network of trails, and interpreted through educational programs. Here, as in the Applegate, community support, public involvement, and volunteerism have become essential ingredients in the organization's successful track record.[14]

In both cases, a number of common denominators were operating to help the process—in fact, they seem to be common in other cases elsewhere, as reviewed by Steven Yaffee.[15] What tends to bring people and organizations together is a commonly perceived problem or threat. In landscape management this can be unchecked urban sprawl, the shortage of a common resource (water, wood, work), the potential extinction of a threatened species, the expansion of invasive species, or increased risk of natural disasters (flooding, fire, landslides). If the problem cannot be successfully dealt with by the individual or a single organization, the stage is set for joining with others who are equally concerned. It is then important to identify the appropriate geographic scale for which a joint effort makes sense. This may be a watershed, a transportation corridor, or a wider region that shares a common denominator. Intimately associated with the geographic dimension is the opportunity for individual and community involvement. The project has to be on a scale that invites participation and a sense of ownership in the total venture. A common sense of place is often what motivates people to see beyond their individual interests and to invest in a joint cause. Funding opportunities and public pressure will facilitate the process, and so will technology—especially the electronic networks that serve rapid, orchestrated, and transparent communication. Another remarkably effective tool is the computer-based geographic information system (GIS), a powerful technology capable of combining information, displaying maps, and graphically portraying possible scenarios in easily perceivable ways. (For most of us, it is difficult to imagine the potential impacts of alternative management decisions, especially those that may be 50 to 100 years down the line; but a three-dimensional image, even if virtual, greatly helps to visualize the eventual outcomes at different scales.) However, if there is nobody who can get the ball rolling, all these factors may not be enough. Ultimately, it takes the initiative and leadership of several visionaries who are willing to launch a program, and who are capable of enlisting other influential partners for shared responsibility, motivating the public, guiding the process over critical hurdles with professional competence and political savvy, and maintaining the momentum.

Familiarity with these common ingredients doesn't automatically make for a successful recipe, but learning from them and applying them in the context of local conditions may point the way in wresting the possible from the impossible and turning it into the actual.

It won't have surprised the reader that one of the examples above has taken us back to the Snoqualmie River valley—the valley where in earlier chapters we have acquainted ourselves with the river, its riparian cottonwoods, and the dynamics of natural processes. People are part of this valley, too, and have an allegiance to its green landscape, its forested hills, and the permanent backdrop of the rocky ramparts of the Cascade Range. Preserving this piece of earth as a multifunctional landscape with a diversity of small and temporary solutions to ever-changing problems, and this in the spirit of an enlightened collaboration, is the hope of several coalitions like the ones described here. Science is part of it, but the main driving force is the public. Or, to put it more generally, the forests themselves may seem too large, too amorphous, and too remote in ownership to fit in our personal sphere. Yet ultimately we are major stakeholders in the landscape too, and there are many ways we can engage in very tangible local projects and make our voices heard in influencing its long-term management—especially in this domesticated nature of ours.

22 / THE ESSENCE OF TREES

Most of this book has been devoted to a discussion of trees in the plural, in the aggregate, and in natural populations, forests, and plantations—as a consequence of its genetic and evolutionary bias and the emphasis on underlying processes. But let us not ignore the tree as an individual, with the ingredients that give it such an iconic presence among organisms in our daily life. What is it that makes a tree a tree and captures our fascination? What image could more powerfully convey a sense of this than the above picture of that colossal oak at Ludwigsruhe on a hill above the Jagst Valley in southern Germany?[1] What more impressive statement of bold individuality against the collective anonymity of the neighboring hardwood stand? No words can do justice to the singular silhouette of this giant. No knowledge of genetics or physiology is needed to feel awed by this living monument that has faced the elements for hundreds of years and survived. Even the untrained eye will perceive a repetitive theme that reverberates through the towering hierarchy of stem, branches, branchlets, and twigs. Every unit on this tree is unmistakably part of the whole. The little twists and angles in the twigs add up at an ever increasing scale to shape the ultimate form, the unique profile, the Gestalt of the tree.

Tree growth is modular and iterative. Its basic unit, as in all plants, is a phytomer, a unit composed of a shoot segment with a leaf and an axillary bud (fig. 22.1). The bud contains a meristem with another phytomer in primordial form. Once this primordium elongates into another full-fledged phytomer, the process repeats itself, adding building block after building block to develop a simple plant body. Yet plants are more complex than that. Even small annuals like *Arabidopsis* have a stem with many small branchlets. And since each branchlet is subtended by a leaf, it evidently developed from an axillary meristem, whereas the stem originated from a terminal or apical meristem. And in order for the plant to gain an erect stature, the apical meristem had to exert a regulatory, dominating function over the axillary meristems, a process called *apical dominance*. A gradient in apical dominance would then allow a hierarchal architecture to emerge, with branchlet length diminishing toward the apex. Finally, allowing successive phytomers to rotate their orientation along the stem's axis would result in a three-dimensional plant body. Add some roots and turn some shoots into flowers and you have what it takes to build a dandelion, a tulip, or a corn plant. But not quite a tree.

Tree growth adds one more dimension to those of an annual plant, namely that of secondary growth. Not only does the tree preserve the first year's structure, it bulks it up through radial growth. This occurs through the activity of another meristem, the vascular cambium. In contrast to the point-like apical and axillary meristems, it is a laminar or sheet-like meristem that connects the shoot's vascular bundles and turns them into a vascular cylinder, adding xylem on the inside and phloem on the outside. Through stepped-up lignification of this sheath, this turns the plant into a woody body, capable of bearing the added weight and staying upright. Then, year after year, it keeps adding

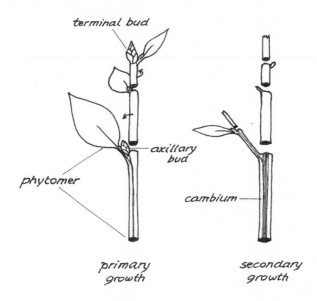

terminal bud

axillary
bud

phytomer

cambium

primary
growth

secondary
growth

22.1 Primary and secondary shoot growth of a woody plant. Rotation of successive phytomers places leaves in different positions above each other according to the phyllotaxy of the species.

one annual sheath after another, gaining height and volume, reaching toward the light and shading out smaller neighbors. This outer, living sheath is carried by an ever-increasing core of dead wood. In fact, by the time a tree reaches the size of that magnificent oak above, as much as 90 percent of it will be dead tissue. In the same way, one of those 4,000-year-old bristlecone pines may in essence be a dead, woody sculpture sustaining a tiny strip of peripheral living matter that connects a few needle bundles with a root below: leaves hanging on to mummified ancestral cells that even in their death provide essential support for life in the sun. In this, the tree is a perfect example of a lasting legacy in a very physical sense.

Plant growth is a celebration of decentralization, and trees push it to its extreme. The dispersed meristems in this open growth system provide a mechanism to deal flexibly with contingencies. Rather than being constrained by the dictates of a centralized body plan, as in animals, meristems in different parts of the crown can be selectively activated or inactivated. Those in the sun can be favored to elongate while those in the shade may remain dormant. Loss of an apical meristem through frost or insect damage can be compensated for by activation of the nearest axillary meristem. Or, in extremis, loss of the entire aerial structure through fire may release root suckers, as in aspen, or root-collar sprouts, as in oaks. And for trees in a hurry, where not a moment must be lost, as in early-successional alders, birches, poplars, and willows, this differential activation may play out throughout the entire growing season so as to maximize gains where they count most. Trees are stuck where they grow. They cannot move to another location (although parts of them may). But they can improve their lot by directing their growth in a favorable direction, toward an opening, away from the wind, or by exploiting a patchy substrate through differential root growth.

If a tree's open growth allows opportunistic flexibility, it still must follow basic rules, and we can decipher some of them just by simple observation—without knowing anything about DNA or gene expression. A first rule says that growth has to stick to the same type of phytomer throughout the entire tree. That's a simple logic, but when put to work through continual repetition it has a profound effect on the appearance—the Gestalt—of the entire tree. Ashes look slimmer than oaks for several reasons, but largely because they are constructed by the repetitive use of a comparatively slim phytomer. Cottonwoods look even slimmer than ashes because indeterminate growth allows them to use their slim phytomers in larger numbers per season. Lombardy poplars look columnar because their angle of bud insertion is narrower than normal, resulting in a narrow branch angle at each successive phytomer. Magnolias develop a broad crown because the wide angle of first-order twigs is repeated in second-, third-, and fourth-order branches, and so on. (In fact, this principle is of some practical use when you are picking a small tree in a nursery, because its early branching pattern is a reasonable predictor of its later shape.)

Another rule regulates the degree by which successive phytomers rotate their position along the shoot's axis; this is an inflexible rule, and it forms the basis of *phyllotaxy*, a reliable ordering principle in plant taxonomy. For example, ashes, maples, and horse chestnuts always have two buds per phytomer; these are opposite one another and generate opposite leaves, and successive leaf pairs are at 90 degrees from each other to minimize mutual shading. By contrast, oaks, cottonwoods, and magnolias have phytomers with single buds which, in successive leaves, form a spiral around the shoot, with an angular deflection characteristic for each genus. Buds may elongate or stay dormant, but their position is governed by the taxon's basic program.

If rotational symmetry and repetitive building blocks lay the basis for a tree's growth, there is a third mechanism that is even more decisive in influencing its final form, and this is the degree to which the tree's terminal dominates its lateral branches, which is referred to as *apical control*. The stronger the control, the more a tree's form approaches that of a spire, with a single central trunk and short radial branches— as can be seen in subalpine fir or Engelmann spruce. The weaker this control, the closer the tree form approximates an umbrella, with a short trunk that divides into multiple stems and broadly arching branches, as in sycamores, acacias, or savanna trees.

Together, these three mechanisms and their many combinations are sufficient to explain most of the great diversity of tree forms, from redwoods to scrub oaks.[2] They determine a basic theme for each species, within which each individual plays a unique variation.

It is the abnormal that often helps us appreciate and understand the normal. The basic rules of allometry let us expect height/diameter relationships in a tree to fit within a certain envelope.[3] Thus, the unusually stocky trunk of that Euphrates poplar in northwest China (fig. 20.1) struck us as calling for some explanation. Or take weeping beeches, columnar oaks, "Camperdown" elms, corkscrew hazels, dwarf conifers—they all are off the chart of their species' architectural norm. Standing out as aberrations from their clan, they draw attention and at some point convinced an enterprising nurseryman to propagate them, thereby raising their fitness value way beyond what raw nature would have granted—one of the benefits of living in what Pollan has called second nature. Thus, the easy clonability of Port Orford cedar (*Chamaecyparis lawsoniana*), a forest tree of coastal Oregon and northern California, has over the years resulted in more than eighty recognized cultivars, ranging from columnar to weeping and dwarf forms, with anything from yellow to variegated to bluish foliage.[4] Or take the many cultivars of Japanese maples (*Acer palmatum*) with such descriptive names as "Dissectum," "Albomarginatum," "Linearilobum," "Atropurpureum," and more. Closer inspection of such deviants points to the critical detail that gives them their unusual form or color. In most cases it is a simple deficiency or change, presumably caused by a mutation and generating a stunted phytomer, or a steeply inserted bud, or insufficient phototropism, or faulty pigmentation, that cumulatively, through repeated action, turns a normal phenotype into a freak. In an annual plant they would have been overlooked. But repetitive error, superimposed on its precursors year after year, couldn't be ignored. Grasping how these variations depart from the theme of their species will also allow us to better see the functionality of the normal. Not surprisingly, their uniqueness has given many of them favored status among gardeners, landscape architects, and estate owners. What would the ornamentals industry do without them? Anomaly has its attractions, and just as the different dog breeds say something about their owners, so do the trees in a garden.

Perhaps the best proof for the basic simplicity of tree growth, the iterative use of a modular unit, is the way simple computer programs can generate remarkably realistic tree designs. For example, fractal theory[5] allows you to draw two-dimensional trees and arrive at contrasting silhouettes that are simply derived from two basic branching patterns (fig. 22.2). Using the same algorithm but going 3-D and refining it through rules derived from those at work in black cottonwood produces a fairly realistic skeleton of a young tree. An even fuller portrait can be obtained by attaching leaves, obeying the species' specific rules on phyllotaxy and leaf orientation (fig. 22.3).[6]

But impressive as these representations are, they still fall short of the real thing. Just as a plastic Christmas tree remains a plastic tree, these models can't get away from their mathematical origin. What they lack is a way to sufficiently allow for the unpredictable impact of a fickle environment. How would you go about properly programming the effect on a riparian cottonwood of an unusually dry summer in its fifteenth year in such a way as to distinguish it from an equivalent summer hitting it in its thirtieth year, after two moderately dry summers preceding it, or in combination with a 20 percent defoliation by the cottonwood leaf beetle? How would the tree be affected by the level of the nearby stream, or by a neighboring tree on its south side? Moreover, when we say impact, we typically refer to more than a single effect—and in fact

22.2 Two-dimensional fractal trees with monopodial (left) and dipodial (right) branching patterns. *(Reprinted from Chen et al., 1994, with permission from Elsevier Science B.V.)*

to an interaction of responses, sometimes early shedding of leaves, sometimes compensatory growth, sometimes shifting allocation of energy to storage or to the mobilization of defense compounds. Just as the flow of time is unidirectional, so is the sequence of environmental experiences, and it is peculiar to each tree. Yes, there is the underlying genetic program, the theme of its species. But the way it individually meets its singular sequence of contingencies has no counterpart in any other tree. Just as every human has a unique face, distinct from any other face on this planet, so does every tree. And a tree has a vastly larger structure with which to show that face, with all its asymmetries, warts, and wrinkles. Individuality is what we expect from a tree. The peculiar marks and scars left by a long life and all that came with it—storms, snow, drought, woodpeckers, insects—give testimony to the inevitable hand of chance. Expressive in an old oak, it is even more so in the scattered clumps of whitebark pines growing in the Cascades at the upper tree line. Candelabra crowns, broken branches, twisted trunks with patches of missing bark, polished by ice storms—woody sculptures, but still alive and facing the elements, and inspiring to all who seek the mountain environment to get a feel of untamed nature.

From another perspective, what would all that architecture be without the vertical dimension? In the living world there is no substitute for

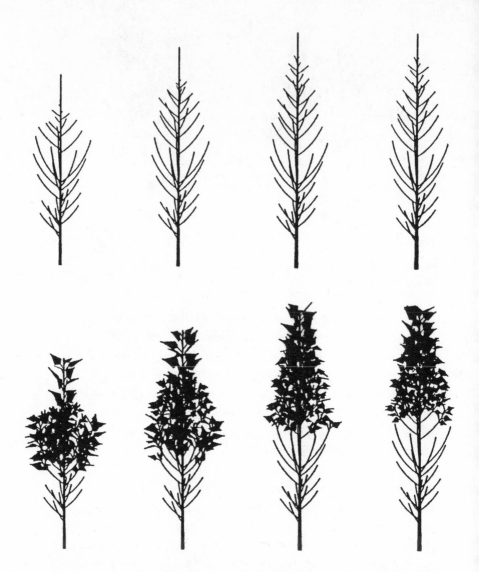

22.3 Fractal tree models of young black cottonwoods at four different stages in their second growing season, with and without leaves. *(Reprinted from Chen at al., 1994, with permission from Elsevier Science B.V.)*

absolute size, and here trees have an uncontested claim. And in proving it they draw thousands of visitors to the Californian redwoods and to the Douglas fir groves on Vancouver Island year after year. Yet what the human eye perceives in looking up into these giants is, thanks to the curvature of the lens, a shortened version of the real thing. This is why we tend to move back and away from the tree to get a better sense of its true size. But even that is not enough. An ambitious photographer, James Balog, has recently taken up this challenge and has captured what we are missing. In climbing a neighboring tree of one of these redwoods and then slowly lowering himself from the top by a rope while taking horizontal photos of his tall object, he was able to assemble a vertical collage of images that were free of the usual distortion. Printed as a foldout among many others in a magnificent book, it opens our eyes to the amazing heights some of these conifers have conquered and filled out. It also helps us understand why these tall trees stick so close to the vertical in their growth, and to a balanced radial symmetry—at these dimensions, gravity punishes even minor deviations.

In other trees, especially broadleaves, it is less the height than the volume of the crown that confers to them their impressive presence. Never does this become more obvious than when an old horse chestnut or a London plane tree is removed from a park or a town square. No one is ever prepared for the huge empty space, the gaping vacuum left behind. The remarkably small pile of disassembled wood seems a final insult to the original edifice. Its lofty architecture had engulfed an enormous amount of space, even beyond its crown, creating an organic oasis in the midst of the city that one felt would last forever. No wonder people will go to the barricades to save such a treasured icon of their daily experience from the chainsaw.

Trees are ideally suited to bring nature to the city. They are large enough to generate a natural presence, and this primarily in vertical space, demanding less real estate than a lawn. Here, the broadleaves have it all: variable crown shapes, leafy canopies that spend shade in summer, color in fall, transparency in winter. And thanks to angiosperm diversity, there is a long list from which suitable species can be selected. However, as any city arborist will tell you, there is an equally long list of biological or practical shortcomings that significantly shrink the number of real choices. As a consequence, the tendency is to look for the ideal city tree that meets all the specs—aesthetics, climatic tolerance, pest resistance, and maintenance. Special cultivars have proved their worth under these exacting conditions, are being vegetatively propagated, and are finding their way into many urban and suburban agglomerations. Streets with uniform "green wallpaper" are becoming more commonplace. Yet precisely here, let me plead for more sensitivity to trees' natural heritage, which has been a major topic throughout this book, and speak up for their remarkable genetic diversity within a species. To me, nothing gives a more sterile effect than an entire avenue of clonal replicates, all the same shape, all copying their neighbors' branching, all leafing out in synchrony, all responding to the same cues in unison like a string section to the maestro's baton. It is even more deplorable in street trees that are meant to stay there for a long time. More to the point, the argument for diversity goes beyond aesthetics, because it is equally valid on biological grounds to mitigate biotic risks. What this means is that in the future the development of suitable urban trees should be pursued with greater emphasis on the use of seedling progenies from selected parents rather than on mass propagation of asexual propagules from selected individuals. In other words, let us celebrate genetic diversity and the polymorphism it generates, bringing out each tree's uniqueness within a context that also emphasizes the subtle differences among individuals that are so pleasing to the eye. It may be more costly in the short term but in the long run will bring richer returns, and this in multiple currencies. With this in mind, I consider the inherent difficulty of vegetatively propagating such species as oaks, beeches, sycamores, and horse chestnuts as having positively contributed to the biotic diversity and aesthetics of our urban streets and parks.

Indeed, a park in the city may be the place where we treasure the ultimate tree-ness of trees most intensely, because this is where they occur as individuals, removed from their natural habitat. What then is their essence? Have I identified and described the essential features that define a tree? Do we see the tree as a perennial structure of phytomers with dispersed meristems and variable apical control? Or are we caught by its size and longevity? Or are we fascinated by its functioning—as a piece of organic architecture that has listened to the repetitive message of a genetic recipe, year after year, executing it under the dictates of the seasons and building a wooden structure, a record of its individual life history, open to be deciphered? Are we still missing something? Could it be expressed in another language?

Here, at the end, I gladly relinquish the field and point the reader to those who inspire us with their arboreal themes in other ways—in music, on canvas, in print, and in poetry.

23 / OUTLOOK

We are now back at the old cottonwood, where our journey in the arboreal world began. In the meantime the old tree has lost its one remaining crown segment to a violent December storm. No longer a statue of
liberty, it has been reduced to a splintered snag and is on its way to becoming part of the history of the forest community it helped establish.
While it will still be feeding countless creatures for years to come and
contributing to the chemical balance sheet of the locale through its
decomposing processes, it has ceased to disseminate seeds and branch
fragments to its riparian environment. Yet it has left an imprint, a genetic legacy that will continue through the vegetation pulses along the
ever-changing river. What fraction of its DNA will still be around by the
end of the century? The next millennium? Which genes will be the ones
to have persisted and mingled with those from the ancient poplar archive, or with some recent upstarts from upriver? What have we learned
to make predictions about the likely fate of specific suites of traits in
cottonwoods and their general adaptive strategies? Are we any wiser in
our decisions on what to conserve and what to bend to our needs, our
whims?

Studying nature is a humbling experience. Things turn out to be
more complicated than expected. Most working hypotheses test negative. The promising ones invariably generate not just one but multiple
follow-up hypotheses. Our image of the phenomenon we study remains
a sketch, an outline. In the end we are sketchers, not painters, and any
painting should be viewed with a skeptical eye. Perhaps someone got
carried away.

Studying nature also means aiming at a moving target. Change is
the rule. Evolution is open-ended and now proceeding at an even faster

pace, given our heavy hand on the environment. Every human generation is facing a new context, a new set of contingencies. This may be viewed as a liberating experience, freeing us from past dogmas and false certainty. After all, it is uncertainty that drives research, raises questions, and keeps us probing for the unknown.

There are more unknowns than ever, as Pascal's metaphor succinctly conveyed, namely, that if all the existing knowledge formed a sphere and its surface were touching the unknown surrounding it, then the interface with the unknown would be increasing at the same pace as the growth of the known. A refreshing concept that sees no end to the mining of the unknown. Tacitly, the inexhaustible unknown also elevates the question above the answer.

Daunting as the study of nature may be, there is also an encouraging aspect about it. After all, the history of our planet is the story of a grand experiment in progress over millions of years. Shifting continents, mass extinctions of entire life forms, ice ages and interglacials alternately shrinking long inhabited life zones and generating new ones, pest outbreaks causing severe population decreases, mutations randomly throwing errors into well-scripted recipes of organisms' development—life in its manifold trajectories continuing to course through this probabilistic landscape, faced with ever-new challenges. The plant world alone is a rich complex of ongoing experiments. Just think of the side-by-side reproductive trials playing out in the green world: unabashed self-fertilization, flagrant inbreeding, uninhibited cloning, promiscuous hybridization, reckless transfer of genes among totally unrelated individuals, all probing to push the envelope of life within cell walls. No wonder there isn't a perfect tree out there after 250 million years of trial and error, only works in progress. No wonder there isn't a plant community out there in perfect harmony with its environment, only a transitory assemblage of migrants, each with an individual agenda of its own. What we treasure as a timeless cathedral of an old-growth forest is but a single frame in a long movie still rolling on.

But as open-ended as this experiment is and as late as we have come to be part of it, we must still find ways to know some of its rules if we want to engage ourselves as collaborative participants aiming for joint benefits. Perhaps it may be from this angle that we can approach the study of trees with less trepidation.

What we know about trees is sketchy at best, and there are good reasons why this is so. Trees are among the most challenging organisms for study, especially if we aren't satisfied with shortcuts and want to go for the real thing in its real environment in real time. Not only are we confronted with an enormous physical body of great complexity, but it is one that was built up under ever-changing conditions, year after year. And this body is not isolated, but interlaced with a myriad of other organisms at scales from the macro- to the microscopic, each with its own life cycle and each capable of having a decisive influence on its host's fate. Who rules whom? In this literal jungle of millions of interactions, which are the ones deserving our attention? Moreover, all this complexity is already there at the level of the individual tree. What about neighboring trees, shrubs, nesting birds, the whole community?

Multiple approaches of study will be needed to penetrate this thicket. For simplicity, we may see them at three different scales. At a first level is the most basic unit, the individual tree. Ideally, to learn more about it, we should be able to replicate it through asexual propagation. That way we can study it in multiple copies under a range of indoor and outdoor environments, and in parallel fashion from different angles by different disciplines. We can then also include it in experiments at a second scale, in artificial communities that hold a finite number of genotypes under more or less controlled conditions. These can be common gardens, short-rotation field trials, or even commercial plantations. Their simplified environmental variables will allow tests for cause–effect relationships of interest to be conducted more quickly and reliably. Insights gained at this level will help sharpen the focus on traits and processes at a third level of scale, namely in an intact forest community. Here, the spectrum of variables increases dramatically so that unless their study is guided by specific hypotheses the tendency will be to study too much in too many ways. For example, if one chooses a forest community in which a study species from the first or second level serves as a foundation species (a species that structures a community by creating locally stable conditions for other species), this will concentrate attention on components and processes for which prior and independent information is already available. In turn, that will help one formulate successive hypotheses of more incisive value. In other words, rigorous study of a few tractable networks will be more useful than aiming too soon at some presumed completeness—even if we allow for some emergent properties (properties at higher levels of scale, not predictable from those at lower levels) to surprise us. This concept has been the landmark of the pioneering studies by Whitham and coworkers and has prompted them to propose a new framework for community and ecosystem genetics.[1]

What we need is many more experiments out there on the ground. There is only so much we can glean from descriptive studies, encompassing as they may be. A complete inventory of a local forest community tells us what is there, but not how it got there, nor what may happen if one of its components were to vanish, nor how the next generation will fare under current, let alone changed conditions. To get a handle on the genetic and evolutionary components of forest ecosystems—a long-neglected aspect of earlier ecological research—we need experiments that disconnect extant genotypes and/or their offspring from their present environment and challenge them with new variables. We also must be able to impose experimental treatments on extant populations in situ to test their adaptability. Finally, we need to change existing genotypes in deliberate ways, through breeding and genetic engineering, and to then study their altered phenotypes under field conditions. Moreover, these field tests should be established in locations that will serve as proxies for anticipated climatic changes. In sum, the key genetic insights we need to guide our environmental and management decisions can only be gained through strategic experimentation. And, as with all experiments, some will hopefully fail. From them we will learn how to conduct follow-up work.

Clearly, such research takes time and is multidimensional. Success depends on continuity and multidisciplinary integration. To say the obvious, what may be learned from corn in a year may take ten years or more with a tree. And if it takes a dozen specialists to shed light on the fascinating complexity of a cornfield, a tree plantation—not to mention a whole forest community—demands no less.

Perhaps it is at this juncture where the merging of different investigative traditions will help us launch productive new ventures in tree research. Continuity is more firmly rooted in European and Asian cultures, where institutions have had a longer history. Continuity means a commitment to keep records, keep people, take care of field installations over time, update equipment, collect data, and disseminate information. And continuity also hinges on maintaining some insulation of institutions from the politics of the day. But it often comes with institutional inertia, inefficiency, and lack of flexibility. Multidisciplinary integration, on the other hand, depends on a regard for the diversity of disciplines involved in research and the need for their mutual interaction. Here, entrenched institutional traditions can be the enemy of progress. New coalitions, ad-hoc teamwork, novel tools, and instant funding sources may help to break new ground. It is this flexibility and responsiveness to new opportunities, combined with merit-based competitive funding, that have been the hallmarks of American research—critical elements in its leading position in the natural sciences and its continued attraction of international talent. However, this creative opportunism, with its drive to quickly capture promising research territory through innovative alliances and grant moneys, has often come at the expense of maintaining existing studies. Discontinuities in personnel, data, and field installations have been responsible for untold losses in information and past investments, especially in forestry research. Just as climate research hinges on long-term continuity of effort and integration of multiple disciplines, so do the ambitious programs aimed at a better understanding of trees, their long life cycles, and their critical role in complex forest communities.

The nature of funding also has a significant influence on the nature of research. "Top-down" funding—that is, allocation of money to institutions or research alliances, which then distribute it to their members—gives recognition to the institutions and enhances the continuity of their programs. The drawback here is that the ultimate allocation of funds to researchers depends on how well the trickle-down process functions to promote good science. Here, the risk is that of favoring the programmatic tried-and-true over new, innovative initiatives. By contrast, "bottom-up" funding is investigator-driven and gives primacy to the individual researcher. It rewards innovative thinking, and is willing to face the risk that a project may defy conventional paradigms and won't fit into existing programs of perceived promise. The challenge is to find the right mix of the two approaches, perhaps one in which two- or three-year projects by individual or small-team investigators can be fitted flexibly into a larger, multidisciplinary program of longer vision. These short-term projects may successfully link some researchers and turn into long-term alliances. Others may prove to be unproductive and fall by the wayside. The overall program may be seen as having ad-hoc status but, based on its scientific productivity, may gradually receive some funding to sustain its coordinating effort and provide continuity for key personnel, facilities, and materials. Keeping it lean will be a continual challenge, so as not to waste funds on an ever-growing overhead. At the same time, there is no denying that with tree research one important need is the maintenance of valuable germ plasm in space and time.

Of course, the nature of research funding tends to reflect the education of those at the controls. The better they understand the nature of science, and the freer they are from being held back by special interests and political pressure, the more likely they are to sustain research ventures of merit. Here I see an urgent need for a tighter integration among the traditional fields of ecology, evolution, genetics, and molecular biology. We clearly have to educate a new generation of scientists that are competent not only within their own domain but also comfortable with acquiring the vocabulary of neighboring disciplines and applying their tools in new contexts. Laboratory culture has a long history in science, and so does field research, especially in the natural sciences. But for studying trees and forest communities, we need scientists who see the links between the two in new, creative ways. The sooner their broadened perspectives filter to the top of the decision-making process in program funding, the better for the future of forest tree research.

Ultimately, funding comes from the people. How can scientists more effectively engage the public in our scientific enterprise and jointly work toward a more rational society? Clearly, the more persuasive and transparent the process, the more likely it is to meet with understanding and support. The more remote and cryptic—"Sorry, this is too complicated to explain"—the more we feed suspicions about an enterprise that seems to be driven largely by curiosity, academic ambition, or corporate gain. Trust is at the heart of it. And as we know, trust is hard to gain and easy to lose. It calls for a sustained effort in public outreach through lectures, field tours, open-house events, and one-on-one contacts. This personal element is particularly critical because in many contexts, for example in genetic engineering, lack of scientific comprehension may explain only part of the public's mistrust. Candid discussions about ethical concerns, conflicts of interest, acceptable versus unacceptable risks, and likely benefits and their social consequences are equally needed. Aiming our efforts at a generally educated citizenry will be the best approach to influence public attitudes and policies.

There is already a large constituency out there that is receptive to new information, including competent professionals, knowledgeable gardeners, botanically interested naturalists, tree enthusiasts, and those deeply concerned with climate change. I here appeal to them to play a part in clearing up the web of myths, misunderstandings, and traditional beliefs among their friends. Often it is in the straightforward comments of an informed neighbor that scientific concepts sound most persuasive. In garden terms, genetics is also less abstract, because it is visible in the new varieties of fuchsias or more colorful petunias appearing in nurseries every year. Obviously, some breeding or other genetic manipulation must have happened to bring these novelties to the market.

Evidently, nature holds a vast reservoir of hidden diversity that can be tapped with the appropriate tools. Some of these new tools are more precise and extend the long history of plant domestication into more refined territory. Trial and error have always been an inevitable part of the history of plant domestication. And even with the more precise tools available today there is a continued need for experimentation to further push the envelope, whether this may be to bring the taste back to modern apples or to develop strains of rice that are less dependent on fertilizer. The increased insight we now have into the inner workings of these crop plants helps to make these experiments more predictable. Potential risks and their mitigation can be better anticipated, if not entirely eliminated. Similar experimentation is necessary in order to take a careful look at forest trees and their diverse functions. They too harbor vast reservoirs of diversity—more than other plants—and much of it will have to do with their growth and development, their productivity, their tolerance of pests, and their adaptability to the climate. And since that climate is in the process of more rapid change than some tree populations may be able to cope with, experimental studies are more essential than ever.

One might argue, of course, that nature has undergone many changes in the past and has come up with viable solutions time and again. But nature has plenty of time and is generous with space in its own experiments, as we have learned from the scale of past epidemics and devastations by fire or flood. In the more densely populated world of today, a better understanding of the natural processes—and how they can be aligned with societal needs for mutual benefit—should be of value to all who are interested in the type of environment we hand down to our grandchildren.

The call for involvement of our more practically oriented citizenry in promoting the need for this research also seems appropriate since we scientists are often inadequately motivated or equipped to act as scientific salesmen. Most of us feel most comfortable with cultivating our peers, preferring to delegate public outreach to the communicators and science reporters. In a recent *Science* editorial, Alan Leshner has pointed to this barrier as a major weakness at the interface of science and society. He considers public outreach to be largely an acquired skill, and argues that more effort should be devoted to educating graduate students and postdoctoral fellows in public communication. He points to existing funding sources that support such programs but, just as importantly, sees a need for better recognition of these activities in the academic reward system for promotion and tenure.[2] Just as politics shouldn't be left to the politicians, engaging in a dialogue with the public should be part of our mission. Moreover, to the extent that our research is enabled through public funding, it is a question of simple accountability.

In the end, the most promising approach is to get the next generation on board at an early age. Their native curiosity deserves it—but you have to reach their teachers first. There are countless opportunities to insert science in a class, on Arbor Day, on field trips, and in day or summer camps. And here I can argue from personal experience that there is hardly another setting in which you can do this more successfully than in the riparian environment along an active river. Here you can tap into physics, hydrology, geology, chemistry, terrestrial ecology, and aquatic fauna—or you can study many aspects of their interaction and dynamics over time in relation to season and weather. Importantly too, this is a setting where continual change is evident even to the uninitiated, making studies more exciting. You can make one-time observations, conduct monitoring, or carry out experiments, and either treat it as an add-on to a given course or else firmly build it in as an integral component of the curriculum. In addition, at the high school level you may even get a joint involvement of teachers interested in combining courses in biology with mathematics and communications. The possibilities are endless.

Summing up, and to have my last word as an unabashed advocate of the Salicaceae, there is no other group of trees that can match poplars and willows for their suitability in this context. Their abundance in the riparian setting, their diversity, rapid growth, phenotypic plasticity, and ease of vegetative propagation for experimentation make them ideal objects for study of the arboreal world in riverine environments. Add to this their relatively short life cycle, in which the different phases in their life history can easily be related to the recurrent pulses of physical change in their environment, and you have an impressive range of possibilities that help students in moving from the purely descriptive to focusing on the underlying processes.

The field environment in its full complexity is by far the best classroom in which to enlist young minds in the scientific process. It invites observation, reveals patterns, encourages interpretation, rewards reflection, and always has some surprises. Where would we be without the surprises?

NOTES

Epigraphs: The Dawkins quote is from *The Blind Watchmaker*, 1. The Haller quote is from *Historia stirpium indigenarum Helvetiae*, II (1768:130; translation in Agnes Arber, *The Mind and the Eye*, 46).

Preface

1 Readers interested in greater in-depth treatment of *Populus* will find more information in *Biology of* Populus (Stettler et al.) and in *Poplar Culture in North America* (Dickmann et al.). Those interested in the broader field of forest-tree genetics are referred to the comprehensive recent text, *Forest Genetics* (White et al.).

Chapter 1. The Tree

1 On the multiple uses of black cottonwood by the native people, see Gunther, *Ethnobotany of Western Washington*, 26; Pojar and MacKinnon, *Plants of the Pacific West Coast*, 46; and Parish et al., *Plants of Southern Interior British Columbia*, 28.

2 Dickmann, in his "Overview of the Genus *Populus*," gives some examples of poplar's role in mythology and poetry and describes the many historical uses of the different species by native people. See also Johnston, *Plants and the Blackfoot*, 28; and Meyer and Linnèa, *America's Famous and Historic Trees*, 41–46, for poplars' significance in the Lewis and Clark expedition.

3 There is no shortage of coffee-table books on magnificent trees, and among broadleaves the oaks have a prominent place, as is well illustrated in Lewington and Parker, *Ancient Trees*, and in Pakenham, *Remarkable Trees of the World*. On the cultural history of oaks in the Old and New World, see Hageneder, *The Spirit of Trees*, and Logan, *Oak*.

Chapter 2. The River

1 Measured by a permanent gage (No. 12144500) below Snoqualmie Falls. Real-time data from key gages are recorded and transmitted via satellite to regional centers of water resources, operated by the U.S. Geological Survey (USGS) and available to the public on the Internet at http://nwis .waterdata.usgs.gov, accessed April 14, 2008.

2 Weideman, *Valley Record.*

3 See Kruckeberg, *Natural History of Puget Sound Country,* where an entire chapter (pages 349–381) is devoted to water and river dynamics in the region; the chapter also shows two pictures of the 1990 floods.

4 Leopold, *A View of the River.*

5 Ibid., 256–282. For a lucid reexamination of meander theories, see Hayes, "Up a Lazy River."

6 Weyl, *Symmetry,* 69–73.

7 See Naiman et al., *Riparia,* 91–100, a comprehensive treatment of the riparian environment and its processes, well explained and beautifully illustrated.

8 Ibid., 64–65; also see Collins et al., "Reconstructing the Historical Riverine Landscape of the Puget Lowland."

9 Leopold, *A View of the River,* 280.

Chapter 3. Regeneration

1 Reed, *Factors Affecting the Genetic Architecture of Black Cottonwood,* 60–75; also illustrated in Naiman et al., *Riparia,* 147.

2 Braatne et al., "Life History, Ecology, and Conservation of Riparian Cottonwoods."

3 Data collected as part of a science outreach program by the author and J. Braatne with students of Advanced Placement Biology classes at Mt. Si High School, Snoqualmie, Washington (1997–2002).

4 Dickmann, "An Overview of the Genus *Populus,*" 29.

5 Harlow et al., *Textbook of Dendrology,* 109–112.

6 Darwin, *On the Origin of Species,* chapter 3.

7 The mathematically inclined reader will enjoy the theoretical treatment of the subject by Enquist et al., "Quarter-Power Allometric Scaling in Vascular Plants," and Brown et al., "Toward a Metabolic Theory of Biology," showing how closely empirical data of individual and collective biomass conform to predicted values, based on first principles of physics, chemistry, and biology.

Chapter 4. Water and Nutrient Relations

1 For a general treatment of basic processes in plant physiology, see Taiz and Zeiger, *Plant Physiology.*

2 Braatne et al., "Life History, Ecology, and Conservation of Riparian Cottonwoods," 67–69.

3 See overview in Neuman et al., "Stress Physiology: Abiotic," 423–431.

4 Smit and Stachowiak, "Effects of Hypoxia and Elevated Carbon Dioxide Concentration"; also Smit et al., "Cellular Processes Limiting Leaf Growth," and Smit et al., "Root Hypoxia Reduces Leaf Growth."

5 Harrington et al., "Biology of Red Alder," 12.

6 Doty et al., "Identification of an Endophytic *Rhizobium* in Stems of *Populus.*"

Chapter 5. Perpetuate and Proliferate!

1 Galloway and Worrall, "Cladoptosis: A Reproductive Strategy in Black Cottonwood."

2 For spring phenology and its high heritability in black cottonwood, see Dunlap and Stettler, "Genetic Variation and Productivity of *Populus trichocarpa.*" This trait is often used in commercial nurseries to screen vegetatively propagated beds of cultivars for asynchronous individuals (contaminants from other beds, or handling errors in propagation); it has proved to be a simple, reliable measure of quality control for various conifers and broadleaf trees.

3 Castiglione et al., "RAPD Fingerprints for Identification of Elite Poplar Clones."

4 Harper's *Population Biology of Plants,* 26; this is a classic treatise of plant population biology, based on rigorous experimentation conducted by the author and his collaborators over many years.

5 See overview by Harrington et al., "Biology of Red Alder."

Chapter 6. Clones

1 Harlow et al., *Textbook of Dendrology,* 229.

2 See Peterson and Peterson, *Ecology, Management, and Use of Aspen and Balsam Poplar,* 6; this is a comprehensive, well-illustrated monograph of the life history, biology, ecology, management, and use of the two species in Canada.

3 More detailed comments on Eckenwalder's "Systematics and Evolution of

Populus," as presented in Table 6.1, are given in chapter 9. Here, the table serves to give an overview of the different poplar species and their taxonomic relationships.

4 Mitton and Grant, "Genetic Variation and Natural History of Quaking Aspen."

5 Peterson and Peterson, *Ecology, Management, and Use of Aspen and Balsam Poplar*, 107.

6 Ibid.; pages 23–24 show illustrations of spatial distribution and trait distinctions of clones.

7 Ibid., 51.

Chapter 7. Why Sex?

1 Matt Ridley's *The Red Queen: Sex and the Evolution of Human Nature* is still one of the most engaging and witty books on the subject, written for a general audience; see its chapter 3, "The Power of Parasites." A more recent text, *Evolutionary Analysis,* by Freeman and Herron (2004), offers a well-developed modern treatment of all aspects of organic evolution, richly illustrated with much current evidence; see pages 274–285 for the adaptive significance of sex.

2 Van Valen, "A New Evolutionary Law."

3 Richard Dawkins, as quoted in Ridley, *The Red Queen,* 66.

4 Reproductive fitness, or Darwinian fitness, is the relative contribution of an individual to the progenies in the next generation—that is, its proportionate genetic representation in the gene pool of the next generation—as compared to that of all other conspecific members it competes with.

5 Guries and Stettler, "Pre-fertilization Barriers to Hybridization, in the Poplars"; see also review by Knox, "Pollen-Pistil Interactions."

6 Freeman and Herron, *Evolutionary Analysis,* 376–377 and 439–443.

7 Bernasconi et al., "Evolutionary Ecology of the Prezygotic Stage."

8 Ottaviano et al., "Pollen Tube Growth Rates in *Zea mays.*"

9 Stettler and Guries, "The Mentor-Pollen Phenomenon in Black Cottonwood."

10 Stettler (unpublished results).

11 Dawson and Geber, "Dimorphism in Physiology and Morphology"; also Grant and Mitton, "Elevational Gradients in Adult Sex Ratios"; for an in-depth review see Geber et al., *Gender and Sexual Dimorphism in Flowering Plants.*

12 Reviewed in Farmer, "The Genecology of *Populus.*"

13 Stettler, "Variation in Sex Expression of Black Cottonwood and Related Hybrids."

Chapter 8. Password?

1 Lanner, "Needed: A New Approach to the Study of Pollen Dispersion."
2 Originally formulated by Mayr, in "Speciation Phenomena in Birds."
3 Villar et al., "Pollen-Pistil Interactions in *Populus*"; see also Knox, "Pollen-Pistil Interactions," for a more general treatment.
4 Stettler, "Irradiated Mentor Pollen: Its Use in Remote Hybridization of Black Cottonwood."
5 Hogenboom, "Incongruity"; this reproductive concept, based on the developmental disharmony at many gene loci, is used to distinguish it from reproductive *incompatibility*, based on one or two loci.
6 Guries and Stettler, "Pre-fertilization Barriers to Hybridization in the Poplars."
7 Stettler et al., "Interspecific Crossability Studies in Poplars."
8 Stanton and Villar, "Controlled Reproduction of *Populus*."
9 Ceccarelli, in *Shaping Science with Rhetoric*, examined three cases of texts that were intended to inspire interdisciplinarity in the natural sciences. Her insightful treatment of Dobzhansky's 1937 book also gives an excellent portrait of the period, its scientific camps, and the key players involved. A more complete review of that synthetic effort and its significance, as seen in retrospect by many biologists, can be found in Mayr and Provine, *The Evolutionary Synthesis*.

Chapter 9. Natural Hybridization

1 Stebbins, *Variation and Evolution in Plants*, chapter 7. For recent reviews on the role of hybridization in plant evolution see Coyne and Orr, *Speciation*, chapter 9; and Rieseberg and Willis, "Plant Speciation."
2 Harlow et al., *Textbook of Dendrology*, 231–233.
3 Rood et al., "Natural Poplar Hybrids from Southern Alberta"; and the review in Braatne et al., "Life History, Ecology, and Conservation of Riparian Cottonwoods in North America."
4 Keim et al., "Genetic Analysis of an Interspecific Hybrid Swarm of *Populus*."
5 Anderson, *Introgressive Hybridization*, another treatise by a field-oriented plant evolutionist from the Stebbins era.

6   Reviewed in Soltis and Soltis, "The Role of Genetic and Genomic Attributes in the Success of Polyploids"; and Rieseberg and Willis, "Plant Speciation."

7   Dobzhansky, *Evolution, Genetics, and Man,* 183. For a review of the different historic and current species concepts see Coyne and Orr, *Speciation,* chapter 1.

8   Eckenwalder, "Systematics and Evolution of *Populus."*

9   The story of Soviet genetics from 1937 to 1964 under the influence of a political ideologue, Trofim D. Lysenko, as written by Medvedev in *The Rise and Fall of T. D. Lysenko,* is not only of historical interest but also a timeless warning about the social consequences that occur when science becomes the handmaiden of politics.

10 Eckenwalder, "Natural Intersectional Hybridization between North American Species of *Populus."*

11 Eckenwalder, "Systematics and Evolution of *Populus."*

12 Argus, "Infrageneric Classification of *Salix* (Salicaceae) in the New World"; also Dickmann and Kuzovkina, Poplars and Willows in the World.

13 Ibid., 1.

14 Reviewed in Whitham et al., "Ecological and Evolutionary Implications of Hybridization"; see also Whitham et al., "Plant Hybrid Zones Affect Biodiversity"; and "A Framework for Community and Ecosystem Genetics."

15 Whitham et al., "Ecological and Evolutionary Implications of Hybridization."

16 Floate et al., "Cottonwood Hybrid Zones as Centres of Abundance for Gall Aphids."

17 Whitham et al., "Plant Hybrid Zones Affect Biodiversity."

18 Harlow et al., *Textbook of Dendrology,* 294; for examples describing introgression in the oaks, see Kremer et al., "Nuclear and Organelle Gene Diversity in *Quercus robur* and *Q. petraea"*; and Whittemore and Schaal, "Interspecific Gene Flow in Oaks."

Chapter 10. Common Gardens

1   Clausen et al., "The Concept of Species Based on Experiment."

2   Ibid., 103.

3   Ibid., 105.

4   French, "Jens Christian Clausen," 81–82.

5   Carnegie Institution of Washington, *Year Book,* 20–21.

6   Clausen et al., *Experimental Studies on the Nature of Species. III.*

7   From Clausen et al., *Experimental Studies on the Nature of Species. I.*

8   Clausen et al., *Experimental Studies on the Nature of Species. III.*

9   Huxley, "Clines: An Auxiliary Taxonomic Principle."

10   Stebbins, *Variation and Evolution in Plants*, 48; on page 45 there is also a summary graph of the *Achillea lanulosa* results recorded at the Stanford garden.

Chapter 11. Transplanted Trees

1   Matyas, "Climatic Adaptation of Trees"; see also Davis and Shaw, "Range Shifts and Adaptive Responses to Quaternary Climate Change."

2   Langlet, in his "Two Hundred Years of Genecology," covers this early period in greater detail.

3   Wright, *Introduction to Forest Genetics*, 267.

4   Ibid., 267. For a more recent account of Scots pine genetic variation see Giertych and Matyas, "Genetics of Scots Pine."

5   Turesson, "The Scope and Import of Genecology"; also Langlet, "Two Hundred Years of Genecology."

6   See Morgenstern, *Geographic Variation in Forest Trees*, for some examples and photos.

7   Zobel and Talbert, *Applied Forest Tree Improvement*, chapter 3.

8   Farmer, "The Genecology of *Populus*."

9   Dunlap, *Genetic Variation in Natural Populations of* Populus trichocarpa.

10   See Dunlap and Stettler, "Variation in Leaf Epidermal and Stomatal Traits of *Populus trichocarpa*," the last in a series of papers on those studies.

11   See Abrams, "Genotypic and Phenotypic Variation as Stress Adaptations in Temperate Tree Species," and references therein for further examples.

12   Unpublished report by P. Berrang and D. Ecker, U.S. Forest Service, Prineville, OR.

Chapter 12. Getting Closer to the Genes

1   Lewontin, *The Genetic Basis of Evolutionary Change*, 23.

2   For those interested in the gel electrophoresis technology and procedures, see the detailed descriptions in Freeman and Herron, *Evolutionary Analysis*, 132–133.

3   Critchfield, *Geographic Variation in* Pinus contorta.

4   See Wheeler and Guries, "Biogeography of Lodgepole Pine," for details about data collection and interpretation.

5   Avise, *Phylogeography*, 12.
6   Wheeler and Guries, "Population Structure, Genic Diversity, and Morphological Variation in *Pinus contorta* Dougl."
7   Hamrick and Godt, "Effects of Life History Traits on Genetic Diversity in Plant Species."
8   Harper et al., "The Shapes and Sizes of Seeds."
9   Ager and Stettler, "Local Seed Variation in Ponderosa Pine."
10 Lewontin, "Directions in Evolutionary Biology."

Chapter 13. Migrant Trees

1   Wheeler and Guries, "Biogeography of Lodgepole Pine," and "Population Structure, Genic Diversity, and Morphological Variation in *Pinus contorta* Dougl."
2   Cwynar and MacDonald, "Geographical Variation of Lodgepole Pine in Relation to Population History."
3   Ibid.
4   For example, Huntley and Webb, *Vegetation History*.
5   Whitlock, "Vegetational and Climatic History of the Pacific Northwest."
6   Davis, "Quaternary History of Deciduous Forests of Eastern North America and Europe."
7   Ibid.; see also Huntley and Webb, *Vegetation History*; Delcourt and Delcourt, *Long-Term Forest Dynamics of the Temperate Zone*; and MacDonald, "Fossil Pollen Analysis and the Reconstruction of Plant Invasions."
8   Clark et al., "Reid's Paradox of Rapid Plant Migration"; and McLachlan et al., "Molecular Indicators of Tree Migration Capacity under Rapid Climate Change."
9   McLachlan and Clark, "Reconstructing Historical Ranges with Fossil Data."
10 Brubaker et al., "Beringia as a Glacial Refugium for Boreal Trees and Shrubs."
11 Wheeler and Guries, "Biogeography of Lodgepole Pine."
12 Alberts et al., *Molecular Biology of the Cell*, 386.
13 Neale et al., "Paternal Inheritance of Chloroplast DNA in Douglas-Fir."
14 Avise, *Phylogeography*, 15.
15 Ibid., 3.
16 In his *The Seven Daughters of Eve*, Bryan Sykes tells an engaging story of that history and in the process familiarizes the reader with the way molecular tools have helped to elucidate it.

17 Kremer et al., "Nuclear and Organelle Gene Diversity in *Quercus robur* and *Q. petraea*"; and Whittemore and Schaal, "Interspecific Gene Flow in Oaks."

18 Petit et al., "Identification of Refugia and Post-Glacial Colonisation Routes of European White Oaks Based on Chloroplast DNA."

19 Ibid.

20 Petit et al., "Glacial Refugia: Hotspots but Not Melting Pots of Genetic Diversity."

21 Liepelt et al., "Wind-Dispersed Pollen Mediates Postglacial Gene Flow among Refugia."

22 Reviewed by Mitton and Williams, "Gene Flow in Conifers."

Chapter 14. Adaptation and Its Limits

1 Davis et al., "Evolutionary Responses to Changing Climate."

2 Millar and Brubaker, "Climate Change and Paleoecology."

3 Cuffey et al., "Large Arctic Temperature Change at the Wisconsin-Holocene Glacial Transition."

4 Lorius et al., "The Ice-Core Record: Climate Sensitivity and Future Greenhouse Warming."

5 Greene, "Looking for a General for Some Modern Major Models."

6 For example, Ruddiman, *Earth's Climate: Past and Future*.

7 Overpeck et al., "Arctic Environmental Change of the Last Four Centuries."

8 Kennett, "The Younger Dryas Cooling Event: An Introduction."

9 Overpeck et al., "Arctic Environmental Change of the Last Four Centuries."

10 Diaz and Markgraf, *El Niño and the Southern Oscillation*.

11 Rehfeldt et al., "Genetic Responses to Climate in *Pinus contorta*."

12 Illingworth, "Study of Lodgepole Pine Genotype-Environment Interaction in B.C."

13 Rehfeldt et al., "Genetic Responses to Climate in *Pinus contorta*."

14 Rehfeldt, "Ecological Genetics of *Pinus contorta* from the Rocky Mountains."

15 Rehfeldt et al., "Genetic Responses to Climate in *Pinus contorta*."

16 Rehfeldt et al., "Intraspecific Responses to Climate in *Pinus sylvestris*."

17 Richard Levins (public lecture, 1967).

18 Jacob, "Evolution and Tinkering."

19 Falconer, *Introduction to Quantitative Genetics*.

20 Solomon et al., *Climate Change 2007*.

21 Rehfeldt et al., "Physiologic Plasticity, Evolution, and Impacts of a Changing Climate on *Pinus contorta*."

22 Rehfeldt et al., "Intraspecific Responses to Climate in *Pinus sylvestris*."

23 Ibid.

24 Davis and Shaw, "Range Shifts and Adaptive Responses to Quaternary Climate Change."

25 Ibid.; and Davis et al., "Evolutionary Responses to Changing Climate."

26 Huntley et al., "Predicting the Response of Terrestrial Biota"; see also Jackson and Overpeck, "Responses of Plant Populations and Communities to Environmental Changes"; Westfall and Millar, "Genetic Consequences of Forest Population Dynamics"; and Millar and Brubaker, "Climate Change and Paleoecology."

Chapter 15. Changing Rivers—Changing Landscapes

1 Finch and Ruggiero, "Wildlife Habitats and Biological Diversity in the Rocky Mountains."

2 Described in Rood and Heinz-Milne, "Abrupt Downstream Forest Decline Following River Damming"; also Rood and Mahoney, "Collapse of Riparian Poplar Forests Downstream from Dams"; and Rood et al., "Instream Flows and the Decline of Riparian Cottonwoods."

3 Rood et al., "Instream Flows and the Decline of Riparian Cottonwoods."

4 Rood and Mahoney, "Revised Instream Flow Regulation Enables Cottonwood Recruitment."

5 Rood et al., "Initial Cottonwood Seedling Recruitment Following the Flood of the Century."

6 Summarized in Rood et al., "Managing River Flows to Restore Floodplain Forests."

7 Michener and Haeuber, "Flooding: Natural and Managed Disturbances," in an issue of *BioScience* devoted to Flooding: Natural and Managed.

8 Haeuber and Michener, "Policy Implications of Recent Natural and Managed Floods."

9 Galat et al., "Flooding to Restore Connectivity of Regulated, Large-River Wetlands"; also Sparks et al., "Naturalization of the Flood Regime in Regulated Rivers"; and Molles et al., "Managed Flooding for Riparian Ecosystem Restoration."

10 Haeuber and Michener, "Policy Implications of Recent Natural and Managed Floods."

11 Michener and Haeuber, "Flooding: Natural and Managed Disturbances";
    see also Hart and Poff, "A Special Section on Dam Removal and River
    Restoration"; Hughes et al., *The Flooded Forest*; and Montgomery et al.,
    Restoration of Puget Sound Rivers.
12 Hughes et al., *The Flooded Forest*.
13 Pollan, *Second Nature*.
14 Palmer et al., "Ecological Science and Sustainability for a Crowded Planet";
    see also Kareiva et al., "Domesticated Nature: Shaping Landscapes and
    Ecosystems for Human Welfare."
15 Bawa et al., "Tropical Ecosystems into the 21st Century."
16 Ruddiman, "The Anthropocene Greenhouse Era Began Thousands of Years
    Ago."
17 Millar and Brubaker, "Climate Change and Paleoecology."
18 Ibid.

Chapter 16. The Dawn of Agriculture

1   See Moore et al., *Village on the Euphrates*, for a detailed account of the
    Abu Hureyra project and its findings; also referred to by Diamond, *Guns,
    Germs, and Steel*, 144–145; Ryan and Pitman, *Noah's Flood*, 172–174; and
    Fagan, *The Long Summer*, 85–88.
2   Hillman, "The Plant Food Economy of Abu Hureira 1 and 2," 416–422.
3   Ibid., 335.
4   Moore et al., *Village on the Euphrates*, 119.
5   See Zohary, "The Progenitors of Wheat and Barley"; and a more recent
    review by Doebley, "Unfallen Grains: How Ancient Farmers Turned Weeds
    into Crops"; also Balter, "Seeking Agriculture's Ancient Roots."
6   Zohary and Hopf, *Domestication of Plants in the Old World*, 17–18; for a
    recent overview of plant domestication, its various centers, and its rate of
    progress, see Balter, "Seeking Agriculture's Ancient Roots."
7   Harlan et al., "Comparative Evolution of Cereals"; see also Zohary and
    Hopf, *Domestication of Plants in the Old World*, 19.
8   Diamond, *Guns, Germs, and Steel*, 119–123.
9   Paterson et al., "Convergent Domestication of Cereal Crops."
10 Zohary and Hopf, *Domestication of Plants in the Old World*, 241–242.
11 Elaborated in Diamond's integrative overview in *Guns, Germs, and Steel*,
    284–292.
12 Fagan, in *The Long Summer*, 98–110, gives a vivid portrait of that climatic
    period and its human impact.

13 Ryan and Pitman's *Noah's Flood* is a highly engaging account of their discovery and the earlier events that led to it. There is some controversy about their interpretations, based on follow-up work by others, some of which has, in turn, been contested by Ryan and colleagues; see the review by Richard Kerr, "Support Is Drying Up for Noah's Flood Filling the Black Sea."

14 Ryan and Pitman, *Noah's Flood*, 188–201.

15 Zohary and Hopf, *Domestication of Plants in the Old World*, 243–246.

16 Diamond, *Guns, Germs, and Steel*, 180–186.

Chapter 17. The Farmer's Trees

1 Kislev et al., "Early Domesticated Fig in the Jordan Valley."

2 Zohary and Spiegel-Roy, "Beginnings of Fruit Growing in the Old World"; see also Zohary and Hopf, *Domestication of Plants in the Old World*, 143.

3 Spiegel-Roy and Kochba, "Inheritance of Nut and Kernel Traits in Almond."

4 Zohary and Hopf, *Domestication of Plants in the Old World*, 185.

5 Liphschitz and Waisel, "The Effects of Human Activity on Composition of the Natural Vegetation during Historic Periods."

6 Liphschitz and Waisel, "Dendroarcheological Investigations in Israel."

7 Leopold, "Trees and Streams: The Efficiency of Branching Patterns."

8 Ibid.

9 Frison et al., Populus nigra *Network*.

10 Cottrell et al., "Postglacial Migration of *Populus nigra* L."

11 Ibid.

12 Ibid.

13 Huntley and Birks, *An Atlas of Past and Present Pollen Maps for Europe.*

14 Zohary and Hopf, *Domestication of Plants in the Old World.*

15 Fineschi et al., "Chloroplast DNA Polymorphism Reveals Little Geographical Structure in *Castanea sativa.*"

Chapter 18. From Farmers' Trees to Tree Farms

1 Olson, "Techniques That Might Smile upon Mona Lisa."

2 Marette, *Connaissance des primitifs par l'étude du bois.*

3 Massafra, *Legni da Ebanisteria.*

4 Leopold, *A View of the River,* 100.

5 See Ponticelli's 1986 *Le Origini della Pioppicoltura Italiana* (The Origins of Poplar Culture in Italy) for an authoritative history on the subject.

6 As quoted in Ponticelli, *Le Origini della Pioppicoltura Italiana*, 37.

7 Smith, "Camillo Benso Cavour."

8 Ponticelli, *Le Origini della Pioppicoltura Italiana*, 52.

9 Houtzagers, *Die Gattung* Populus *und ihre Bedeutung*.

10 Ibid.

11 Eckenwalder, "Description of Clonal Characteristics."

12 Ponticelli, *Le Origini della Pioppicoltura Italiana*, chapters 10 to 12.

13 Bisoffi, "Poplar and Willow Culture."

14 Stout and Schreiner, "Results of a Project in Hybridizing Poplars."

15 Zsuffa et al., "Trends in Poplar Culture"; and Bisoffi, "Poplar and Willow Culture."

16 See Newcombe et al., "*Melampsora* × *columbiana*, a Natural Hybrid."

17 Kittelson, *Biology and Control of the Western Poplar Clearwing Moth*.

18 Stanton et al., "Hybrid Poplar in the Pacific Northwest."

19 See Oak Ridge National Laboratory, Plant Genomics Group.

Chapter 19. Poplar—A Model Tree

1 Bradshaw et al., "Emerging Model Systems in Plant Biology"; and Jansson and Douglas, "*Populus:* A Model System for Plant Biology."

2 Mendel, "Experiments in Plant-Hybridization."

3 Boveri, "Ueber mehrpolige Mitosen als Mittel zur Analyse des Zellkerns."

4 Sturtevant, in *A History of Genetics*, chapters 7 and 8, gives a colorful account of that seminal period in the "fly room," written by an insider.

5 Rhee et al., "*Arabidopsis thaliana* Genome Maps."

6 Mandoli and Olmstead, "The Importance of Emerging Model Systems in Plant Biology."

7 Bradshaw et al., "Emerging Model Systems in Plant Biology"; and Jansson and Douglas, "*Populus:* A Model System for Plant Biology."

8 Allard, *Principles of Plant Breeding*, 219–223.

9 Stettler et al., *Biology of* Populus; and Dickmann et al., *Poplar Culture in North America*.

10 Bradshaw and Stettler, "Molecular Genetics of Growth and Development in *Populus*."

11 Scarascia-Mugnozza et al., "Production Physiology and Morphology of *Populus* species."

12 Newcombe et al., "*Melampsora* × *columbiana*, a Natural Hybrid."

Chapter 20. Tree Genomics and Beyond

1 DeSalle and Yudell, "Introduction," in *Welcome to the Genome*, xvii.
2 Ibid., 102–103.
3 Jacob, "Evolution and Tinkering."
4 DeSalle and Yudell, *Welcome to the Genome*, 47–49.
5 Tuskan et al., "The Genome of Black Cottonwood."
6 See Eckenwalder, "Systematics and Evolution of *Populus*."
7 Reviewed by Jansson and Douglas, "*Populus*: A Model System for Plant Biology."
8 Tuskan et al., "The Genome of Black Cottonwood."
9 Alberts et al., *Molecular Biology of the Cell*, 96 ff.
10 DeSalle and Yudell, *Welcome to the Genome*, 119–122.
11 Reviewed in Nester et al., *Agrobacterium tumefaciens*; see also Han et al., "Cellular and Molecular Biology of *Agrobacterium*-Mediated Transformation of Plants."
12 Reviewed in Boerjan, "Biotechnology and the Domestication of Forest Trees"; and Busov et al., "Genetic Transformation: A Powerful Tool for Dissection of Adaptive Traits in Trees."
13 Bradshaw and Strauss, "Breeding Strategies for the 21st Century"; Meilan et al., "Accomplishments and Challenges in Genetic Engineering of Forest Trees"; Strauss and Brunner, "Tree Biotechnology in the Twenty-First Century."
14 Ausubel et al., "Foresters and DNA."
15 Meilan et al., "Modification of Flowering in Transgenic Trees."
16 Flathman and Lanza, "Phytoremediation: Current Views on an Emerging Green Technology."
17 Doty et al., "Enhanced Phytoremediation of Volatile Environmental Pollutants with Transgenic Trees."
18 See Oak Ridge National Laboratory, Plant Genomics Group.
19 For review of gene flow in forest trees and an example of modeling transgene dispersal in hybrid poplar, see Slavov et al., "Gene Flow in Forest Trees."
20 Raffa, "Transgenic Resistance in Short-Rotation Plantation Trees."
21 Bryson et al., "Have You Got a License for That Tree?"
22 Yanchuk, "The Role and Implications of Biotechnological Tools in Forestry"; also Strauss, "Genomics, Genetic Engineering, and Domestication of Crops."
23 National Research Council, *Environmental Effects of Transgenic Plants*.

24 Neale and Savolainen, "Association Genetics of Complex Traits in Conifers"; and Groover, "Will Genomics Guide a Greener Forest Biotech?"

25 Strauss and Bradshaw, *The Bioengineered Forest;* and Burdon and Libby,
Genetically Modified Forests.

26. Whitham et al., "Extending Genomics to Natural Communities and Ecosystems."

Chapter 21. Between Old Growth and Plantations

1 Ruddiman, "The Anthropocene Greenhouse Era Began Thousands of Years
Ago."

2 Kareiva et al., "Domesticated Nature: Shaping Landscapes and Ecosystems."

3 Ausubel et al., "Foresters and DNA."

4 Johnson et al., "Potential Impacts of Genetically Modified Trees on Biodiversity of Forestry Plantations."

5 Ausubel et al., "Foresters and DNA."

6 See Sedjo, "The Role of Forest Plantations in the World's Future Timber
Supply."

7 Ausubel et al., "Foresters and DNA."

8 Wilson, *The Future of Life,* 161.

9 Friedman and Charnley, "Environmental and Social Aspects of the Intensive Plantation/Reserve Debate."

10 Houllier et al., *Future Forest Research Strategy.*

11 Yanchuk, "A Quantitative Framework for Breeding and Conservation of
Forest Tree Genetic Resources"; and White et al., *Forest Genetics.*

12 See the Applegate Partnership website at http://www.arwc.org.

13 Bormann et al., "Adaptive Management of Forest Ecosystems."

14 See Ellis, "The Road Still Beckons"; also the Mountains to Sound website
at http://www.mtsgreenway.org.

15 Yaffee, "Cooperation: A Strategy for Achieving Stewardship across Boundaries."

Chapter 22. The Essence of Trees

1 Drawn by Heather Lewis, after a photo in Hockenjos, *Begegnung mit Bäumen,* 35.

2 For a concise and well-illustrated treatment of tree growth, see Wilson, *The
Growing Tree.*

3 MacMahon and Kronauer, "Tree Structure"; see also Brown et al., "Toward a Metabolic Theory of Biology."

4 Hillier, *Hillier's Manual of Trees & Shrubs*, 468–472.

5 Mandelbrot, *The Fractal Geometry of Nature*; and Chen et al., "A Fractal-Based *Populus* Canopy Structure Model."

6 Balog, *Tree: A New Vision of the American Forest.*

Chapter 23. Outlook

1 Whitham et al., "A Framework for Community and Ecosystems Genetics"; and "Extending Genomics to Natural Communities and Ecosystems."

2 Leshner, "Outreach Training Needed," 161.

GLOSSARY

abscission   The shedding of a plant part; leaf abscission is facilitated by the formation of a separation layer at the base of the petiole.

acclimation   The production of different phenotypes when exposing a genotype to different climatic conditions; for example, cottonwood clones can develop smaller leaves with more stomates per unit of surface in a hot, dry environment than when grown under cool, moist conditions.

adventitious   A structure arising not in its usual place, such as roots arising from stems, or buds arising at other locations than in terminal or axillary structures.

Agrobacterium A common soil bacterium that inserts genes that cause gall formation in the recipient plant. Modified forms of the bacterium are commonly used for genetic transformation of many species of plants, including poplar.

allele   One of several possible mutational forms of a gene (A, a, a_1, a_5, etc.).

allometry   A measure of proportionality that compares how the value of any biological trait of an organism changes as the total size of the organism changes; for example, the proportion of stem diameter to tree mass at different stages of tree growth.

allozyme   see **isozyme**

cambium, vascular cambium   In woody stems, the cambium is the cylindrical meristem that, through cell division, generates xylem (the water-conducting vascular tissue) on the inside, and phloem (the food-conducting tissue) on the outside.

For genetic terms, *A Dictionary of Genetics*, 7th ed. (New York: Oxford University Press, 2006), by Robert C. King, William D. Stansfield, and Pamela K. Mulligan, has been a valuable source; for anatomical terms, *Anatomy of Seed Plants* (New York: John Wiley & Sons, 1960) by Katherine Esau; and for ecological terms, *Forest Ecology*, 3rd ed. (Upper Saddle River, NJ: Prentice Hall, 2004) by J. P. Kimmins.

chloroplast The chlorophyll-containing, photosynthesizing organelle of plants; chloroplasts contain DNA (cpDNA) and multiply during the cell cycle; in angiosperms they are transmitted maternally, in conifers, paternally.

cladoptosis The abscission of viable short shoots from a tree; a mechanism of asexual propagation.

conspecific Belonging to the same species.

cotyledon The seed leaf of an embryo.

cross-pollination, cross-fertilization Mating among different individuals; in contrast to selfing or self-pollination.

cultivar A special form selected from the wild and maintained in cultivation as a clone.

density-dependent selection Selection in which the values for relative fitness depend on the density (stocking) of the population; for example, genotypes that leaf out early will be favored more in a dense stand than under wide spacing.

dioecious Having male and female flowers on separate, unisexual plants.

diploid The chromosome state in which each type of chromosome is represented twice (2n).

electrophoresis The movement of charged molecules in solution in an electric field; in gel electrophoresis the solution is held in a gel that makes it possible to distinguish different proteins (e.g., isozymes) by the position of their distinct bands (see illustration at the beginning of chapter 12).

endosperm The nutritive tissue formed within the embryosac of seed plants and surrounding the embryo in the seed.

epicormic branch A branch growing from a suppressed bud or adventitious bud located in the bark of the stem.

evapotranspiration The loss of soil water through evaporation and plant transpiration.

evolution, organic evolution The cumulative change in the characteristics of populations related by descent, occurring during the course of successive generations; in population genetic terms it is the change in gene frequencies from one generation to the next. See also gene frequency.

evolutionary mechanisms The mechanisms that cause evolutionary change; they include mutation, gene flow, selection, and genetic drift.

$F1_1$, F_2, B_1 First and second filial generations, and first backcross generation in controlled crosses; for example:

$$Parents\ P(A) \times P(B) \qquad \rightarrow F_1$$
$$F_1 \times F_1 \qquad\qquad\ \rightarrow F_2$$
$$F_1 \times P(A)\ or\ (B) \quad \rightarrow B_1$$

fastigiate Crowded close together, erect, as the branching in columnar poplars.

fitness, Darwinian fitness The relative ability of an individual to survive and transmit its genes to the next generation (i.e., in relation to other individuals competing with it).

gallery forest A narrow strip of forest, either natural or planted, commonly found along rivers.

gamete sex cell, that is, an egg cell or sperm; both are haploid (n).

gene expression The display of genetic activity by the synthesis of gene products that affect the phenotype. Some genes are active throughout the life of a cell or organism, others only under certain conditions or at specific times during development.

gene flow The exchange of genes via pollen, seed, or asexual propagules between different populations of the same species.

gene frequency The frequency of an allele in a population. Example: Assume that a population of 100 diploid plants has the following genotypes: 25 *AA*, 50 *Aa*, and 25 *aa*. In the total pool of 200 alleles, there are 100 *A* and 100 *a* alleles; thus, the gene (or allele) frequency of *A* is 50 percent or 0.5, and so is that of *a*. If at the next census, several generations later, the composition of genotypes has changed to 49 *AA*, 42 *Aa*, and 9 *aa*, there would be a total of 140 *A* and 60 *a* alleles in the allelic pool and the gene frequencies would be 0.7*A* and 0.3 *a*. Such a change could have been brought about by selection favoring *AA* and *Aa* genotypes.

genet The collective clonal members of a genotype having arisen from an original zygote; they all have the same genetic constitution.

genetic distance A measure of the allelic substitutions per locus that have occurred during the separate evolution of two populations or species; the greater the genetic distance, the greater the number of loci and alleles at which two populations differ.

genetic drift The random fluctuations ("drifting") of gene frequencies due to sampling errors; its effects are most evident in very small populations.

genetic engineering The use of recombinant DNA methods to modify genes or other DNA, and their asexual insertion back into living organisms. Gene sequences can be derived from the same or different species, or modified/created de novo based on scientific principles.

genome The genetic complement of an individual, containing both nuclear DNA and that of the organelles in the cell (mitochondria and chloroplasts).

genomics The study of the structure and functioning of the genomes of species for which extensive nucleotide sequences are available.

genotype   The genetic constitution of an organism.

germinant   A germinating seedling.

growth chamber   A chamber in which plants are grown in a completely controlled environment.

haploid   The gametic chromosome number, symbolized by n.

heritability   In the broad sense, it is the degree to which a phenotypic trait is genetically determined; the higher the value, the stronger is the genetic (vs. environmental) control of the trait; for example, rust resistance or bud-burst timing in cottonwood have a higher heritability than volume or height growth.

heteroblasty   Having different foliage types on juvenile versus mature plants; for example, narrow versus ovate leaves in black cottonwood.

heterosis   The greater vigor and growth of hybrids compared to their parents.

heterozygous   Having dissimilar alleles at a locus (Aa, or $a_3 a_5$, etc.); an individual with high heterozygosity has many loci at which it is heterozygous.

homozygous   Having identical alleles at a locus (AA, or aa; or at another locus $b_2 b_2$, etc.).

hybrid swarm   A continuous series of morphologically distinct hybrids resulting from hybridization of two or more species, followed by crossing and backcrossing of subsequent generations.

independent assortment   During meiosis, the random distribution to the gametes of genes located on different chromosomes; thus, an individual of genotype $AaBb$ (with A and B loci being on different chromosomes) will produce equal numbers of four types of gametes: AB, Ab, aB, and ab.

indeterminate growth   An apical meristem that produces an unrestricted number of lateral organs indefinitely. In cottonwoods, birches, alders, and several other trees the terminal bud contains three to five primordia of the early leaves, which emerge first; the apical meristem then continues to produce more leaves, the late leaves, as the shoot keeps elongating throughout the growth season.

introgression, introgressive hybridization   The incorporation of genes of one species into the gene pool of another; a common process in areas where the ranges of two species overlap and fertile hybrids are produced; these hybrids tend to backcross with the more abundant species.

isozyme   One of multiple forms of a single enzyme, distinct from the others by one or more amino acids.

linkage   The association of genes (alleles) on the same chromosome. Close linkage tends to keep them together as they are transmitted via gametes to the next generation. For example:

$$—A—b————E—$$
$$—a—B————e—$$

Because of chromosomal breakage and exchange during meiosis, A and b are more likely to end in the same gamete than A and E.

locus (plural, **loci**) The position a gene occupies in a chromosome.

megagametophyte The female gametophyte (haploid) containing the egg cell.

meiosis The process by which sex cells, or gametes, are generated, involving the reduction of the diploid chromosome number to the haploid number and the associated shuffling of genes due to independent assortment and exchange of chromosomal segments.

meristem An actual or potential zone of growth, composed of meristematic cells; these cells can divide and give rise to shoots, roots, and/or radial growth of the stem.

micropyle The canal through which the pollen tube enters the ovule.

mitochondrion A self-reproducing cell organelle that plays an important role in cellular metabolism and has its own DNA (mtDNA); it is transmitted maternally.

monoecious Having male and female organs in separate floral structures on the same plant.

mutation The process by which a gene undergoes a structural change; a modified gene resulting from mutation. Mutations are the ultimate source of all genetic diversity.

niche The functional, adaptational, and distributional characteristics of a species.

ovule The structure in a seed plant that develops into a seed after fertilization of an egg cell within it.

petiole The stem of a leaf.

phenology The study of natural phenomena that recur periodically (e.g., bud burst, leaf fall) and of their relation to climate and changes in season.

phenotype The observable properties of an organism, produced by the genotype in conjunction with the environment; a seedling may have a green phenotype but an Aa genotype with a recessive albino allele (a) that is masked by its dominant normal allele (A).

phenotypic plasticity The capacity of a genotype to adaptively change its phenotype in response to changing environmental conditions; for example, herbivore browsing may cause a genotype to express a gene that is responsible for the production of a defensive compound in new leaves being formed.

photosynthate   The organic compounds produced in photosynthesis from the conversion of light energy.

phototropism   The tendency to grow toward the light.

phyllotaxy   The mode in which the leaves are arranged on the axis of a shoot (opposite vs. alternate); also, the rotational displacement of successive leaves or leaf pairs on a shoot.

pistil   The female organ of a flower.

polymorphism   Of multiple forms; genetic polymorphism is the existence of two or more genetically different classes in the same interbreeding population.

polyploidy   The situation where the number of chromosome sets is greater than two; for example, tetraploid ($2n = 4\times$), pentaploid ($2n = 5\times$), hexaploid ($2n = 6\times$), and so on.

pre-zygotic barrier   A reproductive barrier preventing fertilization, or the formation of a zygote.

propagule   A unit of propagation, for example, a branch fragment, a cutting, a root segment.

provenance   The geographical location, and its physical features, where a specific genotype or population evolved; generally used to describe the location of plant seed collection.

recessive   An allele that does not produce a phenotypic effect when heterozygous with the dominant allele. Many albino mutations (*a*) are recessive and completely green in heterozygous condition (*Aa*); the albino condition will only show up in homozygotes (*aa*) and will be lethal. Some other forms of albinism show up as "golden," in the heterozygotes (*Aa*).

recombination, genetic recombination   The occurrence of progeny with combinations of genes other than those in the parents due to independent assortment and exchange of chromosomal segments in meiosis.

recruitment, seedling recruitment   The successful establishment of seedlings, ensuring natural regeneration of a forest or individual stand.

regulator gene   A gene whose primary function is to control the expression of other, distantly located genes.

root nodule   A specialized root structure containing symbiotic, nitrogen-fixing bacteria or fungi.

rotation   In forest and plantation management, the time span from stand establishment to harvest.

seed orchard   An orchard designed and operated to generate seed for superior planting stock; it is composed of trees selected for their superior performance or the superior performance of their progenies, as tested in field trials.

selection   The process that determines the relative share allotted to different genotypes in the propagation of a population; natural selection occurs through the differential survival and contribution of individuals to the gene pool of the subsequent generation(s).

self fertilization, selfing   The act of a plant producing offspring from the union of its own gametes. This extreme form of inbreeding leads to true-breeding lines with high degrees of homozygosity.

self incompatibility   Mechanisms that prevent self fertilization.

sink strength   A measure of the demand for carbon, water, or nutrients at active growth centers in a plant (developing leaves, roots, reproductive structures). Sometimes, an organ can be both a source and a sink; in a developing leaf, its mature tissue is a source, its growing and expanding tissue a sink.

stoma   (plural, **stomata**) A pore in the epidermis of a leaf; its two guard cells regulate gas exchange and transpiration through opening and closing.

succession, ecological succession   The process by which a series of different plant communities and associated animals and microbes successfully occupy and replace each other over time in a particular location after a disturbance; includes associated changes in soil and microclimate.

taxon   (plural, **taxa**) A unit of classification; for example, a species, a subspecies, a variety, and so on.

transformation (genetic)   The asexual insertion of a new gene into a genome, that gene having been extracted or modified by the use of genetic engineering methods.

transgenic   Containing one or more genes introduced through genetic transformation methods.

zygote   A cell formed by the union of two gametes; for example, a fertilized egg cell.

BIBLIOGRAPHY

Abrams, M. D. "Genotypic and Phenotypic Variation as Stress Adaptations in Temperate Tree Species: A Review of Several Case Studies." *Tree Physiology* 14 (1994): 833–842.

Ager, Alan A., and Reinhard F. Stettler. "Local Seed Variation in Ponderosa Pine." *Canadian Journal of Botany* 61 (1983): 1337–1344.

Alberts, Bruce, Dennis Bray, Julian Lewis, Martin Raff, Keith Roberts, and James D. Watson. *Molecular Biology of the Cell.* 2nd ed. New York: Garland Publishing, 1989.

Allard, Robert W. *Principles of Plant Breeding.* New York: John Wiley & Sons, 1960.

Anderson, Edgar. *Introgressive Hybridization.* New York: Wiley and Sons, 1949.

Applegate Partnership. http://www.arwc.org, accessed April 14, 2008.

Arber, Agnes. *The Mind and the Eye.* Cambridge: Cambridge University Press, 1964.

Argus, G. W. "Infrageneric Classification of *Salix* (Salicaceae) in the New World." *Systematic Botany Monographs.* Ann Arbor, MI: American Society of Plant Taxonomy, Vol. 52 (1997): 1–121.

Ausubel, Jesse H., Paul E. Waggoner, and Iddo. K. Wernick. "Foresters and DNA." In *Landscapes, Genomics, and Transgenic Conifers,* edited by C. G. Williams. Dordrecht: Springer, 2006.

Avise, John C. *Phylogeography: The History and Formation of Species.* Cambridge, MA: Harvard University Press, 2000.

Balog, James. *Tree: A New Vision of the American Forest.* New York: Barnes & Noble, 2004.

Balter, Michael. "Seeking Agriculture's Ancient Roots." *Science* 316 (2007): 1830–1835.

Bawa, K. S. et al. "Tropical ecosystems into the 21st Century." *Science* 306 (2004): 227–228.

Bernasconi, G. et al. "Evolutionary Ecology of the Prezygotic Stage." *Science* 303 (2004): 971–975.

Bisoffi, Stefano. "Poplar and Willow Culture." Editorial, *The Forestry Chronicle* 77 (2001): 182–186.

Boerjan, W. "Biotechnology and the Domestication of Forest Trees." *Current Opinion in Biotechnology* 16 (2005): 159–166.

Bormann, Bernard T., Richard W. Haynes, and Jon R. Martin. "Adaptive Management of Forest Ecosystems: Did Some Rubber Hit the Road?" *BioScience* 57 (2007): 186–191.

Boveri, Theodor. "Ueber mehrpolige Mitosen als Mittel zur Analyse des Zellkerns." *Verhandlungen der physikalisch-medizinischen Gesellschaft. Würzburg* 35 (1902): 67–90.

Braatne, Jeffrey H., Stewart B. Rood, and Paul E. Heilman. "Life History, Ecology, and Conservation of Riparian Cottonwoods in North America." In *Biology of* Populus *and Its Implications for Management and Conservation,* edited by R. F. Stettler et al., pp. 57–86. Ottawa: National Research Council of Canada, 1996.

Bradshaw, H. D., Jr., Reinhart Ceulemans, John Davis, and Reinhard Stettler. "Emerging Model Systems in Plant Biology: Poplar (*Populus*) as a Model Forest Tree." *Journal of Plant Growth Regulation* 19 (2000): 306–313.

Bradshaw, H. D., Jr., and R. F. Stettler. "Molecular Genetics of Growth and Development in *Populus*. IV. Mapping QTLs with Large Effects on Growth, Form, and Phenology Traits in a Forest Tree." *Genetics* 139 (1995): 963–973.

Bradshaw, H. D., Jr., and S. H. Strauss. "Breeding Strategies for the 21st Century: Domestication of Poplar." In *Poplar Culture in North America,* edited by D. I. Dickmann et al., pp. 383–394. Ottawa: National Research Council of Canada, 2001.

Brown, James H., James F. Gillooly, Andrew P. Allen, Van M. Savage, and Geoffrey B. West. "Toward a Metabolic Theory of Biology." *Ecology* 85 (2004): 1771–1789.

Brubaker, Linda B., Patricia M. Anderson, Mary E. Edwards, and Anatoly V. Lozhkin. "Beringia as a Glacial Refugium for Boreal Trees and Shrubs: New Perspectives from Mapped Pollen Data." *Journal of Biogeography* 32 (2005): 833–848.

Bryson, Nancy S., Steven P. Quarles, and Richard J. Mannix. "Have You Got a License for That Tree?" In *The Bioengineered Forest: Challenges for Science and Society,* edited by Steven H. Strauss and H. D. Bradshaw, Jr., pp. 163–180. Washington, DC: Resources for the Future, 2004.

Burdon, Rowland D., and William J. Libby. *Genetically Modified Forests: From Stone Age to Modern Biotechnology.* Washington, DC: Forest History Society, 2007.

Busov, Victor B., Amy M. Brunner, Richard Meilan et al. "Genetic Transformation: A Powerful Tool for Dissection of Adaptive Traits in Trees." *New Phytologist* 167 (2005): 9–18.

Carnegie Institution of Washington. *Year Book* 32 (1933): 20–21.

Castiglione, S., G. Wang, G. Damiani, C. Bandi, S. Bisoffi, and F. Sala. "RAPD Fingerprints for Identification and for Taxonomic Studies of Elite Poplar (*Populus* spp.) Clones." *Theoretical and Applied Genetics* 87 (1993): 194–200.

Ceccarelli, Leah. *Shaping Science with Rhetoric: The Cases of Dobzhansky, Schrödinger, and Wilson.* Chicago: University of Chicago Press, 2001.

Chen, S. G., R. Ceulemans, and I. Impens. "A Fractal-Based *Populus* Canopy Structure Model for the Calculation of Light Interception." *Forest Ecology and Management* 69 (1994): 97–110.

Clark, J. S., C. Fastie, G. Hurtt et al., "Reid's Paradox of Rapid Plant Migration." *BioScience* 48 (1998): 13–24.

Clausen, Jens C., David D. Keck, and William M. Hiesey. "The Concept of Species Based on Experiment." *American Journal of Botany* 26 (1939): 103–106.

———. *Experimental Studies on the Nature of Species. I. Effect of Varied Environments on Western North American Plants.* Washington, DC: Carnegie Institution of Washington, Publ. No. 520, 1940.

———. *Experimental Studies on the Nature of Species. III. Environmental Responses of Climatic Races of Achillea.* Washington, DC: Carnegie Institution of Washington, Publ. No. 581, 1948.

Collins, Brian D., David R. Montgomery, and Amir J. Sheikh. "Reconstructing the Historical Riverine Landscape of the Puget Lowland." In *Restoration of Puget Sound Rivers,* edited by David R. Montgomery et al., pp. 79–128. Seattle: University of Washington Press, 2003.

Cottrell, J. E., V. Krystufek, H. E. Tabbener et al. "Postglacial Migration of *Populus nigra* L.: Lessons Learnt from Chloroplast DNA." *Forest Ecology and Management* 206 (2005): 1–3, 79–90.

Coyne, Jerry A., and H. Allen Orr. *Speciation.* Sunderland, MA: Sinauer Associates, 2004.

Critchfield, William B. *Geographic Variation in Pinus contorta.* Cambridge, MA: Maria Moors Cabot Foundation, Publ. 3, 1957.

Cuffey, K. M., G. D. Clow, R. B. Alley, M. Stuvier, E. D. Waddington, and

R. W. Saltus. "Large Arctic Temperature Change at the Wisconsin–
Holocene Glacial Transition." *Science* 270 (1995): 455–458.

Cwynar, L. C., and G. M. MacDonald. "Geographic Variation of Lodgepole
Pine in Relation to Population History." *American Naturalist* 129 (1987):
463–469.

Darwin, Charles. *On the Origin of Species by Means of Natural Selection.*
London: J. Murray, 1859.

Davis, Margaret B. "Quaternary History of Deciduous Forests of Eastern
North America and Europe." *Annals of the Missouri Botanical Garden* 70
(1983): 550–563.

Davis, Margaret B., and Ruth G. Shaw. "Range Shifts and Adaptive Responses
to Quaternary Climate Change." *Science* 292 (2001): 673–679.

Davis, Margaret B., Ruth G. Shaw, and Julie R. Etterson. "Evolutionary
Responses to Changing Climate." *Ecology* 86 (2005): 1704–1714.

Dawkins, Richard. *The Blind Watchmaker.* New York: W. W. Norton, 1986.

———. *Climbing Mount Improbable.* New York: W. W. Norton, 1996.

Dawson, Todd E., and Monica A. Geber. "Dimorphism in Physiology and
Morphology." In *Gender and Sexual Dimorphism in Flowering Plants,*
edited by M. A. Geber, T. E. Dawson, and L. F. Delph, pp. 175–215. Berlin:
Springer Verlag, 1999.

Delcourt, P. A., and H. R. Delcourt. *Long-Term Forest Dynamics of the
Temperate Zone: A Case Study of Late-Quaternary Forests in Eastern North
America.* New York: Springer-Verlag, 1987.

DeSalle, Rob, and Michael Yudell. *Welcome to the Genome: A User's Guide
to the Genetic Past, Present, and Future.* New York: John Wiley & Sons,
2005.

Diamond, Jared. *Guns, Germs, and Steel: The Fates of Human Societies.* New
York: W. W. Norton, 1997.

Diaz, H. F., and V. Markgraf, eds. *El Niño and the Southern Oscillation:
Multiscale Variability and Global and Regional Impacts.* Cambridge:
Cambridge University Press, 2000.

Dickmann, Donald I. "An Overview of the Genus *Populus.*" In *Poplar Culture
in North America,* edited by Donald I. Dickmann et al., pp. 1–41. Ottawa:
National Research Council of Canada, 2001.

Dickmann, Donald I., Judson G. Isebrands, James E. Eckenwalder, and Jim
Richardson. *Poplar Culture in North America.* Ottawa: National Research
Council of Canada, 2001.

Dickmann, Donald I., and Julia Kuzovkina. Poplars and Willows of the
World with Emphasis on Silviculturally Important Species. FAO

Forestry Working Paper IPC/9-2, Rome, Italy 2008; http://www.fao.org/
forestry/32608/en/, accessed Dec. 1, 2008.

Dobzhansky, Theodosius. *Genetics and the Origin of Species.* New York:
Columbia University Press, 1937.

———. *Evolution, Genetics, and Man.* New York: John Wiley & Sons, 1955.

Doebley, John. "Unfallen Grains: How Ancient Farmers Turned Weeds into
Crops." *Science* 312 (2006): 1318–1319.

Doty, Sharon L. et al. "Identification of an Endophytic *Rhizobium* in Stems of
Populus." *Symbiosis* 39 (2005): 27–36.

Doty, Sharon L., C. Andrew James, Allison L. Moore et al. "Enhanced
Phytoremediation of Volatile Environmental Pollutants with Transgenic
Trees." *Proceedings of the National Academy of Sciences USA* 104 (2007):
16816–16821.

Dunlap, Joan M. *Genetic Variation in Natural Populations of Populus
trichocarpa T. & G. from Four River Valleys in Washington.* PhD thesis,
University of Washington, Seattle, 1991.

Dunlap, Joan M., and Reinhard F. Stettler. "Genetic Variation and
Productivity of *Populus trichocarpa* and Its Hybrids. IX. Phenology and
Melampsora Rust Incidence of Native Black Cottonwood from Four River
Valleys in Washington." *Forest Ecology and Management* 87 (1996): 233–256.

———. "Variation in Leaf Epidermal and Stomatal Traits of *Populus
trichocarpa* from Two Transects across the Washington Cascades."
Canadian Journal of Botany 79 (2001): 528–536.

Eckenwalder, J. E. "Natural Intersectional Hybridization between North
American Species of *Populus* (Salicaceae) in Sections *Aigeiros* and
Tacamahaca. Population Studies of *P.* × *parryi.*" *Canadian Journal of
Botany* 62 (1984): 317–324.

———. "Systematics and Evolution of *Populus.*" In *Biology of* Populus *and
Its Implications for Management and Conservation,* edited by R. F. Stettler
et al., pp. 7–32. Ottawa: National Research Council of Canada, 1996.

———. "Description of Clonal Characteristics." In *Poplar Culture in North
America,* edited by D. I. Dickmann et al., pp. 331–382. Ottawa: National
Research Council of Canada, 2001.

Ellis, James R. "The Road Still Beckons." Remarks delivered to Downtown
Rotary Club of Seattle, August 30, 2006. 13 pp.

Enquist, Brian J., Geoffrey B. West, and James H. Brown. "Quarter-Power
Allometric Scaling in Vascular Plants: Functional Basis and Ecological
Consequences." In *Scaling in Biology,* edited by James H. Brown and
Geoffrey B. West, pp. 167–198. New York: Oxford University Press, 2000.

Fagan, Brian. *The Long Summer: How Climate Changed Civilization*. New York: Basic Books, 2004.

Falconer, D. S. *Introduction to Quantitative Genetics*. New York: John Wiley & Sons, 1989.

Farmer, Robert E., Jr. "The Genecology of *Populus*." In *Biology of Populus and Its Implications for Management and Conservation*, edited by R. F. Stettler et al., pp. 33–55. Ottawa: National Research Council of Canada, 1996.

Finch, D. M., and L. F. Ruggiero. "Wildlife Habitats and Biological Diversity in the Rocky Mountains and Northern Great Plains." *Natural Areas Journal* 13 (1993): 191–203.

Fineschi, S., D. Taurchini, F. Villani, and G. G. Vendramin. "Chloroplast DNA Polymorphism Reveals Little Geographical Structure in *Castanea sativa* Mill. (Fagaceae) throughout Southern European Countries." *Molecular Ecology* 9 (2000): 1495–1503.

Flathman, Paul E., and Guy R. Lanza. "Phytoremediation: Current Views on an Emerging Green Technology." *Journal of Soil Contamination* 7 (1998): 415–432.

Floate, Kevin D., Gregory D. Martinsen, and Thomas G. Whitham. "Cottonwood Hybrid Zones as Centres of Abundance for Gall Aphids in Western North America: Importance of Relative Habitat Size." *Journal of Animal Ecology* 66 (1997): 179–188.

Freeman, Scott, and Jon C. Herron. *Evolutionary Analysis*. 3rd ed. Upper Saddle River, NJ: Pearson Prentice Hall, 2004.

French, C. Stacy. "Jens Christian Clausen, March 11, 1891–November 22, 1969." In *Biographical Memoirs*. National Academy of Sciences, Vol. 58: 75–107. Washington, DC: National Academy of Sciences Press, 1989.

Friedman, Sharon T., and Susan Charnley. "Environmental and Social Aspects of the Intensive Plantation/Reserve Debate." In *The Bioengineered Forest: Challenges for Science and Society*, edited by Steven H. Strauss and H. D. Bradshaw, Jr., pp. 141–162, Washington, DC: Resources for the Future, 2004.

Frison, E., F. Lefèvre, S. de Vries, and J. Turok. Populus nigra *Network*. Rome: Report of the 1st Meeting of the International Plant Genetic Resources Institute, October 3–5, 1995.

Galat, David L., Leigh H. Fredrickson, Dale D. Humburg et al. "Flooding to Restore Connectivity of Regulated, Large-River Wetlands." *BioScience* 48 (1998): 721–733.

Galloway, G., and J. Worrall. "Cladoptosis, A Reproductive Strategy in Black Cottonwood?" *Canadian Journal of Forest Research* 9 (1979): 122–125.

Geber, Monica A., Todd E. Dawson, and Lynda F. Delph, eds. *Gender and Sexual Dimorphism in Flowering Plants*. Berlin: Springer-Verlag, 1999.

Giertych, M., and C. Matyas, eds. "Genetics of Scots Pine." *Developments in Plant Genetics and Breeding*, 3. Amsterdam: Elsevier, 1991.

Grant, M. C., and J. B. Mitton. "Elevational Gradients in Adult Sex Ratios and Sexual Differentiation in Vegetative Growth Rates of *Populus tremuloides* Michx." *Evolution* 33 (1979): 914–918.

Greene, M. T. "Looking for a General for Some Modern Major Models." *Endeavour* 30 (2006): 55–59.

Groover, Andrew T. "Will Genomics Guide a Greener Forest Biotech?" *Trends in Plant Science* 12 (2007): 234–238.

Gunther, Erna. *Ethnobotany of Western Washington*. Seattle: University of Washington Press, 1945.

Guries, R. P., and R. F. Stettler. "Pre-fertilization Barriers to Hybridization in the Poplars." *Silvae Genetica* 25 (1976): 37–44.

Haeuber, R. A., and W. K. Michener. "Policy Implications of Recent Natural and Managed Floods." *BioScience* 48 (1998): 765–772.

Hageneder, Fred. *The Spirit of Trees: Science, Symbiosis, and Inspiration*. New York: Continuum International Publishing Group, 2005.

Hamrick, J. L., and M. J. W. Godt. "Effects of Life History Traits on Genetic Diversity in Plant Species." *Philosophical Transactions of the Royal Society of London*. Series B (1996): 1291–1296.

Han, K.-H., M. P. Gordon, and S. H. Strauss. "Cellular and Molecular Biology of *Agrobacterium*-Mediated Transformation of Plants and Its Application to Genetic Transformation of *Populus*." In *Biology of* Populus *and Its Implications for Management and Conservation*, edited by R. F. Stettler et al., pp. 201–222. Ottawa: National Research Council of Canada, 1996.

Harlan, J. R., J. M. J. De Wet, and E. G. Price. "Comparative Evolution of Cereals." *Evolution* 27 (1973): 311–325.

Harlow, William H., Ellwood S. Harrar, and Fred M. White. *Textbook of Dendrology*. 6th ed. New York: McGraw-Hill, 1979.

Harper, J. L. *Population Biology of Plants*. London: Academic Press, 1977.

Harper, J. L., H. Lovell, and K. G. Moore. "The Shapes and Sizes of Seeds." *Annual Review of Ecology and Systematics* 1 (1970): 327–356.

Harrington, Constance A., John C. Zasada, and Eric A. Allen. "Biology of Red Alder (*Alnus rubra* Bong.)" In *The Biology and Management of Red Alder*, edited by David E. Hibbs et al., pp. 3–22. Corvallis: Oregon State University Press, 1994.

Hart, David D., and N. LeRoy Poff. "A Special Section on Dam Removal and River Restoration." *BioScience* 52 (2002): 653–655.

Hayes, Brian. "Up a Lazy River." *American Scientist* 94 (2006): 490–494.

Hillier, Harold G. *Hillier's Manual of Trees & Shrubs*. 5th ed. New York: Van Nostrand Reinhold, 1981.

Hillman, G. C. "The Plant Food Economy of Abu Hureira 1 and 2." In *Village on the Euphrates: From Foraging to Farming at Abu Hureira*, edited by A. M. T. Moore et al., pp. 327–422. Oxford: Oxford University Press, 2000.

Hockenjos, Wolf. *Begegnung mit Bäumen*. Stuttgart: DRW-Verlag Weinbrenner KG, 1978.

Hogenboom, N. G. "Incongruity: Non-functioning of Intercellular and Intracellular Partner Relationships through Non-matching Information." In *Cellular Interactions: Encyclopedia of Plant Physiology, New Series*, Vol. 17, edited by H. F. Linskens and J. Heslop-Harrison, pp. 640–654. Berlin: Springer-Verlag, 1984.

Houllier, F., J. Novotny, R. Päivinen et al. *Future Forest Research Strategy for a Knowledge-Based Forest Cluster: An Asset for a Sustainable Europe*. Joensuu, Finland: European Forest Institute, 2005.

Houtzagers, G. *Die Gattung* Populus *und ihre Bedeutung*. Hannover: Verlag M. u. H. Schaper, 1941.

Hughes, Francine, Keith Richards, Jacky Girel et al., eds. *The Flooded Forest: Guidance for Policy Makers and River Managers in Europe on the Restoration of Floodplain Forests*. Cambridge: The FLOBAR2 Project, 2003.

Huntley, B., and H. J. B. Birks. *An Atlas of Past and Present Pollen Maps for Europe, 0–13,000 Years Ago*. Cambridge: Cambridge University Press, 1983.

Huntley, B., W. Cramer, A. V. Morgan, H. C. Prentice, and J. R. M. Allen. "Predicting the Response of Terrestrial Biota to Future Environmental Changes." In *Past and Future Rapid Environmental Changes: The Spatial and Evolutionary Responses of Terrestrial Biota*, edited by B. Huntley, W. Cramer, A. V. Morgan, H. C. Prentice, and J. R. M. Allen. Berlin: NATO ASI Series, Vol. I (47), Springer-Verlag, 1997.

Huntley, B., and T. Webb III, eds. *Vegetation History*. Dordrecht: Kluwer Academic, 1988.

Huxley, J. S. "Clines: An Auxiliary Taxonomic Principle." *Nature* 142 (1938): 219.

Illingworth, K. "Study of Lodgepole Pine Genotype-Environment Interaction in B.C." In *Proceedings of the IUFRO Joint Meeting of Working Parties: Douglas-Fir Provenances, Lodgepole Pine Provenances, Sitka Spruce*

Provenances, and Abies *Provenances.* Vancouver, BC, Canada (1978): 151–158.

Jackson, S. T., and J. T. Overpeck. "Responses of Plant Populations and Communities to Environmental Changes of the Late Quaternary." *Paleobiology* 25 (2000): 194–220.

Jacob, François. "Evolution and Tinkering." *Science* 196 (1977): 1161–1166.

Jansson, Stefan, and Carl J. Douglas. "*Populus:* A Model System for Plant Biology." *Annual Review of Plant Biology* 58 (2007): 435–458.

Johnson, Brian, and Keith Kirby. "Potential Impacts of Genetically Modified Trees on Biodiversity of Forestry Plantations: A Global Perspective." In *The Bioengineered Forest: Challenges for Science and Society,* edited by Steven H. Strauss and H. D. Bradshaw, Jr., pp. 190–207. Washington, DC: Resources for the Future, 2004.

Johnston, Alex. *Plants and the Blackfoot.* Lethbridge, AB: Occasional Paper No. 15, Lethbridge Historical Society, 1987.

Kareiva, P., S. Watts, R. McDonald, and T. Boucher. "Domesticated Nature: Shaping Landscapes and Ecosystems for Human Welfare." *Science* 316 (2007): 1866–1869.

Keim, P., K. N. Paige, T. G. Whitham, and K. G. Lark. "Genetic Analysis of an Interspecific Hybrid Swarm of *Populus:* Occurrence of Unidirectional Introgression." *Genetics* 123 (1989): 557–565.

Kennett, J. P. "The Younger Dryas Cooling Event: An Introduction." *Paleoceanography* 5 (1990): 891–895.

Kerr, Richard A. "Support Is Drying Up for Noah's Flood Filling the Black Sea." *Science* 317 (2007): 886.

Kislev, Mordechai E., Anat Hartmann, and Ofer Bar-Yosef. "Early Domesticated Fig in the Jordan Valley." *Science* 312 (2006): 1372–1374.

Kittelson, Neal T. *Biology and Control of the Western Poplar Clearwing Moth,* Paranthrene robiniae Hy. Edwards, *in Hybrid Poplars.* PhD thesis, Washington State University, Pullman, 2006.

Knox, R. B. "Pollen-Pistil Interactions." In *Cellular Interactions: Encyclopedia of Plant Physiology, New Series,* Vol. 17, edited by H. F. Linskens and J. Heslop-Harrison, pp. 508–608. Berlin: Springer-Verlag, 1984.

Kremer, A., R. Petit, A. Zanetto et al. "Nuclear and Organelle Gene Diversity in *Quercus robur* and *Quercus petraea.*" In *Genetic Variation of Forest Tree Populations in Europe,* edited by G. Müller-Starck and M. Ziehe, pp. 141–166. Berlin: Sauerländer Verlag, 1991.

Kruckeberg, Arthur R. *The Natural History of Puget Sound Country.* Seattle: University of Washington Press, 1991.

Langlet, Olof. "Two Hundred Years of Genecology." *Taxon* 20 (1971): 653–722.

Lanner, R. M. "Needed: A New Approach to the Study of Pollen Dispersion." *Silvae Genetica* 15 (1966): 50–52.

Leopold, Luna B. "Trees and Streams: The Efficiency of Branching Patterns." *Journal of Theoretical Biology* 31 (1971): 339–354.

———. *A View of the River.* Cambridge, MA: Harvard University Press, 1994.

Leshner, Alan. "Outreach Training Needed." *Science* 315 (2007): 161.

Levins, Richard. Public lecture, Seattle, Washington, 1967.

Lewington, Anna, and Edward Parker. *Ancient Trees.* London: Collins & Brown, 1999.

Lewontin, Richard C. *The Genetic Basis of Evolutionary Change.* New York: Columbia University Press, 1974.

———. "Directions in Evolutionary Biology." *Annual Review of Genetics* 36 (2002): 1–18.

Liepelt, S., R. Bialozyt, and B. Ziegenhage. "Wind-Dispersed Pollen Mediates Postglacial Gene Flow among Refugia." *Proceedings of the National Academy of Sciences USA* 99 (2002): 14590–14594.

Liphschitz, Nili, and Yoav Waisel. "The Effects of Human Activity on Composition of the Natural Vegetation during Historic Periods." *Proceedings of the 4th Scientific Conference of the Israel Ecological Society,* Tel Aviv (1973): F-4–F-17.

———. "Dendroarcheological Investigations in Israel (St. Catherine's Monastery in Southern Sinai)." *Israel Exploration Journal* 26 (1976): 39–48.

Logan, William Bryant. *Oak: The Frame of Civilization.* New York: W. W. Norton, 2005.

Lorius, C., J. Jouzel, D. Raynaud, J. Hansen, and H. Le Treut. "The Ice-Core Record: Climate Sensitivity and Future Greenhouse Warming." *Nature* 347 (1990): 139–145.

MacDonald, G. M. "Fossil Pollen Analysis and the Reconstruction of Plant Invasions." *Advances in Ecological Research* 24 (1993): 67–110.

MacMahon, T. A., and R. E. Kronauer. "Tree Structure: Deducing the Principle of Mechanical Design." *Journal of Theoretical Biology* 59 (1976): 443–466.

Mandelbrot, B. B. *The Fractal Geometry of Nature.* San Francisco: Freeman, 1983.

Mandoli, Dina F., and Richard Olmstead. "The Importance of Emerging Model Systems in Plant Biology." *Journal of Plant Growth Regulation* 19 (2000): 249–252.

Marette, J. *Connaissance des primitifs par l'étude du bois*. Paris: Éditions A. & J. Picard & Cie., 1961.

Massafra, Maria Grazia. *Legni da Ebanisteria: Coordinate per una trattazione*. Roma: Ministero per i beni e le attività culturali; Istituto centrale per il catalogo e la documentazione, 2002.

Matyas, C. "Climatic Adaptation of Trees: Rediscovering Provenance Tests." *Euphytica* 92 (1996): 45–54.

Mayr, Ernst. "Speciation Phenomena in Birds." *American Naturalist* 74 (1940): 249–278.

———. *Systematics and the Origin of Species*. New York: Columbia University Press, 1942.

Mayr, Ernst, and William B. Provine, eds. *The Evolutionary Synthesis: Perspectives on the Unification of Biology*. Cambridge, MA: Harvard University Press, 1980.

McLachlan, Jason S., and James S. Clark. "Reconstructing Historical Ranges with Fossil Data at Continental Scales." *Forest Ecology and Management* 197 (2004): 139–147.

McLachlan, Jason S., James S. Clark, and Paul S. Manos. "Molecular Indicators of Tree Migration Capacity under Rapid Climate Change." *Ecology* 86 (2005): 2088–2098.

Medvedev, Zhores A. *The Rise and Fall of T. D. Lysenko*. New York: Columbia University Press, 1969.

Meilan, R., A. Brunner, J. Skinner, and S. Strauss. "Modification of Flowering in Transgenic Trees." In *Molecular Breeding of Woody Plants*, edited by A. Komamine and N. Morohoshi, pp. 247–256. Amsterdam: Elsevier Science, 2001.

Meilan, Rick, Dave Ellis, Gilles Pilate, Amy Brunner, and Jeff Skinner. "Accomplishments and Challenges in Genetic Engineering of Forest Trees." In *The Bioengineered Forest: Challenges for Science and Society*, edited by Steven H. Strauss and H. D. Bradshaw, Jr., pp. 36–51. Washington, DC: Resources for the Future, 2004.

Mendel, Gregor. "Experiments in Plant-Hybridization." In *Classic Papers in Genetics*, edited by James A. Peters, pp. 1–20. Englewood Cliffs, NJ: Prentice-Hall; English translation, 1959 (original publication, 1865).

Meyer, J. G., and Sharon Linnèa. *America's Famous and Historic Trees*. Boston: Houghton Mifflin, 2001.

Michener, William K., and Richard A. Haeuber. "Flooding: Natural and Managed Disturbances." *BioScience* 48 (1998): 677–680.

Millar, Constance I., and Linda B. Brubaker. "Climate Change and

Paleoecology: New Contexts for Restoration Ecology." In *Foundations of Restoration Ecology*, edited by D. Falk, J. Zedler, and M. Palmer, pp. 315–340. Washington, D.C.: Island Press, 2006.

Mitton, J. B., and M. C. Grant. "Genetic Variation and Natural History of Quaking Aspen." *BioScience* 46 (1996): 25–31.

Mitton, J. B., and C. G. Williams. "Gene Flow in Conifers." In *Landscapes, Genomics, and Transgenic Conifers*, edited by C. G. Williams, pp. 147–168. Dordrecht: Springer, 2006.

Molles, Manuel C. Jr., Clifford S. Crawford, Lisa M. Ellis, H. Maurice Valett, and Clifford N. Dahm. "Managed Flooding for Riparian Ecosystem Restoration." *BioScience* 48 (1998): 749–756.

Montgomery, David R., Susan Bolton, Derek B. Booth, and Leslie Wall, eds. *Restoration of Puget Sound Rivers*. Seattle: University of Washington Press, 2003.

Moore, A. M. T., G. C. Hillman, and A. J. Legge. *Village on the Euphrates: From Foraging to Farming at Abu Hureyra*. Oxford: Oxford University Press, 2000.

Morgenstern, E. Kristian. *Geographic Variation in Forest Trees: Genetic Basis and Application of Knowledge in Silviculture*. Vancouver: University of British Columbia Press, 1996.

Mountains to Sound. http://www.mtsgreenway.org, accessed April 14, 2008.

Naiman, Robert J., Henri Decamps, and Michael E. McClain. *Riparia: Ecology, Conservation, and Management of Streamside Communities*. Amsterdam: Elsevier Academic Press, 2005.

National Research Council. *Environmental Effects of Transgenic Plants: The Scope and Adequacy of Regulation*. Washington, DC: National Academy Press, 2002.

Neale, D. B., N. C. Wheeler, and R. W. Allard. "Paternal Inheritance of Chloroplast DNA in Douglas-Fir." *Canadian Journal of Forest Research* 16 (1986): 1152–1154.

Neale, D. B., and O. Savolainen. "Association Genetics of Complex Traits in Conifers." *Trends in Plant Science* 9 (2004): 325–330.

Nester, Eugene, Milton P. Gordon, and Allen Kerr, eds. Agrobacterium tumefaciens: *From Plant Pathology to Biotechnology*. St. Paul, MN: American Phytopathological Society Press, 2005.

Neuman, Dawn S., Michael Wagner, Jeffrey H. Braatne, and Jon Howe. "Stress Physiology: Abiotic." In *Biology of* Populus *and Its Implications for Management and Conservation*, edited by R. F. Stettler et al., pp. 423–458. Ottawa: National Research Council of Canada, 1996.

Newcombe, G., B. Stirling, S. K. McDonald, and H. D. Bradshaw, Jr. "*Melampsora* × *columbiana*, a Natural Hybrid of *M. medusae* and *M. occidentalis.*" *Mycological Research* 104 (2000): 261–274.

Oak Ridge National Laboratory, Plant Genomics Group. http://www.esd.ornl .gov/PGG/htm, accessed April 14, 2008.

Olson, Elizabeth. "Techniques That Might Smile upon Mona Lisa." *New York Times*, January 1, 2005: B1.

Ottaviano, E., M. Sari-Gorla, and D. Mulcahy. "Pollen Tube Growth Rates in *Zea mays:* Implications for Genetic Improvements of Crops." *Science* 210 (1980): 437–438.

Overpeck, J., K. Hughen, D. Hardy et al. "Arctic Environmental Change of the Last Four Centuries." *Science* 278 (1997): 1251–1256.

Pakenham, Thomas. *Remarkable Trees of the World*. New York: W. W. Norton, 2002.

Palmer, M. A. et al. "Ecological Science and Sustainability for a Crowded Planet: 21st Century Vision and Action Plan for the Ecological Society of America." Washington, DC: Ecological Society of America, 2004; available at http://esa.org/ecovisions/, accessed April 14, 2008.

Parish, Roberta et al. *Plants of Southern Interior British Columbia*. Vancouver, BC: Lone Pine Publishing, 1996.

Paterson, Andrew H., Yann-Rong Lin, Zhikang Li et al. "Convergent Domestication of Cereal Crops by Independent Mutations at Corresponding Genetic Loci." *Science* 269 (1995): 1714–1718.

Peterson, E. B., and N. M. Peterson. *Ecology, Management, and Use of Aspen and Balsam Poplar in the Prairie Provinces*. Edmonton, AB: Forestry Canada, Northwest Region, Northern Forestry Centre, Special Report 1, 1992.

Petit, Remy J., Itziar Aguinagalde et al. "Glacial Refugia: Hotspots but not Melting Pots of Genetic Diversity." *Science* 300 (2003): 1563–1565.

Petit, Remy J., Simon Brewer et al. "Identification of Refugia and Post-Glacial Colonisation Routes of European White Oaks Based on Chloroplast DNA and Fossil Pollen Evidence." *Forest Ecology and Management* 156 (2002): 49–74.

Pojar, Jim, and Andy MacKinnon. *Plants of the Pacific West Coast*. Vancouver, BC: Lone Pine Publishing, 1994.

Pollan, Michael. *Second Nature: A Gardener's Education*. New York: Dell Publishing, 1992.

Ponticelli, Paolo. *Le Origini della Pioppicoltura Italiana. Dove, quando e perché*. Bologna: Edagricole, 1986.

Raffa, Kenneth F. "Transgenic Resistance in Short-Rotation Plantation Trees: Benefits, Risks, Integration with Multiple Tactics, and the Need to Balance the Scales." In *The Bioengineered Forest: Challenges for Science and Society*, edited by Steven H. Strauss and H. D. Bradshaw, Jr., pp. 208–227. Washington, DC: Resources for the Future, 2004.

Reed, John P. *Factors Affecting the Genetic Architecture of Black Cottonwood Populations*. MS Thesis, University of Washington, Seattle, 1995.

Rehfeldt, Gerald E. "Ecological Genetics of *Pinus contorta* from the Rocky Mountains (USA): A Synthesis." *Silvae Genetica* 37 (1988): 131–135.

Rehfeldt, Gerald E., Nadejda M. Tchebakova, Yelena I. Parfenova, William R. Wykoff, Nina A. Kuzmina, and Leonid I. Milyutin. "Intraspecific Responses to Climate in *Pinus sylvestris*." *Global Change Biology* 8 (2002): 912–929.

Rehfeldt, Gerald E., William R. Wykoff, and Cheng C. Ying. "Physiologic Plasticity, Evolution, and Impacts of a Changing Climate on *Pinus contorta*." *Climatic Change* 50 (2001): 355–376.

Rehfeldt, Gerald E., Cheng C. Ying, David L. Spittelhouse, and David A. Hamilton, Jr. "Genetic Responses to Climate in *Pinus contorta*: Niche Breadth, Climate Change, and Reforestation." *Ecological Monographs* 69 (1999): No. 3.

Rhee, S. Y., S. Weng, D. Flanders et al. "*Arabidopsis thaliana* Genome Maps 9." *Science* 282 (1998): Special Section, October 23.

Ridley, Matt. *The Red Queen: Sex and the Evolution of Human Nature*. New York: Penguin Books USA, 1993.

Rieseberg, Loren H., and John H. Willis. "Plant Speciation." *Science* 317 (2007): 910–914.

Rood, S. B., J. S. Campbell, and T. Despins. "Natural Poplar Hybrids from Southern Alberta. I. Continuous Variation for Foliar Characteristics." *Canadian Journal of Botany* 64 (1986): 1382–1388.

Rood, S. B., and S. Heinze-Milne. "Abrupt Downstream Forest Decline Following River Damming in Southern Alberta." *Canadian Journal of Botany* 67 (1989): 1744–1749.

Rood, S. B., A. R. Kalischuk, and J. M. Mahoney. "Initial Cottonwood Seedling Recruitment Following the Flood of the Century of the Oldman River, Alberta, Canada." *Wetlands* 8 (1998): 557–570.

Rood, S. B., and J. M. Mahoney. "Collapse of Riparian Poplar Forests Downstream from Dams in Western Prairies: Probable Causes and Prospects for Mitigation." *Environmental Management* 14 (1990):451–464.

———. "Revised Instream Flow Regulation Enables Cottonwood

Recruitment along the St. Mary River, Alberta, Canada." *Rivers* 7 (2000): 109–125.

Rood, S. B., J. M. Mahoney, D. E. Reid, and L. Zilm. "Instream Flows and the Decline of Riparian Cottonwoods along the St. Mary River, Alberta." *Canadian Journal of Botany* 73 (1995): 1250–1260.

Rood, S. B., G. M. Samuelson, J. H. Braatne, C. R. Gourley, F. M. R. Hughes, and J. M. Mahoney. "Managing River Flows to Restore Floodplain Forests." *Frontiers in Ecology and Environment* 3 (2005): 193–201.

Ruddiman, W. F. *Earth's Climate: Past and Future.* San Francisco: W. H. Freeman, 2001.

———. "The Anthropocene Greenhouse Era Began Thousands of Years Ago." *Climatic Change* 61 (2003): 261–293.

Ryan, William B. F., and Walter C. Pitman. *Noah's Flood: The New Scientific Discoveries about the Event That Changed History.* New York: Simon & Schuster, 1998.

Scarascia-Mugnozza, G. E., T. M. Hinckley, R. F. Stettler, P. E. Heilman, and J. G. Isebrands. "Production Physiology and Morphology of *Populus* Species and Their Hybrids under Short Rotation. III. Seasonal Carbon Allocation Patterns from Branches." *Canadian Journal of Forest Research* 29 (1999): 1419–1432.

Sedjo, R. A. "The Role of Forest Plantations in the World's Future Timber Supply." *Forestry Chronicle* 77 (2001): 221–226.

Slavov, Gancho T., Stephen DiFazio, and Steven H. Strauss. "Gene Flow in Forest Trees: Gene Migration Patterns and Landscape Modelling of Transgene Dispersal in Hybrid Poplar." In *Introgression from Genetically Modified Plants into Wild Relatives,* edited by H. C. M. den Nijs, D. Bartsch, and J. Sweet, pp. 89–106. Wallingford, UK: CABI Publishing, 2004.

Smit, Barbara A., D. S. Neuman, and M. Stachowiak. "Root Hypoxia Reduces Leaf Growth. Role of Factors in the Transpiration Stream." *Plant Physiology* 92 (1990): 1021–1028.

Smit, Barbara A., and M. Stachowiak. "Effects of Hypoxia and Elevated Carbon Dioxide Concentration on Water Flux through *Populus* Roots." *Tree Physiology* 4 (1988): 153–165.

Smit, Barbara A., M. Stachowiak, and E. Van Volkenburgh. "Cellular Processes Limiting Leaf Growth in Plants under Hypoxic Root Stress." *Journal of Experimental Botany* 40 (1989): 89–94.

Smith, D. M. "Camillo Benso Cavour." *Encyclopedia Britannica* 5 (1965): 122.

Solomon, Susan et al., eds. *Climate Change 2007: The Physical Science Basis.*

Contribution of Working Group I to the Fourth Assessment Report of the
Intergovernmental Panel on Climate Change. Cambridge: Cambridge
University Press, 2007.

Soltis, Pamela S., and Douglas E. Soltis. "The Role of Genetic and Genomic
Attributes in the Success of Polyploids." *Proceedings of the National
Academy of Sciences USA* 97 (2000): 7051–7057.

Sparks, Richard E., John C. Nelson, and Yao Yin. "Naturalization of the Flood
Regime in Regulated Rivers." *BioScience* 48 (1998): 706–720.

Spiegel-Roy, P., and J. Kochba. "Inheritance of Nut and Kernel Traits in
Almond (*Prunus amygdalus* Batsch)." *Euphytica* 30 (1981): 167–174.

Stanton, Brian, Jake Eaton, Jon Johnson et al. "Hybrid Poplar in the Pacific
Northwest." *Journal of Forestry* 100 (2002): 28–33.

Stanton, Brian J., and Marc Villar. "Controlled Reproduction of *Populus*." In
Biology of Populus *and Its Implications for Management and Conservation*,
edited by R. F. Stettler et al., pp. 113–138. Ottawa: National Research
Council of Canada, 1996.

Stebbins, G. Ledyard, Jr. *Variation and Evolution in Plants*. New York:
Columbia University Press, 1950.

Stettler, R. F. "Irradiated Mentor Pollen: Its Use in Remote Hybridization of
Black Cottonwood." *Nature* 219 (1968): 746–747.

———. "Variation in Sex Expression of Black Cottonwood and Related
Hybrids." *Silvae Genetica* 20 (1971): 42–46.

Stettler, R. F., and R. P. Guries. "The Mentor-Pollen Phenomenon in Black
Cottonwood." *Canadian Journal of Botany* 54 (1976): 820–830.

Stettler, R. F., R. Koster, and V. Steenackers. "Interspecific Crossability
Studies in Poplars." *Theoretical and Applied Genetics* 58 (1980): 273–282.

Stettler, Reinhard F., Harvey D. Bradshaw, Jr., Paul E. Heilman, and
Thomas M. Hinckley, eds. *Biology of* Populus *and Its Implications for
Management and Conservation*. Ottawa: National Research Council of
Canada, 1996.

Stout, A. B., and E. J. Schreiner. "Results of a Project in Hybridizing Poplars."
Journal of Heredity 24 (1933): 218–219.

Strauss, Steven H. "Genomics, Genetic Engineering, and Domestication of
Crops." *Science* 300 (2003): 61–62.

Strauss, Steven H., and H. D. Bradshaw, Jr., eds. *The Bioengineered Forest:
Challenges for Science and Society*. Washington, DC: Resources for the
Future, 2004.

Strauss, Steven H., and Amy M. Brunner. "Tree Biotechnology in the Twenty-
First Century: Transforming Trees in the Light of Comparative Genomics."

In *The Bioengineered Forest: Challenges for Science and Society,* edited by Steven H. Strauss and H. D. Bradshaw, Jr., pp. 76–97. Washington, DC: Resources for the Future, 2004.

Sturtevant, A. H. *A History of Genetics.* New York: Harper & Row, 1965.

Sykes, Bryan. *The Seven Daughters of Eve.* New York: W. W. Norton, 2001.

Taiz, Lincoln, and Eduardo Zeiger. *Plant Physiology.* 4th ed. Sunderland, MA: Sinauer Associates, 2006.

Turesson, G. "The Scope and Import of Genecology." *Hereditas* 4 (1923): 4.

Tuskan, G. A., S. DiFazio, S. Jansson et al. "The Genome of Black Cottonwood, *Populus trichocarpa* (Torr. & Gray)." *Science* 313 (2006): 1596–1604.

Van Valen, L. "A New Evolutionary Law." *Evolutionary Theory* 1 (1973): 1–30.

Villar, Marc et al. "Pollen-Pistil Interactions in *Populus.*" *Sexual Plant Reproduction* 6 (1993): 249–256.

Weideman, Paul. *The Valley Records* (Snoqualmie 77: 23), November 29, 1990.

Westfall, Robert D., and Constance I. Millar. "Genetic Consequences of Forest Population Dynamics Influenced by Historic Climatic Variability in the Western USA." *Forest Ecology and Management* 197 (2004): 159–170.

Weyl, Hermann. *Symmetry.* Princeton, NJ: Princeton University Press, 1952.

Wheeler, Nicholas C., and Raymond P. Guries. "Biogeography of Lodgepole Pine." *Canadian Journal of Botany* 60 (1982a): 1805–1814.

———. "Population Structure, Genic Diversity, and Morphological Variation in *Pinus contorta* Dougl." *Canadian Journal of Forest Research* 12 (1982b): 595–606.

White, T. L., W. T. Adams, and D. B. Neale. *Forest Genetics.* Wallingford, UK: CABI Publishing, 2007.

Whitham, T. G., S. P. DiFazio, J. A. Schweitzer, S. M. Shuster et al. "Extending Genomics to Natural Communities and Ecosystems." *Science* 320 (2008): 492–495.

Whitham, T. G., K. D. Floate, G. D. Martinsen, E. M. Driebe, and P. Keim. "Ecological and Evolutionary Implications of Hybridization: *Populus*-Herbivore Interactions." In *Biology of* Populus *and Its Implications for Management and Conservation,* edited by R. F. Stettler et al., pp. 247–275. Ottawa: National Research Council of Canada, 1996.

Whitham, T. G., G. D. Martinsen, K. D. Floate, H. S. Dungey, B. M. Potts, and P. Keim. "Plant Hybrid Zones Affect Biodiversity: Tools for a Genetic-Based Understanding of Community Structure." *Ecology* 80 (1999): 416–428.

Whitham, T. C. et al. "A Framework for Community and Ecosystem Genetics: From Genes to Ecosystems." *Nature Reviews. Genetics* 7 (2006): 510–523.

Whitlock, C. "Vegetational and Climatic History of the Pacific Northwest during the Last 20,000 Years: Implications for Understanding Present-Day Biodiversity." *Northwest Environmental Journal* 8 (1992): 5-28.

Whittemore, A. T., and B. A. Schaal. "Interspecific Gene Flow in Oaks." *Proceedings of the National Academy of Sciences USA* 88 (1991): 2540-2544.

Wilson, B. F. *The Growing Tree.* Amherst: University of Massachusetts Press, 1970.

Wilson, E. O. *The Future of Life.* New York: Random House, 2002.

Wright, Jonathan W. *Introduction to Forest Genetics.* New York: Academic Press, 1976.

Yaffee, Steven L. "Cooperation: A Strategy for Achieving Stewardship across Boundaries." In *Stewardship across Boundaries,* edited by Richard L. Knight and Peter B. Landres, pp. 299-324. Washington, DC: Island Press, 1998.

Yanchuk, Alvin D. "A Quantitative Framework for Breeding and Conservation of Forest Tree Genetic Resources in British Columbia." *Canadian Journal of Forest Research* 31 (2001): 566-576.

———. "The Role and Implications of Biotechnological Tools in Forestry." *Unasylva* 52 (2001): 53-61.

Zobel, Bruce, and John Talbert. *Applied Forest Tree Improvement.* New York: John Wiley and Sons, 1984.

Zohary, D. "The Progenitors of Wheat and Barley in Relation to Domestication and Agriculture Dispersal in the Old World." In *The Domestication and Exploitation of Plants and Animals,* edited by P. J. Ucko and G. W. Bimbleby, pp. 47-66. London: Duckworth, 1969.

Zohary, Daniel, and Maria Hopf. *Domestication of Plants in the Old World.* Oxford: Clarendon Press, 1988.

———. *Domestication of Plants in the Old World.* 3rd ed. Oxford: Oxford University Press, 2000.

Zohary, D., and P. Spiegel-Roy. "Beginnings of Fruit Growing in the Old World." *Science* 187 (1975): 319-327.

Zsuffa, L., E. Giordano, L. D. Pryor, and R. F. Stettler. "Trends in Poplar Culture: Some Global and Regional Perspectives." In *Biology of Populus and Its Implications for Management and Conservation,* edited by R. F. Stettler et al., pp. 515-539. Ottawa: National Research Council of Canada, 1996.

INDEX

Note: page numbers in *italics* refer to figures and tables; those followed by "n" indicate endnotes.

A

Abies alba (silver fir), 124

Abu Hureyra site (Syria), 152–55

Acer palmatum (Japanese maples), 231–32

Achillea borealis, 89–90

Achillea lanulosa, 90–92, *91*, 253n10(ch10)

Achillea millefolium complex, 89–90

adaptation: of aspen leaves, *44*; climate warming and, 135–38; to climatic conditions, 86, 126–29, *129*; cues and responses, *133*; limits of, 133–35; provenance test and, 130–33, 136–37; regeneration and, 18–19; stomatal density, 101–2; trees and, ix; to water regime fluctuations, 27–30. *See also* phenotypic plasticity; selection; variation and diversity

Ager, Alan, 112

agriculture, development of. *See* domestication and early agriculture

Agrobacterium, 205

Aigeiros poplars, *46*, 77

Alaska, 70

Alberta, 71, 143–46

alleles: rare, 107; recessive, 56, 134

allozyme analysis: overview, 104–5; comparison among plant groups, 110–11; limitations of, 113–14; lodgepole pine study, 105–10, *106*; other conifers, 110; usefulness of, 110

almond culture, 162–63

Alnus rubra (red alder), 30, 37–38

amino acids, 200–201

Anderson, Edgar, 74, 251n5(ch9)

apical control, 231

apical dominance, 228

apical meristems, 228, 230

Arabidopsis, 56, 200, 202–3

archeological research, 152–55, 163–64

Armenia, 76

asexual reproduction and clones (vegetative propagation): age of genets, 36–37, 45; aspens and, 44–50; clumps, clonal, 33–36; genetic engineering and, 206–7;

catkins: bisexual, 59; in hybrids, 71; maturation, 58; sexual reproduction and, 52–53, 54, 58; shedding of, 54
Cavour, Camillo Benso di, 177–78
Ceccarelli, Leah, 251n9
cellulosic ethanol plants, 186
channel migration, 14–15, 16
chestnut, European (*Castanea sativa*), 171–72
China, 169, 207–8
Chinese aspen (*Populus adenopoda*), 73
chromosome recombination, 53, 55–56, 68
chrysomelid beetles, 78–79
city trees, 235–37
cladoptosis, 35
Clausen, Jens, 86–93
clearwing poplar moth, 184
climate science, 127–28
climate warming, 135–38, 186
climatic conditions: common-garden experiment on, 87–92; as ecological change agent, 127; fluctuation patterns, 126–29, *129*; intraspecific adaptations to, 86; moisture and temperature regime, 99–100, 128–29; timing of growth period, 99; in Younger Dryas period, 154
climatic (ecological) races, 90, 91–92
clines, 92
clones. *See* asexual reproduction and clones (vegetative propagation)
cold tolerance, 131–32
Collins, Francis, 199–200
Columbia River, 184–85

columnar poplars, 164–70, *168*
common-garden experiments, 87–92, 100–103, 240–41
communities, artificial, 240–41
community coherence and migration, 118
competition: columnar form and, 167; in cottonwood stands, 23–25; lodgepole pines and, 23–24; pioneer species and, 18, 24; in sexual reproduction, 55–57
computer models of tree growth, 232, 233, 234
conservation biology, 150
coppicing, 176
corn, hybrid vigor in, 192
cottonwoods (overview), 5–7, 23–25, 144–46. *See also* black cottonwood (*Populus trichocarpa*); poplars (genus *Populus*); *particular topics*
crossing. *See* hybrids and hybridization
crown volume, 6, 164–65, 167, *168*, 235
Cwynar, Les, 116

D
Darwin, Charles, 24, 62
Darwinian fitness, 54, 250n4(ch7)
date palms, 162
da Vinci. *See* Leonardo da Vinci
Dawkins, Richard, 54, 68, 200, 215
defense mechanisms, 47–48, 78–79
diameter-to-height proportion, 22, 207–8, *208*, 231
Diamond, Jared, 159
Dickmann, Donald I., 76, 247n2
dimorphism, sexual, 6, 58–59, 113

diploidy, 53, 55–56, 105, 134

diversity. *See* variation and diversity

DNA: complementary double-stranded (cDNA), 204; finger-printing, 36; of mitochondria and chloroplasts, 120–25, 170, 171–72; nuclear, 121; recombination, 53, 68, 121, 197

DNA sequencing, 200–203. *See also* genomics

Dobzhansky, Theodosius, 62–63, 66–67, 69, 75, 89, 251n9

domestication and early agriculture: overview, 151; Abu Hureyra site (Syria), 152–55; assemblages of domesticates, 157; Black Sea flood and migration, 158–59; chestnuts, 171–72; columnar poplars, 164–70, *168*; mutations and selection, 155–57; sedentary lifestyle and, 157–58; tree domes-tication, beginnings of, 161–64

Doty, Sharon, 30–31, 209

Douglas fir (*Pseudotsuga menziesii*), 50, 96

Drosophila (fruit fly), 89, 189, 190, 200

drought-responsiveness in hybrids, 192

Dunlap, Joan, 100

E

eastern cottonwood (*Populus del-toides*): climate, leaf size, and taxonomy, 100; in Europe, 73, 178; hybrids, 66, 191–96; in hybrid zone, 71

Eaton, Jake, 181

Eckenwalder, James, 76–77

ecological genetics, 94

ecological (climatic) races, 90, 91–92

Ecological Society of America, 150

ecological succession, 5–6, 15, 44

ecosystem evolution, process of, 8, 20–23, 78–80

ecotypes, 88, 92

electrophoresis, 105, 107, 110, 113

embryos, 56–57, 64, 66

Enquist, Brian J., 248n7(ch3)

enzymes. *See* allozyme analysis

epicormic branches, 29–30

ethanol, 186

Euphrates poplar (*Populus euphratica*), 154–55, 164, 207–8, 208

Euphrates River, 152

Europe: columnar poplars and, 169–70; eastern cottonwood, introduction of, 73; floods in, 147; forests in, 217, 219; Italian uses of poplar, 173–80; multipurpose for-ests in, 219–20; oak phylogeogra-phy, 122–24; provenance research in, 95–96

European aspen (*Populus tremula*), 43–44, 73

European black poplar. *See* black poplar (*Populus nigra*)

European chestnut (*Castanea sativa*), 171–72

European Forest Genetic Resources Program (EUFORGEN), 169–70

European white oak, 172

Euxine Lake, 158–59

evolution: domestication and human influence, 155–59; hybrid-ization and, 74–75; mechanisms

of, 67–68; Modern Synthesis, 62–
63, 66–67, 104; rate of, in poplars,
202. *See also* genes and genetics

F

Fagan, Brian, 257n12(ch16)
Farmer, Robert, 99
fertilization, 54–55, 55, 57, 63–64,
74–75
field testing of GE trees, 210–14
figs, 162
fire, 23–24, 44, 230
Fisher, Ronald, 66–67
fitness. *See* adaptation; selection
flavone glycosides and flavonol
glycosides, 79
floodplain forests, 149
floods: adaptation to, 28–29; Black
Sea (Mini Ice Age), 158–59; dams
and, 144–46, *145*; greenhouse experiments, 28–29; habitat change
from, 15; as human disasters, 147;
river processes and, 10–11
Food and Agriculture Organization
(FAO), UN, 180
forests: overview, 215–16; artificial
communities, 240–41; con-
tinuum, integration of, 222–23;
multipurpose, 219–21; new
partnerships, 223–25; old-growth,
221–22; plantation forestry, 216–
19; recreational, 221; Snoqualmie
River Valley, 225–26. *See also*
plantations
Forest Service (USDA), 224
fractal models, 232, 233, 234
Frankia spp., 30
Fremont cottonwood (*Populus
fremontii*), 73, 79

fruit fly (*Drosophila*), 89, 189, 190,
200
fruit trees, earliest cultivation of,
162–63
functional genomics, 203–5

G

gall aphids, 79
gamete, 59–60
gel electrophoresis, 105, 107, 110, 113
gene chips, 204–5
genecology, 96–97
gene flow: columnar poplars and,
169; definition of, 67; density-
dependent selection and, 131–32;
GE cultivars and, 211; hybridization and, 74
genes and genetics: adaptation and,
ix–x; association genetics, 213;
common-garden experiment and,
87–88; ecological genetics, 94;
hybridization and, 74; Modern
Synthesis, 62–63, 66–67, 104;
passwords, 61–66; phenotype and
genotype, link between, 104–5;
polymorphisms, genetic, 50–51.
See also genomics; phenotypic
plasticity
genetic drift, 67–68, 116
genetic engineering. *See* genomics
genets, 36–37, 44–45. *See also*
asexual reproduction and clones
genomics: field testing, 209–12;
functional, 203–5; genetic engineering, 205–9; human genome,
199–200; impact of, 213–14; regulation and guidelines, 212–13;
sequencing, 200–203
geographic ranges. *See* allozyme

analysis; common-garden experiment; glacial refuges and postglacial migration; provenance research

germination, 19–20, 20, 156

glacial refuges and postglacial migration: overview, 115–16; chestnut and, 171–72; columnar poplars in Europe, 170; lodgepole pine and, 106, 108, 116–17; Mini Ice Age and human migration, 158–59; palynology, 117–20; phylogeography and organellar DNA, 120–25, 123

global warming, 135–38, 186

Godt, M. J. W., 110–11

Goethe, Johann von, 176

Gordon, Milton, 205

grapevine cultivation, 162

growth systems, 228–33, 229, 233, 234

Guries, Ray, 65, 105–8, 116–17, 120

H

Haeuber, R. A., 148

Haldane, J. B. S., 66–67

Hall, Havrey M., 89

Hamrick, J. L., 110–11

haploidy, 53, 105

haplotypes, 121, 170, 172

Harper, John L., 36, 249n4(ch5)

hawkweed (*Hieracium* sp.), 189

height: cold tolerance vs. height dominance, 131–32; diameter-to-height proportion, 22, 207–8, 208, 231; fitness and growth in, 130–31

Herron, Jon C., 250n1

heteroblasty, 27

heterosis, 192

heterozygosity: allozyme analysis and, 105, 107–8; crossing and, 193; levels of, 203; maladaptive mutations and, 134; tree domestication and, 161–62

Hieracium sp. (hawkweed), 189

Hiesey, William M., 86–93

Hillman, Gordon, 154

homozygosity, 105, 134, 193

Hughes, Francine, 149

human genome, 199–200, 201

Huxley, J. S., 92

hybrid analysis: F_1 hybrids, 191–93; F_2 hybrids, 193–96, 195, 197; limits of, 196–98

hybrids and hybridization: in animals and plants, contrasted, 69; European breeding and selection programs, 73; experimental matings, 64–66; first crosses, backcrosses, and advance-generation hybrids, 71–73; genetic significance and evolutionary consequences of, 74–75; identification of, 70, 71; insect preferences and, 78–80; with introduced non-native poplars, 73–74; introgressive hybridization, 74, 75, 79, 80; inviability, 65, 80; mechanisms to prevent, 63–66; plantations, 178–79, 180, 182, 185; reciprocal crosses, 66; sterility, 65, 70; taxonomy and, 75–78; zones of, 71–73, 78–81

hybrid vigor, 192

hydrographs, 11, 12

hydrologic cycle, 11–12

hypoxia, 28

Mississippi River, 16, 147
model organisms, 188–91
Modern (Evolutionary) Synthesis, 62–63, 66–67, 104
moisture: drought-responsiveness in hybrids, 192; germination and, 20; growing season and, 99–100; temperature and, 128–29
Mona Lisa, 173–74
Monceau, Duhamel du, 95, 178
monoecious species, 37, 112–13
Moore, Andrew, 153
Morgan, T. H., 62, 89, 189
multipurpose forests, 219–21
mutations: columnar form, 164–65; definition of, 67; domestication and, 155–57; genotype and mutant phenotypes, 104; maladaptive, 134; neofunctionalization, 202; sexual reproduction and, 55–56

N
Nägeli, Karl von, 189
Naiman, Robert J., 248n7(ch2)
narrowleaf cottonwood (*Populus angustifolia*), 71–72, 73, 79
natural selection. *See* selection
Nepal, 166
Nester, Eugene, 205
Nisqually River Valley, 100–103, 201
nitrogen-fixing symbionts, 30–31
Norway spruce (*Picea abies*), 96

O
Oak Ridge National Laboratory, 201
oaks (*Quercus*): cpDNA differentiation in European white oak, 172; long life of, 7–8; phylogeography

of, 122–24; *Q. semecarpifolia* in Nepal, 166
old-growth forests, 221–22
olives, 162
Olmstead, Richard, 190
Oregon: Applegate Partnership, 223–24; Boardman plantations, 181–84; Columbia River plantations, 184–85; environmental gradient west to east, 180–81
outcrossing: genetic diversity and, 111; monoecious, 112–13; obligate, 59, 60; tree domestication and, 161–62

P
paintings on poplar wood, 173–75
paleoecology, 114–16, 117–20, 127, 150
palynology, 117–20
parasites and sexual reproduction, 53–54
parks, urban, 221, 236–37
Pascal, Blaise, 239
Pemphigus betae (gall aphids), 79
Peterson, E. B., 249n2(ch6)
Peterson, N. M., 249n2(ch6)
phenolic compounds, 78–79
phenotypic plasticity: clonal propagation and, 33; growth and allocation adjustments, 30; leaf size and, 27; resprouting and, 27; stomatal density and, 102
photoperiod and phenology, 99
photosynthesis: adjustment of photosynthetic demand, 30; chloroplasts and, 120–21; columnar form and, 167; heat buildup and, 26; hybrids and, 193
phyllotaxy, 230–31

phylogeography, 120–25, *123*, 171–72

phytomers, 228, 230

phytoremediation, 209

Picea abies (Norway spruce), 96

Pinus contorta. See lodgepole pine

Pinus ponderosa (ponderosa pine), 96, 102, 111–13, 125

Pinus sylvestris (Scots pine), 95–96, 132, 137

pioneer species: channel migration and, 15; cloning and, 37; competition among, 18, 24; succession and, 6, 8

Pitman, Walter C., 158, 258n13(ch16)

plantation forestry, 216–19

plantations: Boardman, Oregon, 181–84, 186; GE cultivars and, 212; for hybrid analysis, 194–95; markets, 184–86; in Po Valley, Italy, 177–80

point bars, 13, *14*, 15, 18

Pollan, Michael, 149, 231

pollarding, 176

pollen: irradiated, 57, 64–65; output, with gender dimorphism vs. bisexuality, 58; paleoecological analysis of, 117–20, 171–72

pollination: in sexual reproduction, 54–55, *55*; by zoonotic agents, 66, 77, 78–80

pollutants and genetic engineering, 209

polygenic model of trait variation, 196

polymorphisms, genetic, 50–51. *See also* variation and diversity

polyploidy, 74, 134, 202

ponderosa pine (*Pinus ponderosa*), 96, 102, 111–13, 125

poplars (genus *Populus*): aspens and white poplars within, 44; classification of, 46–47; DNA sequencing, 201–3; early cultivation of, 163; hybrids, uses of, x, 180, 183–86; as model organisms, 187–91; revised taxonomy of, 76–78; willows compared to, 77–78. *See also particular species*

population bottlenecks, 134

Populus genus. *See* poplars

Populus section, classification of, 46

P. adenopoda (Chinese aspen), 73

P. alba (white poplar), 73, 169, 175

P. angustifolia (narrowleaf cottonwood), 71–72, 73, 79

P. balsamifera (balsam poplar), 70–71

P. deltoides. See eastern cottonwood

P. euphratica (Euphrates poplar), 154–55, 164, 207–8, *208*

P. fremontii (Fremont cottonwood), 73, 79

P. nigra. See black poplar

P. serotina Hartig, 178

P. tremula (European aspen), 43–44, 73

P. tremuloides. See aspen

P. trichocarpa. See black cottonwood

P. x canadensis, 73, 178, 192

Po Valley (Padana), Italy, 175–80

primary growth, 228, *229*

propagules, asexual, 36

protein variation. *See* allozyme analysis

provenance research: adaptation and, 130–33; allozyme analysis vs., 109; climate warming modeling with, 136–37; history of,

ABOUT THE AUTHOR

With a forestry degree from his native Switzerland and a Ph.D in Genetics from UC Berkeley, Reinhard Stettler has spent a lifetime studying plant growth and development and the diversity of forest trees. He taught and conducted research at the University of Washington for more than three decades and has published widely in scientific and technical literature. Broadly interested in biology, literature, art, and anthropology, he has been a visiting lecturer in Germany, Italy, China, Switzerland, and the Netherlands and is the recipient of several national and international awards.